London is a living architectural ........ portable guide will help you to find your way around one of the world's most exciting cities, offering architectural experiences and insights into London's finest contemporary architecture.

- features more than 400 buildings including key venues from the 2012 Olympic Park
- provides a superb full colour photographic record of the capital aids navigation of the city's greatest architectural sights with a clear map-based format
- considers each district in turn, identifying the buildings most worthwhile visiting, and providing essential information and insights into each

Jam packed with the authors' intimate architectural experience and knowledge of London's buildings, the accompanying commentary is both lively and entertaining, providing all the information that any architectural explorer will need to appreciate and experience London's contemporary architecture.

**Kenneth Allinson** AADipl RIBA is the author of *The Wild Card of Design* (1992), *Getting There by Design* (1996), and *Architects and Architecture of London* (2008), as well as earlier editions of this guide. During his career Ken worked for and with, among others, Richard Rogers, John Winter, Archigram Architects, Terry Farrell, YRM and DEGW. He has taught design and professional practice at the UCL, Greenwich and Oxford Brookes Universities, has run his own practice consultancy and is currently a director of Architectural Dialogue. Together with Victoria Thornton he was a founding Trustee of Open House London. He is currently preparing a theoretical work entitled *Meetings With Buildings*.

**Victoria Thornton** OBE is founding director of Open-City, founder of the Open House worldwide initiative and of Architectural Dialogue. In 2003 the RIBA awarded an Honorary Fellowship to Victoria Thornton in recognition of her contribution to architecture and the education of future generations and in 2005 she received an honorary MA degree from London Metropolitan University. She is also a fellow of the RSA and completed an MA relating to European architecture policy and young people (2009). In 2012 Victoria received the Order of the British Empire (OBE) in the New Year's Honours list for services to architecture and architecture education.

# LONDON'S CONTEMPORARY ARCHITECTURE

## An Explorer's Guide

A map-based guide for
pavement-walking
architectural enthusiasts
to recent and accessible
London works, with occasional
references to other, nearby
significant buildings of all ages
that you might also be inclined to
enjoy.

## 6th Edition

**Kenneth Allinson**

**Victoria Thornton**

Routledge
Taylor & Francis Group

LONDON AND NEW YORK

First edition published 1994
by Architectural Press, Elsevier.

This edition published 2014
by Routledge
2 Park Square, Milton Park, Abingdon, Oxon, OX14 4RN

and by Routledge
711 Third Avenue, New York, NY 10017

Routledge is an imprint of the Taylor & Francis Group, an informa business

British Library Cataloguing in Publication Data
A catalogue record for this book is available from the British Library

Library of Congress Cataloging-in-Publication Data
Allinson, Kenneth, author.
London's contemporary architecture : an explorer's guide / Ken Allinson and Victoria
Thornton. -- Sixth Edition.
pages cm
Includes index.
"First edition published 1994 by Architectural Press, Elsevier."
1. Architecture--England--London--History--20th century--Guidebooks. 2. Architecture-
-England--London--History--21st century--Guidebooks. 3. London (England)--Buildings,
structures, etc.--Guidebooks. I. Thornton, Victoria, author. II. Title.
NA970.A4 2014
720'.94210904--dc23
2013043821

ISBN13: 978-0-415-82502-3 (pbk)
ISBN13: 978-1-315-77643-9 (ebk)

Publisher's note
This book has been prepared from camera-ready copy provided by the authors.

Printed by Bell and Bain Ltd, Glasgow

In memory of John Winter

# Contents

# This 6th Edition

## Who is this guide for?

The principal aim of this, the sixth guide to *London's Contemporary Architecture*, is to point the reader toward what is recent, worthy and reasonably accessible. Above all, the guide's aim is to get readers onto the street to experience architecture 'in the flesh'.

Wholly private and inaccessible buildings, i.e. where little or nothing can be seen, have been omitted, as have speculative projects. However, some buildings in construction at the time of writing have been included where these are deemed to be of significance and due for completion before or soon after publication.

Where well-designed buildings of *any* date are nearby, we have (presuming the reader is also interested in good architectural design of any period) made reference to the more significant of them (we wish there was space for more). Not all buildings from previous editions have been included.

The purpose of the maps is to indicate locations, but also to suggest that buildings can be visited as related groups.

We are grateful to all those architects, photographers, building managers and agents who have kindly supported this guide by providing information, graphic material and photographs. We have attempted to make attributions wherever possible and apologise, in advance, for any errors or omissions. Where attributions of photos have not been made, they are from public sources or belong to the authors.

Definitely for Abi, who is so curious & inquisitive!

Victoria T. X

9

# Using the Guide

## How to use the guide

Most of the architecture you will want to visit is in a relatively small and central area (see map opposite), usually with Zones 1,2 and 3 and what is referred to as the Inner Circular Road (i.e., the 80/20 Rule applies).

**A.** The City of London – the historic core of the metropolis – is, despite its monoculture, surprisingly rich in architectural interest to a degree that will surprise many foreign visitors. The peripheral fringe areas make an intriguing contrast and have, more recently, been witness to the overspill from traditional City boundaries.

**B.** East London and Docklands has many buildings of interest because of the last 30 years of regeneration. This continues as a key area for London's planners.

**C.** Apart from the City, the West End (developed from the late 17th century onward) is the most obvious and easiest area to explore. You will find this subdivided into two parts, A (East) and B (West), but it should be treated as a whole.

**D.** Then comes North, West and South Central London: areas embracing a ring of what were once village areas such as Camden, Angel, Fulham, Notting Hill, etc. The area south of the Thames has recently become especially interesting, particularly along the river itself and around places such as Elephant & Castle and Nine Elms. Surprisingly, West London has relatively fewer contemporary works of special interest.

**E.** Beyond this – but still within the M25 that circles London – are suburban areas where there are fewer buildings that you may consider worth travelling to. Our qualification is that enhanced transport links are making travel to outlying areas ever easier.

The typical listing for a building dating from 2000 onward would be as follows: building name; architect, address and year of completion; nearest transport (e.g. Tube, Rail, Overground or DLR). However, we do advise using the London Transport (TFL; http://www.tfl.gov. uk) website and the apps that are available (e.g. Citymapper).

### 1. City Information Point
Make Architects, 2008
St Paul's Churchyard, EC4
Tube: St Paul's

Since it would be unfair to ignore notable and nearby buildings of any other date (prior to 2000), we have also indicated these, but with grey headings, as follows:

### 2. Bracken House
Hopkins Architects, 1991
Friday Street, EC4
Tube: St Paul's

Transport is noted as **Tube, Rail, DLR or Overground**. The latter refers to a popular circular service run by Transport For London since 2007 (it is on Tube maps) and is not to be confused with traditional overground Rail services (also noted as Rail on Tube maps).

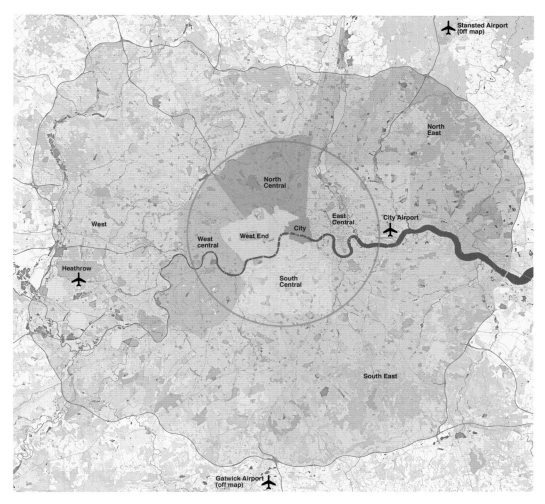

We have organised the guide as a series of distinct areas that begin with the City of London – London's historic core – and work out from there. Most of what you will want to see will be within travel zones 1 to 2 (rarely more than zone 3). Areas within zone 3 more or less includes the Inner London ring road and the area marked in orange in the above map. (Motorways do not penetrate further than this ring.)

The central area has been subdivided into smaller areas and a map provided for each.

You will, of course, find that some buildings are located near or on a boundary we have defined between one area and another.

Where necessary, we suggest use of the A–Z street guides or similar phone app equivalent.

London's four airports are: Heathrow (to the west, within the M25, marked on the above map and accessible by Rail from Paddington or by Tube); City Airport (located in East London at the east end of the Royal Docks and accessible by DLR); Gatwick (to the south of London, just outside of the M25, not indicated on the map and best accessed by train from Victoria Station); and Stansted (located to the north-east of London, off the M11, also not indicated on the map and accessed by Rail from Liverpool Street Station).

For travel assistance and the Tube travel zones see:
http://www.tfl.gov.uk/gettingaround/1106.aspx
and
http://www.london-tubemap.com/fare_zone.php
and
http://wikitravel.org/en/London

# A Patterned Metropolis

Generalisations are intended to be sufficiently valid to be heuristically beneficial. It is with this in mind that we can claim there is a simple pattern to London's urban topography. The easiest way to explain this is as a narrative of the kind Victor Hugo once gave of Paris and which inspired John Summerson to give a similar one for London.

Summerson began his story 2000 years ago, looking down from an air-balloon upon a green, wooded landscape and a meandering river. And then the Romans arrive, trundling up from the south coast, finding a river crossing and making a settlement: *Londinium*, with a fortress where Wood Street now stands and a temple where, it is said, St Paul's Cathedral is now located.

The Romans left, and the natives returned, eventually reclaiming the settlement, rebuilding a bridge across the river and constituting a trading town that grew in prosperity – until, that is, new invaders arrived: the Normans, descendants of Viking warriors who had settled in France and now came to England in order to lay claim to the English crown.

Conscious of the fact that the last English king had been crowned in a 7th-century monastery dedicated to St Peter and located upon unhealthy marshes adjacent to the River Thames at what is now Westminster, the Normans came around London and settled there. Meanwhile, they constructed a threatening fortress on the river and at the eastern edge of the existing settlement: the Tower of London. Thus, some 1000 years ago the fundamental pattern of London's urban topography had been set in place: a royal palace and a monastery in the west, and an independent trading settlement in the east, with its own significant church – St Paul's Cathedral – and an impressive fortress representing the power of the monarch watching over the pretensions to independence enjoyed by London's citizens.

At Westminster the monarchy gathered a court of nobles around itself, later a Parliament and then a governmental administration, all in the same area. Meanwhile, the historic city prospered and carried on life very much as a state within a state. This trading wealth and associated influence gathered momentum in the seventeenth century, blossoming into the beginnings of a global trading empire.

At the beginning of that period London suffered its famous fire (in 1666), which consumed two-thirds of the old city. King and courtiers had grand plans for rebuilding, but the citizens didn't wait: they got on with rebuilding their dense, noisy and polluted city – now as brick town-houses, with minimal timber. However, the most affluent took the opportunity to move westward into new suburban areas owned by aristocratic courtiers eager to capitalise upon urban expansion.

Inigo Jones (1573-1652), masque designer and architect to Charles I, who introduced Renaissance 'regularity' to London in the mid-17th century.

The novelty of this new era was a regularity imposed upon speculative property

development by Charles I and his favoured architect, Inigo Jones (at Covent Garden, during the 1640s). However, subsequent urban regularity was arguably the product of a more or less common taste, together with strict building regulations drawn up by architects, thus engendering that late 16th to early 19th century regularity we label as 'Georgian': squares and row upon row of terraced speculative town-houses – a 'vertical' kind of living that amused foreign visitors and later bored the Victorian era.

On the opposite, eastern, side of the historic core there was an entirely different kind of development. Ship traffic came up the River Thames from this direction, as far as London Bridge. As a result, everything to do with shipping traffic, ship repair, warehousing and the industries thriving upon a closeness to where goods came in and departed were located in this area: what became known as an East End set in contrast to the West End.

With the prospect of employment came immigration and dense populations of the poor who breathed in the coal-fire smoke that had served Londoners since the Middle Ages and which the prevailing south-west wind blew in their direction. A simple pattern was set that, more or less, has persisted into the 21st century: in the west, near to where monarchs reside and the government sits, are the healthiest and wealthiest in the United Kingdom; to the east, in areas of industrial employment, immigration and poor living conditions has been witness to the deprivation side-by-side huge docks and warehouses, mostly constructed in a period between the 1790s and the late 1820s.

By the 1850s the United Kingdom had 7000 miles of railway track, some of it pushing its way toward and into London. Within the metropolis the Metropolitan Line arrived in 1863, carrying traders and bankers from their residences in the west into the City. The horse-drawn omnibus was followed by motorised buses and, finally, the motor-car. London, founded upon the benefits of general trade, slavery and sea power, now had the opportunity to spread as never before – so much so that expansion had to be contained within a 'green-belt' and then a ring motorway (the M25).

At the heart of what became a city of over 8 million people and the largest in Europe, there was still a simple twin-poled organisation set alongside the River Thames (by now polluted and stinking). Today, that river has been cleaned up and the embankments have become promenades that – particularly on the south side – stretch for long distances up and down river. What was once the life-blood of the capital now serves as a symbolic artery about which the beast of the metropolis pulses.

In part, that change has come about because of a de-industrialisation of London and the closure of docks that began in 1970, in the process engendering enormous physical and social problems over the East End. Regenerating that area has been going on ever since – hence

Canary Wharf, built in the late 1980s – and the site of the Olympic Park for the 2012 Games (at Stratford, directly north of Canary Wharf). That regeneration need has altered the character of London, but without changing a polarisation between the governmental West End and the trading function of the City (where only 8500 people now reside).

If you were to go to Tower Hill and look about you the signs of this 2000-year history would be all around (as well as fine work from Stanton Williams Architects, with a restaurant from Tony Fretton Architects just out of view, by the river): a Medieval wall on Roman foundations; the Tower of London; the former Port of London Authority building, with a huge statue of Neptune on top; a war memorial by Edwin Lutyens to sailors who died in WWI; the Mayor's city Hall, designed by Norman Foster; office buildings where people still trade; Trinity House, a building of 1796, representing the organisation managing the lighthouses around Britain's shores since the 16th century; St Katharine's Dock, the last, smallest and most expensive of the great docks, built in the 1820s; a highway system that suddenly changes, marking a shift from the historic street pattern of the City to the eastern fringe historically occupied by immigrants and now dominated by the Bangladeshi community.

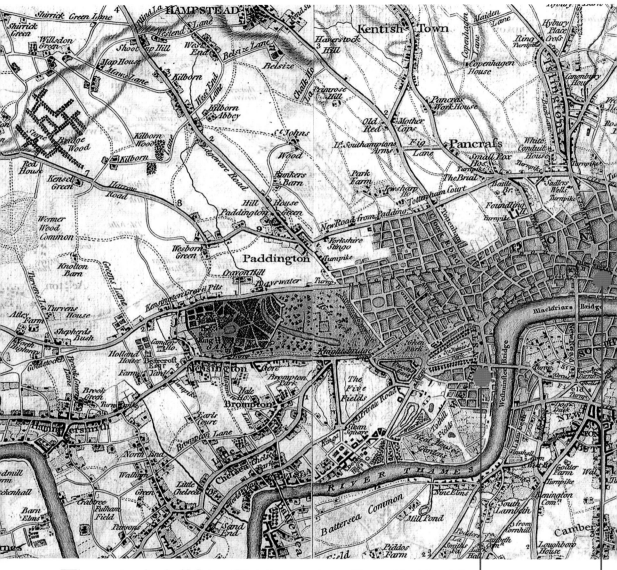

The monastery church of St Peter, at Westminster marshes, on Thorney Island, founded in the 7th century. and now opposite the Houses of Parliament. The first English king to be crowned here was Edward the Confessor (1042). The Norman invaders continued this tradition, since when the church has enjoyed national significance.

The Cathedral of St Paul on Ludgate Hill, in the City. This was again founded in the 7th-century and (unverified) tradition has it that the building is located on the site of a Roman temple to Diana. The route between St Peter's and St Paul's (along the Mall, the Strand and Fleet street) is an occasional ceremonial way which, again, follows a traditional route between Westminster – where the monarchy, Parliament and government come together – and the City of London. Historically, the City has subsisted as a semi-independent state-within-a-state – a status continued in its economic role and in many ceremonial traditions.

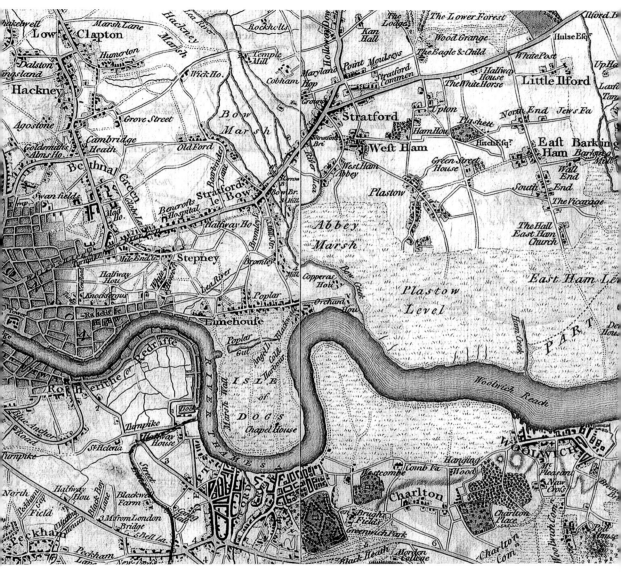

Toward the end of the Enlightenment London was the capital city of a United Kingdom on the brink of forming an empire that, just after WWI, controlled almost one-third of the globe's population. When Cary drew his map, London was a city of 900,000 people: a brick-and-stone city without walls, surrounded by market gardens and brick fields whose fires glowed at night. At its heart was the Thames and the two churches serving as the principal reference points of London's urban topography and power politics – now represented by the City of London's economic power, and the monarchical and political powers concentrated at Westminster. Note that the map shows a burgeoning development of the West End, well before the 19th-century development of Kensington and Chelsea (now London's most affluent areas). Also note that the great docks had not yet been constructed (c.1790-1830) and shipping had clear travel up to London Bridge. A bridge at Westminster had been completed in 1750, and a third, Blackfriars, in 1769. Additionally, note the developments on the south side of the River Thames and the roads linking all three and a river crossing in use at Lambeth since the Middle Ages.

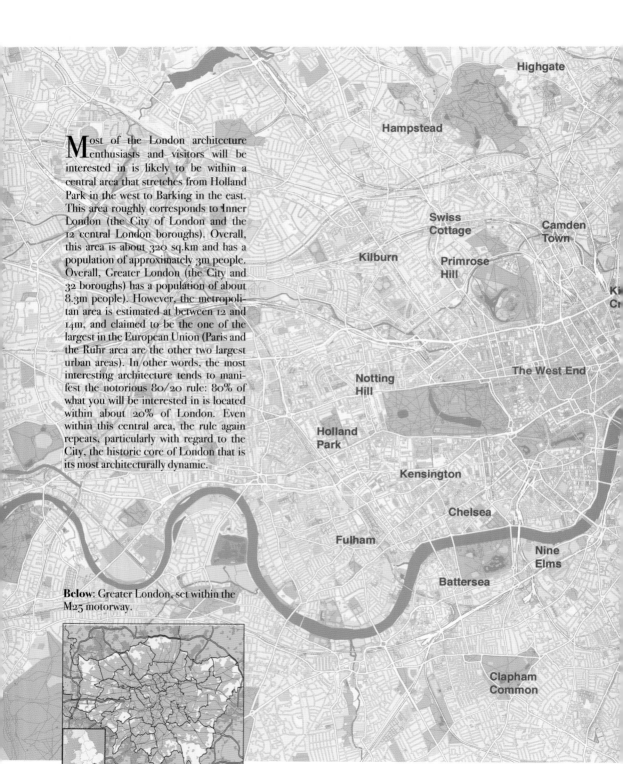

Most of the London architecture enthusiasts and visitors will be interested in is likely to be within a central area that stretches from Holland Park in the west to Barking in the east. This area roughly corresponds to Inner London (the City of London and the 12 central London boroughs). Overall, this area is about 320 sq.km and has a population of approximately 3m people. Overall, Greater London (the City and 32 boroughs) has a population of about 8.3m people). However, the metropolitan area is estimated at between 12 and 14m, and claimed to be the one of the largest in the European Union (Paris and the Ruhr area are the other two largest urban areas). In other words, the most interesting architecture tends to manifest the notorious 80/20 rule: 80% of what you will be interested in is located within about 20% of London. Even within this central area, the rule again repeats, particularly with regard to the City, the historic core of London that is its most architecturally dynamic.

**Below**: Greater London, set within the M25 motorway.

Highgate

Hampstead

Swiss Cottage

Camden Town

Kilburn

Primrose Hill

Ki Cr

Notting Hill

The West End

Holland Park

Kensington

Chelsea

Fulham

Nine Elms

Battersea

Clapham Common

# A Contemporary Context

The previous version of this guide was published in 2009 and much has changed since we handed that work over to the publishers in late 2008. In fact, it is surprising how architectural cares, concerns and fashions shift so rapidly. For example, recent years have particularly been witness to a fashion for subtle proportions and the use of brickwork. We see this in many new apartment buildings, in schools, office buildings and, generally, as a new care given to careful proportionality. On the other hand, there are still enthusiasms for curves (e.g. Hadid at the Serpentine), 'stealth' and 'crystalline' geometries (e.g. Wilkinson Eyre Architects at the Royal Docks, Herzog & de Meuron at the Tate Modern, and O'Donnell & Tuomey for the LSE), and variations on surface patterning correlated with offset openings and even structural grids.

Among the 'grand old men' of the profession (sorry, they do continue to be men), Baron Rogers of Riverside (Rogers Stirk Harbour+Partners) continues to consistently employ a 'served-and-servant' equation that has served them well for decades (from the Lloyds '86 building to the remarkable Leadenhall skyscraper); the Sir Michael Hopkins' team continues with an equally consistent and recognisably individuated approach to the practice's output (e.g. the municipal offices at Wembley and a library in Stratford); and the office of Baron Foster of Thames Bank provides a prolific if more varied body of work (from the ME hotel to the City's Willis building). Grimshaw and Farrell also continue to provide London with new buildings (although Farrell is now more notable as a master planner).

Among the next generation now dominating the profession in London are substantial practices such as Eric Parry, John McAslan+Partners, Lifschutz Davidson Sandilands, Feilden Clegg Bradley, Bennetts Associates, Stanton Williams, AHMM and Allies & Morrison (with

the latter being among the most stylistically consistent). Just behind them, Maccreanor Lavington, Haworth Tompkins, Hawkins Brown and Sergison Bates are representative of admirably sober concerns while, in contrast, the work of firms such as dRMM, Amanda Levete, Will Alsop, Egret West and Zaha Hadid are (for disparate reasons) distinctly more exuberant. And then there are firms such as Make Architects – who have an individuated and bold approach that, as they say, takes no prisoners – or the ever-impressive body of works from Alison Brooks, Duggan Morris, 6A Architects, Niall McLaughlin, Tim Ronalds and similar architects.

Another contrast is the difference between sleek, carefully-fashioned buildings – whether from Allies & Morrison or Foster – and a taste for heavily textured, shabby-chic interiors which manifest boredom with the paradigm of polished, unscratched, low-tolerance constructions (one thinks of Village Underground or interiors within the Tea Building, such as the Pizza East restaurant, Shoreditch House, etc.)

In other words London, as ever, is not a consistent scene of architectural discourse and activity. If there is a consistent note it is perhaps the long-term erosion of the architect's project authority. Nowadays the game is about branding.

Overall, however, the message is a good one: you, as architect, enthusiast or visitor to London can go out onto its streets and play your own, personal game of 'joining-the-dots' in order to construct personal architectural meanings from this richly varied body of contemporary work. It is then possible that, like us, you will wonder in amazement at the peculiarity of an urban beast that seems to have a life all of its own and whose architecture complements the city's cultural diversity – beneath which is a simple polar underpinning at the heart of the city's urban geography.

# Indicative
# changes

This sixth edition of **London's Contemporary Architecture** marks a 20-year period since the first publication in 1994), toward the end of a deep recession not dissimilar to the post-financial crisis period experienced from 2008. In the intervening years London's architects experienced an unprecedented boom period. Now, once again the capital is flourishing. In part, the reason for the city's unique economic status is that London has become a safe haven for foreign capital. In the period up to mid-2013 more than three-quarters of new homes in the city centre were being sold to overseas buyers, off plan, with more than half going to those in the Far East. Other investors typically came from the Middle East, such as Qatar. Their investments include Harrods, Canary Wharf Tower, the Shard, Sainsbury, Camden Market, the former US embassy in Grosvenor Square, the Shell Centre, the London Stock Exchange, One Hyde Park apartment block, Chelsea Barracks and the Athletes' Village at the 2012 Games – all of which is, bizarrely, as much a defence strategy as a property investment (Qatar remembers the invasion of Kuwait and optimistically expects the UK government to protect its former protectorate).

However inflows into London include people as well as capital. London is increasingly a multicultural city. Since the late 1980s – when planners were still enabling suburban housing typologies in central areas such as Surrey Quays – London has been experiencing massive population growth and a desire to live centrally. The population is now 8.3m; by 2019 it is expected to be 9m (although this is hardly more than the population in 1939). Over the next twenty years the number of households is expected

to increase by nearly 700,000, generating an estimated annual net housing requirement for 32,600 homes (in addition to a need for schools, hospitals, shops, jobs and workplaces, etc.). As a consequence, official policy has been forced to increase planning densities.

As an example of this shift, in the mid-1990s only about 25% of British housing was apartments; the remainder was traditional terraced and semi-detached suburban housing. Since then the situation has been reversed: most of what we now build are apartments. And many terraced, former Victorian family homes are now apartment buildings.

Housing developments are now taking place all over London. Smaller infill projects are everywhere and tall housing blocks are becoming commonplace (at the time of writing we are told that over 230 buildings of twenty stories or more are in the planning pipeline). We not only see major developments in Docklands, but in locations such as Battersea and Nine Elms, Kings Cross and Elephant & Castle, Kilburn, Stratford, etc. And this housing is increasingly expensive, subjecting inner London areas such as Brixton, Peckham, Hackney and Walthamstow to the forces of gentrification. Meanwhile, the domestic tastes of Londoners have dramatically altered. If one examines 1980s Docklands housing you will see new apartment blocks trying to look like old ones and new terraced housing at no more than three storeys, with small windows; no one wanted to live in tall buildings. Today, the most desirable residence is a glazed penthouse with wide terraces, at the top of a tower overlooking the River Thames.

While housing demand dominates the entirety of London, areas such as the Square Mile and Canary Wharf are enjoying a renewed appetite for tall office buildings. Three new ones stand out, literally and metaphorically: Renzo Piano's Shard; Rogers Stirk Harbour+Partners' 'Cheesegrater' in Leadenhall; and Rafael Vinoly's 'Walkie Talkie' in Fenchurch Street. Meanwhile, the City is manifesting two other significant changes since the 1980s and 1990s: the efforts of City planners to reintroduce retail space and set the City in competition with Canary Wharf (as at Jean Nouvel's One New Change), and a host of supplementary developments that include hotels, cafés, bars, restaurants, clubs and, surprisingly, even new residences. The most prominent of the latter (adding to a City population concentrated in the Barbican area) is The Heron residential tower designed by David Walker. (The traditional London leasehold system mitigates against a mix of offices – which might have a comparatively short life-span – and residences, which one expects to last much longer.)

The City fringes also continue to change. While architects are still in Clerkenwell, to the north-east, development continues on the south bank of the River Thames near to the Tate Modern (where the Herzog & de Meuron extension is being completed), and the Shoreditch area has also experienced a new spurt of development since the opening of the Shoreditch Overground station, opposite AHMM's remarkably successful Tea building. The City continues to push out in every direction, horizontally as well as vertically.

All this growth and development is totally dependent upon London's infrastructure. For example, diversification of development away from the City and Docklands is being fed by the new Crossrail network which began construction in 2009 and will be complete by 2018, having constructed 42km of tunnels through the heart of London. Each of Crossrail's trains will be 200m long (twice as long as an Underground train) and carry 1500 people. Up to 24 of these will run each hour, supplementing the London rail network capacity by 10%. And, of course, investors have been busy acquiring property along the route since before construction began.

At the opposite end of the transport scale is bicycles. Cycling has increased 175% since 2001 and is ever more popular (by the end of 2013 there were 11,000 Barclays ('Boris') hire bikes in London). However, cycling remains more dangerous than it needs to be – hence efforts to improve routes and junctions, and realise some key ambitions: a better London for everyone; a 'Tube' network of routes for bicyclists ('a Crossrail for bikes'); safer streets for bikes; and more people travelling by bike.

By the time we publish a seventh edition of this guide London will probably feel the same, but will be looking very different.

# The City:
# London's
# Historic Core

St Paul's Cathedral

Bank

Leadenhall
Building

Willis
Building

Lloyds '86
Building

Tower 42

Barbican

Moorhouse

Gherkin

Broadgate

Image courtesy of Rogers Stirk Harbour+Partners

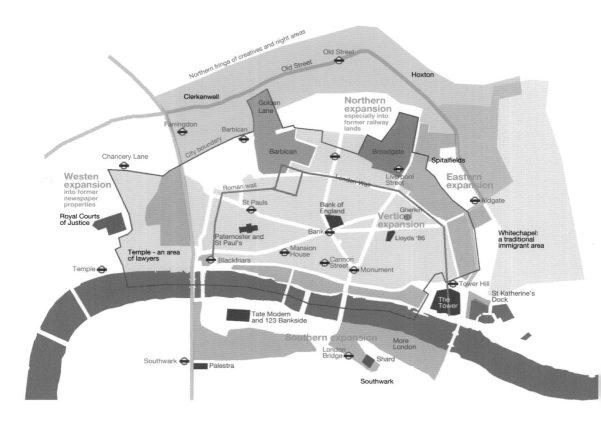

The symbol and geographical heart of the City is at Bank – the location of the Bank of England. Traditionally, one was meant to have a respectable address that lay within a ten-minute walk of Bank – which is, more or less, the distance to the old Roman wall that wrapped the City from the Tower of London to Blackfriars (built about AD 200 and mostly demolished in the 18th and 19th centuries).

For most of its history City inhabitants turned their backs on the River Thames, its shipping and warehouses. This introverted character did not alter until the mid-1980s when, during the so-called 'Big Bang' of banking deregulation, the City expanded in every direction: pushing out, going upward and even leap-frogging across the River Thames. Today, the inner heart of the City is a conservation area of office buildings littered with old graveyards and churches, many of them by Wren and built between 1670 and 1700. And, around that heartland is a series of fringe areas with quite different characters. Overall, the area is increasingly like a set of concentric circles centred on Bank.

• The eastern geographic boundary is Farringdon Road, beyond which is Fleet Street, an area occupied by lawyers since the Middle Ages (Temple). When the newspapers left in the 1970s and 1980s, the sites of printing works became office buildings (what estate agents incongruously like to call 'Mid-Town').

• To the north-west is Smithfield and Clerkenwell – land of architects, designers and furniture showrooms. The Barbican and Golden Lane estates are here.

• Further around, to the north-east, is Broadgate and the peculiarity of Shoreditch and Hoxton: a mostly run-down area of high rents the government and estate agents would like to label 'Tech-City'. The Sunday Colombia flower market is in this area.

• Hoxton quickly becomes a traditional area of immigration that forms the eastern boundary between the bankers and a Bangladeshi community – an area including Spitalfields and Brick Lane.

• Following around, we come to the Tower of London and St Katharine's Dock, and then – across the River Thames – More London and a strip of regeneration that includes Southwark Cathedral and the Tate Modern, bringing us back to Blackfriars Bridge.

Photo: courtesy of Bennett Associates ( Peter Cook)

**Above**: New Street Square, Fetter Lane, by Bennett Associates – an instance of westward expansion and one of the City's more outstanding recent developments (2009). The Square is located on the edge of the district of lawyers that sits between the City and the West End, comprising disparate buildings by the same architect, set around a simple urban square. It has been noted that some ground-floor areas are unnecessarily grand and largely empty entrance lobbies that achieve very little for anyone (and for which the architect was not responsible), but this is otherwise an admirable urban development. Beware of security guards eager to inform you that a photograph can't be taken within the boundaries of the development – what looks public but is, in fact, private, as are many such developments in London. In fact, there is no curtailment of photographing as such. Simply walk to the perimeter, to a public pavement, and photograph from there. (Yes, it is all rather silly.)

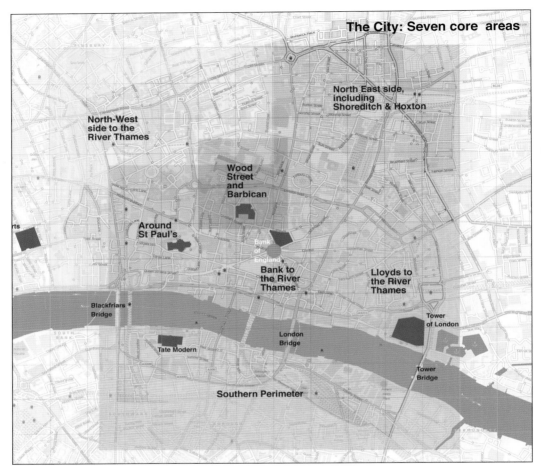

The City: Seven core areas

We have divided the area in and around the City of London into eight subgroups and provided a small local map for each area. The south, north-east and west are mixed fringe areas.

**Note**: being adjacent to one another, these areas can overlap and are simply meant to identify an area's character and groupings of buildings.

**1. Around St Paul's**
Including Paternoster, One New Change, etc.

**2. Wood Street and the Barbican**
This group is centred where the old Roman fort was located and includes buildings by Rogers, Foster, Farrells, Grimshaw, etc., including the Barbican and Golden Lane housing (where most of the City population lives).

**3. Bank to the River Thames**
From the geographical heart of the City to the river.

**4. Lloyds to the River Thames**
This area is centred on a group of tall buildings near to the Lloyds '86 building, going down to the River Thames.

**5. North-East Side**
The northern edges of the City and its expansion to the north-east around Broadgate, toward Spitalfields.

It is centred on the Broadgate development and on the Shoreditch triangle.

**6. Shoreditch and Hoxton**
The fringe area to the very north-east of the City, centred on 'The Shoreditch Triangle'.

**7. North-West Side to the River Thames**
This is really an extension of the northern part of the City, as it runs into Islington and Hackney boroughs. It also extends westward into Fleet Street and Smithfield areas.

**8. Southern Perimeter**
This group covers the exceptional extension of office buildings over the river, especially to Bankside 123 and to More London. It includes the Tate Modern on the west side and the mixed former docklands area of Butlers Wharf to the east of Tower Bridge.

Around St Paul's Cathedral

Wood Street and the Barbican

Bank to the River Thames

Lloyds to the River Thames

North-East Side

Shoreditch and Hoxton

North-West Side to the River Thames

Southern Perimeter

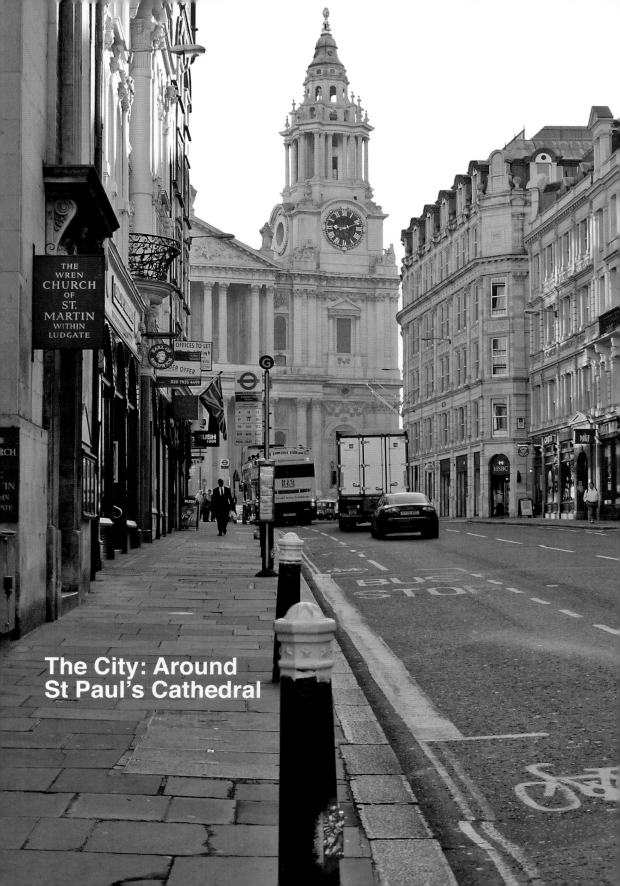

The City: Around
St Paul's Cathedral

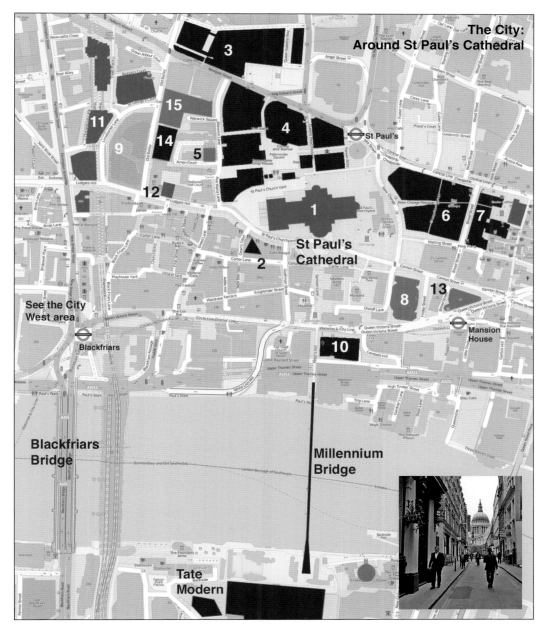

St Paul's

St Paul's
Cathedral

See the City
West area

Blackfriars

Mansion
House

Blackfriars
Bridge

Millennium
Bridge

Tate
Modern

Most things in this area have to do with St Paul's and its dome – a more potent symbol to Londoners than, say, the Houses of Parliament. From this area one can go in three principal directions: south, across the Millennium Bridge, to the Tate Modern and other buildings in that area, south of the River Thames; north-east, to the Wood Street area; or eastward, toward the Bank group.

Going westward leads into Fleet Street and the Inns of Court. Going north leads to Smithfield and Clerkenwell (an area dense with architectural practices).

It is worth noting that 'the Square Mile' is currently linked to one in six jobs in the capital; that 9200 people currently live within the City boundary and that 340,000 people work there.

## 1. St Paul's Cathedral
Christopher Wren, 1700
Ludgate Hill, EC4
Tube: St Paul's

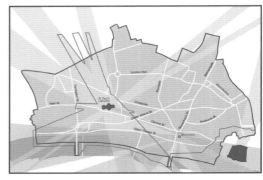

London has many important buildings of historic importance, but one of them – St Paul's Cathedral – is also of deep contemporary significance. Until comparatively recently, the church dominated London's skyline – hence protection by a series of 'strategic viewing corridors' and height controls all around its location, all set within a 'view management framework' that look toward its dome (diagram right). The St Paul's Heights, for example, restricts buildings to between 20 and 52m above datum. (The very top of the dome is approximately 128m above datum.)

Overall, City controls on development embrace conservation areas, ancient monuments, parks, 'river prospects', etc., and adopt a picturesque approach to protecting the character of the City. These are incorporated within the 'London View Management Framework'. The degree to which these views are respected is a moot point (the most notable recent example being the Shard, which sits in the corridor from Parliament Hill, right behind the dome). On the other hand, some architects take an inventive attitude to these controls. The overall form of Jean Nouvel's One New Change building, for example, is derived from the Heights (along with the site boundaries, daylight guidelines and rights of light issues), filling the allowable volume to the maximum and thus engendering what Nouvel enthusiastically likened to a 'stealth' geometry. Another example is the Rogers Stirk Harbour+Partners Leadenhall 'Cheesegrater', which leans backward in order to retain a view from the east (in the process engendering some interesting pigeon deposit issues!).

## 2. City Information Point
Make Architects, 2008
St Paul's Churchyard, EC4
Tube: St Paul's

The simple City Information Point outside of St Paul's was Make's first London building after Ken Shuttleworth walked away from the Foster office. Though rather sub-Libeskind and dramatically different to any aspect of St Paul's, it holds its own very well and is a fine building. Nouvel possibly thought so when designing One New Change in a similar 'stealth' geometry. (One wonders why architects are so fascinated by these military associations.)

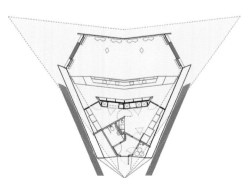

## 3. Merrill Lynch
Swanke Hayden Connell and David Walker Architects, 2001
2 King Edward Street, EC1
Tube: St Paul's

The Merrill Lynch complex is an admirable scheme compromised by security constraints that stop one doing what the design intended, namely walking through the lobby and along a small rear alley that sits behind (and runs parallel to) the retained buildings on Holborn Viaduct (still with shops below small rooms used for meetings). The scheme also retains a rather large Post Office building on King Edward Street (opposite 'Postman's Park' – one of the City's hidden-away green spaces). When completed the complex (designed to, if necessary, be broken up into discrete buildings) was the best example in the City of how to provide huge trading floors (at the time, the largest in Europe) without going high (which, in any case, it couldn't do because of the proximity to St Paul's). This was one of the first London office buildings to have a now *de rigueur* roof terrace for entertaining. Try walking all around and into the rear street (if only as far as the entrance lobby); or use a shop or café to walk through; however, don't take photos once you are within the site boundary – the security guards get alarmed.

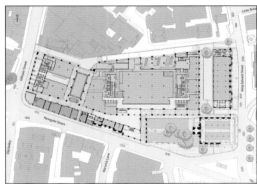

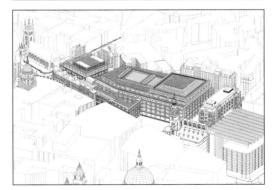

## 4. Paternoster Square

Various architects, 2001
Paternoster Square, EC4
Tube: St Paul's

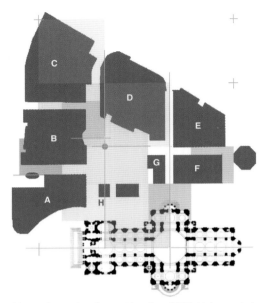

Paternoster was the child of Prince Charles, intended to show what was possible and demonstrate his care and concern for St Paul's. As you can imagine, it was long in gestation, finally realised as a masterplan designed by Sir William Whitfield (a rather good architect who diplomatically remarked: "I set out to do something that was fundable, buildable and lettable. Of course it's a compromise in some respects, but if it weren't, nothing would have been built at all").

The architects called upon included Allies and Morrison, Rolfe Judd, Eric Parry (with Sheppard Robson), MJP (whose Warwick Place is possibly the best building here) and Whitfield himself (with Sheppard Robson and Sidell Gibson). The masterplan (which includes Wren's resurrected Temple Bar gateway, once sat across Fleet Street) is actually quite good, but the whole enterprise has a tired feel about it and, along the south frontage facing onto St Paul's, Whitfield's Juxon House is alarmingly under-scaled, as if five-eighths full size (no doubt in conformance with today's floor-to-ceiling conventions in office buildings). Only Heatherwick's sculptural vent (west side), and the Parry and MacCormac buildings have something fresh to say. Having said that – and despite the project's history – Paternoster is quite a pleasant place and one suspects its urbane gamesmanship receives more respect than most architects are willing to admit.

Compare with New Street Square, Paddington Basin, Regent's Place, Canary Wharf, Broadgate, More London, etc., all of which are similar private developments offering ostensibly public space. Kings Cross is a modified version of such developments, demonstrating more effort to intermix private and public ownership and adoption of spaces.

**Above:** the master plans put together. Whitfield demonstrates a whole series of geometrical relationships that are, in turn, rooted in the geometries of St Paul's. **A.** Whitfield's Juxon House. **B.** the MJP building (Warwick Court). **C.** by Rolfe Judd. **D.** Eric Parry's Stock Exchange building (King Edward Court). **E.** Allies and Morrison (St Martin's Court; not A&M at their best). **F.** Whitfield, with Siddell Gibson. **G.** Whitfield & Sidell Gibson, **H.** Wren's Temple Bar gateway (1672).

**Above:** Paternoster from the dome of St Paul's. **A.** is the MJP Architects building, Warwick Court (quite unlike most City office buildings and more like their Oxbridge work). **B.** is by Eric Parry: 10 Paternoster Square, (a design that reminds one of Terragni, in fascist Italy). **C.** is Sir Christopher Wren's late 17th-century Temple Bar gateway building (in Fleet Street until demolished in 1878). **D.** is Sir William Whitfield's Juxon House. Compare the latter with Whitfield's 1960s work for the Institute of Chartered Accountants (supplementing the work of John Belcher, Beresford Pite and, especially, John James Joass) in Great Swan Alley, EC3. The principal criticism of this view has been that no one seemed to remember the roofs.

## 5. Amen Lodge

Warwick Lane, EC4
Norman Bailey & Partners, 1961
Tube: St Paul's

On the west side of Paternoster, corner of Warwick Lane, Ave Maria Lane and Amen Corner, there is a much-admired building attributed to an architect better known for cinemas. For some reason Pevsner describes it as 'Brutalist' (i.e., he didn't like it).

**Top left**: view to Temple Bar. **Above**: axial view to the dome of St Paul's. **Left**: section through MJP's Warwick Court. **Bottom left**: plan of Warwick Court. **Bottom right**: Thomas Heatherwick's sculptural ventilation shaft.

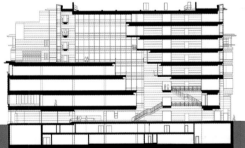

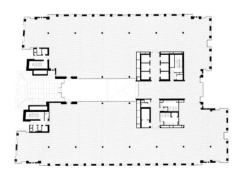

### 6. One New Change

Ateliers Jean Nouvel, 2011
Cheapside and New Change, EC4
Tube: St Paul's

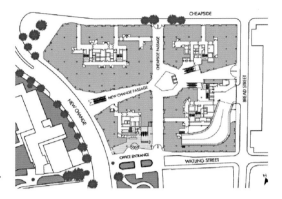

In Dickens' lifetime Cheapside was the most important shopping street in London. Now, the City would like to see it return to something like its former status. Why? If for no other reason than the success of the retailing at the City's competitor in Docklands: Canary Wharf. And what more logical place to introduce such retail content than adjacent to St Paul's?

The brief for the competition on this site required a mix of retail, offices and a public viewing deck – all of it within the tight height controls around St Paul's Cathedral. Nouvel won by offering a design that (so the story goes) fitted the allowable building envelope to the millimetre and conceiving of a glass cladding that would wrap up the sides and over the top of his 'stealth' building.

In plan, the scheme fills an entire urban block but makes a major nod in reference to the Cathedral: a 'slot' in the western side that orients the entire building toward the dome of St Paul's. This is both the scheme's success and weakness.

The scheme is almost diagrammatic, reliant upon one or two gestures, ignoring the other references all around which it might have acknowledged. And its appearance is rather daunting. However, it is hard not to the overall success, especially the shopping content (although a cruciform plan is less than ideal) and the uniqueness of an upper-level public deck. In between, there is a set of huge U-shaped floor plates which, frankly, are rather ordinary and witness to a loss of nerve manifest as an irrelevant atrium to the upper parts.

The cladding does not, in fact, wrap the entire building and over a roof that necessarily becomes the scene of vents, residual green areas and four gigantic concealed service cranes that emerge from individual silos to cantilever 43m out toward the perimeter.

The finishes employed are not uninteresting, including polished plaster offset against expanded metal. In addition, the cladding is a technical achievement that incorporates 4300 unique panels within an overall total of 6500 units.

Overall, Nouvel's design provides 52,024 sqm of accommodation, of which 20,500 sqm is retail space and 30,700 sqm is offices.

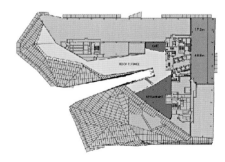

Go there on a sunny, warm day when you can enjoy the restaurants, cafés and a very pleasant view ... then perhaps go over to the Cathedral, climb to the top, and look down upon the roof-level of One New Change.

**Above**: ground floor; mid-floor; mid-floor with financial services layout; roof plan.

**Above**: One New Change from St Paul's. **Below**: St Paul's from One New Change, looking back west, through the 'slot'.

## 7. Bow Bells House
David Walker Architects, 2008
46-52 Cheapside, EC2
Tube: St Paul's

## 8. Bracken House
Hopkins Architects, 1991
Friday Street, EC4
Tube: St Paul's

Bow Bells House sits adjacent to the Wren church (St Mary Le Bow, 1683) and, on the west side, One New Change. It typifies Walker's current work: simple, elegant, with clean proportions and slim details (and utterly different to its other neighbour, One New Change). Walker is an interesting architect to follow in the City: Deutsche Bank (with Swanke Hayden), Merrill Lynch (ditto), One Coleman Street, Riverbank House and the latest: The Heron residential tower. Unfortunately, like most 'shell' archi-tects, Walker gets pushed aside by others undertaking the inter-nal fit-outs.

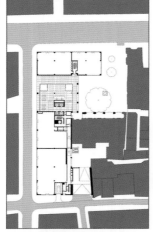

The adjacent Bow Bells church (by Wren) has an impres-sive spire that con-trasts with a somewhat ordinary interior.

An adaptation of the offices and printing works of the Financial Times, a building originally designed by Albert Richardson (1952). Only the two office wings were retained and the central area replaced by new open spaces around a central lift core (providing about 23,500 sqm of floor space). The interesting part of the architecture is the 'load-bearing' façade and the fineness of its detailing. Everything here is 'what–you–see–is–what–you–get', even the stone-bearing pillars. Overall, the building is a fine example of contexturalism, referencing the history of the building, the retained (north and south) parts

and an historical context whilst informing Prince Charles that a contempo-rary façade *can* be load-bearing and interesting. The building's style (and its concerns) may no longer be in topical, but this remains an intrigu-ing achievement. Look closely.

Photo courtesy of David Walker (Timothy Soar)

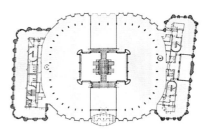

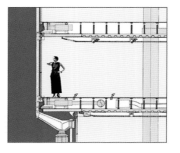

## Ludgate Hill

Ludgate Hill is a sub-area in this grouping near to St Paul's. To the west we have Paternoster and Bailey's 1961 building, then Avery's 7–10 Old Bailey, adjacent to McMorran & Whitby's Old Bailey extension; then a new site at One and Two Ludgate Hill, from Fletcher Priest and the German-English firm of Sauerbruch & Hutton; then a string of SOM buildings from the early 1990s through to 2007. It's quite a mix and typical of London.

### 9. Ludgate Hill
Fletcher Priest Architects / Sauerbruch & Hutton, 2014
Ludgate Hill, EC1
Tube: St Paul's

Two new office blocks from two well-known practices: Sauerbruch & Hutton (who designed the rear block, No.2) and Fletcher Priest (No.1), who now have quite a few buildings in the City. Although each building looks different to its twin, the interiors are (as one might expect) very similar (providing about 2100 sqm). Both play façade games with deep fins. FP provide a 10s variation of the podium+(squat) tower equation with deep white fins claimed to match in with the deep façades of older neighbours. SH (also providing a 10s building) give us their usual highly coloured branding, but now as motorised 'active' fins. In between is an oddly named 'piazzetta'.

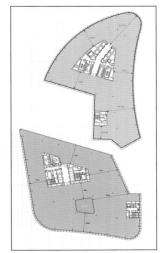

The building is in construction at the time of writing. It will be SH's first in London, but joins a growing list of FP buildings in the City (such as One Wood Street).

### 10. Salvation Army Global HQ
Sheppard Robson, 2005
Queen Victoria Street, EC4 (Millennium Bridge Approach)
Tube: St Paul's or Mansion House

How times have changed: a shrunken HQ, but with a café, etc. in the basement and offices above, all constrained within the St Paul's heights and paid for by selling off part of the site, to the east.

## 11. Limeburner Lane
SOM, 1993–2007
Limeburner Lane/Fleet Place, EC1
Tube: St Paul's

A curious run of buildings (see 11a to 11d on the map on page 37) that begin on the south-west corner of Ludgate Hill with one of the worst Po-Mo buildings in London, then crosses the road to a design whose stone façade looks as if it were from 1910, then continues to a neighbour at 10 Fleet Place (a 10s, 16,700 sqm black building) and then further up Limeburner Lane to other buildings at Fleet Place, e.g., the white-framed no. 1 Fleet Place. The most recent building is no.5 (2007). They are an eclectic bunch and (apart from 10 Fleet Place) tend to slip off SOM's current portfolio. These contrasts, from one SOM building to another, will soon be contrasted again by neighbours designed from Sauerbruch & Hutton and Fletcher Priest. Fashions in architecture change fast.

## 12. St Martin Ludgate
Christopher Wren, 1684
Ludgate Hill, EC1
Tube: St Paul's

This is a rather a neglected church, but you have to see it as one of a long series that Wren's office churned out after the Great Fire of 1666. Set it into that context – every site and situation a unique challenge – and this church (possessing the opposite of St Paul's grandeur) comes to life (if you work at it!). The contrasts are the likes of St Stephen Walbrook and St Lawrence Jewry, both fully restored. The basic plan is not so dissimilar to St Stephen Walbrook. However, this church is land-locked and only has access to daylight at the rear. Otherwise the plan has, of course, to strive toward a westward orientation (on that point compare with Wrens St Stephen Walbrook and Hawksmoor's St. George, in Bloomsbury).

## 13. 30 Cannon Street
Whinney, Son & Austen Hall, 1997
30 Cannon Street, EC4
Tube: St Paul's

This five-storey 1977 office building (formerly Credit Lyonnais) was designed by Whinney, Son & Austen Hall and sits opposite Bracken House on the site of a Wren church bombed in WWII. It has been argued

that the building's raked and prefabricated, glass-reinforced cement façade (mimicking earlier load-bearing façades of the type constructed by Seifert) is a lot more interesting than Bracken could ever be. However, one suspects its theatricality is the stuff of Hopkins' nightmares.

## 14. Central Criminal Court Extension
McMorran & Whitby, 1972
Old Bailey, EC1
Tube: St Paul's

A deceptive building – fascinating, like the efforts of this practice on the Police Station in Wood Street and the building adjacent to the Reform Club in Pall Mall. We admit: they are an acquired taste.

## 15. 7–10 Old Bailey
Avery Associates Architects, 2009
7–10 Old Bailey, EC1
Tube: St Paul's

Brian Avery can always be counted upon to attempt to slip something idiosyncratic into his designs, especially if they have anything to do with daylight issues and its arcane dimensions. Here, Avery uses the cut-backs required on the rear façade (overlooking Amen Court and abutting the Roman wall) to insert an atrium featuring a reflective curved wall that draws daylight in and reflects (as a 'periscope') the image of St. Paul's. Games are also played on the front façade. (Also see RADA and Avery's building at Victoria Station.)

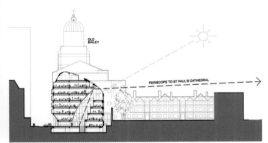

**Wood Street
and
the Barbican**

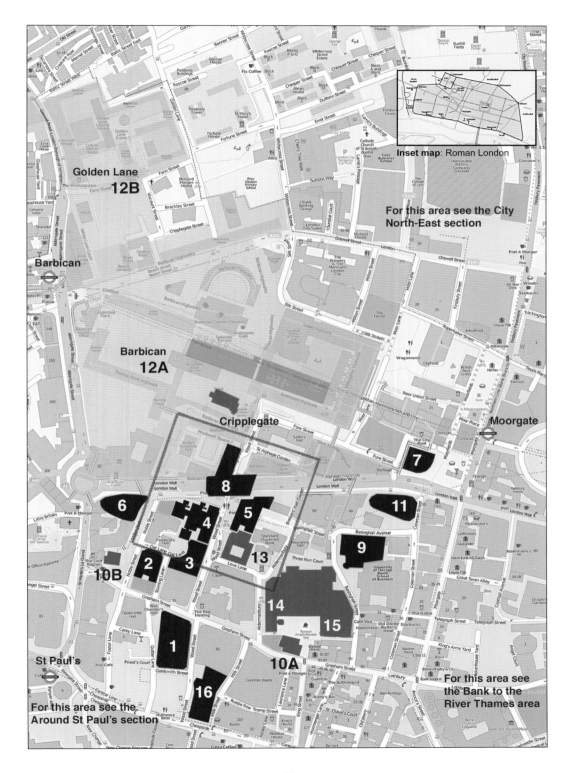

Inset map: Roman London

# The City: Wood Street and the Barbican

## 1. 10 Gresham Street

Foster + Partners, 2000
10 Gresham Street, EC2
Tube: St Paul's, Barbican or Bank

This is an 11-storey, block-filling office building with a large central atrium, notable at the time for a change in the Foster language: a neo-Mies aesthetic, now with aluminium sections instead of steel; and wood blinds instead of aluminium. Elegant proportions, with escape stairs marking the corners.

## 2. 25 Gresham Street

Grimshaw, 2002
25 Gresham Street, EC2
Tube: St Paul's, Barbican or Bank

A small but interesting office building, largely because of the side rather than frontal access beneath an acrobatic cantilever over the edge of the historic St John Zachary Gardens (a church burnt down in the Great Fire of 1666). In contradistinction to 10 Gresham, for example, one approaches from either side, enters a glass lift, comes out onto glass floors, looks back over where one has come from (over the City), and turns around into the office space: simple, but no one else does it. (Note the slate +'spiders' cladding detail.)

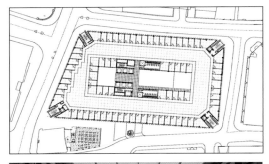

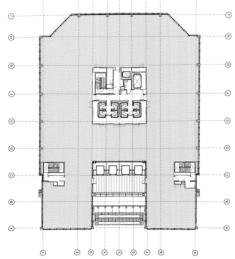

Photo courtesy of Foster + Partners

### 3. 100 Wood Street
Foster + Partners, 2000
100 Wood Street, EC2
Tube: St Paul's, Barbican or Bank

This is a dual-faced (20,000 sqm) building that admirably deals with unequal street demands to east and west and, for that very reason, is an inconsistent architecture rarely publicised by the Foster office. Another reason is perhaps the vaguely Jim Stirling gamesmanship on the west side – intended to allow sunlight onto an old graveyard, now a place for lunch-time sandwiches and trysts. The structure here is acrobatic, but notice how it appears to be entirely theatrical and structurally redundant. The vaguely 1950s offset structure of the east side was quite novel in 2000 (see, for example, Parry's later building in Finsbury Square).

### 4. 88 Wood Street
Rogers Stirk Harbour+Partners, 2000
88 Wood Street, EC2
Tube: St Paul's, Barbican or Bank

The Wood Street frontage pretends to be eight storeys, as others in the street, but the building rapidly climbs upward to 18 storeys (of about 24,000 sqm). The language is familiar: simple rectangular floor plates, with peripheral elevator and escape stair towers articulating the building. And the detailing is, as usual, immaculate. It's a formula that works, over and again, adapting itself to a wide variety of sites and even building usages (see, for example, the Neo housing behind the Tate Modern). The entrance lobby is unusually grand (from end to end), but the oddity is the continued symbolic use of air vents: red for foul being vented out; blue for fresh air being drawn in, etc. One can, in other words, trace these architectural values a long way back.

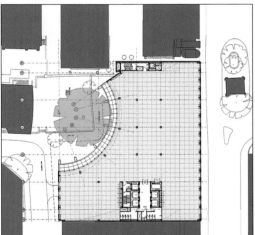

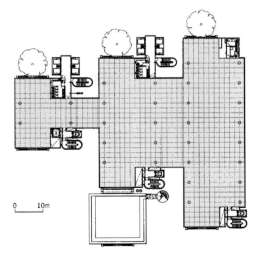

0      10m

## 5. Aldermanbury Square
Eric Parry Architects, 2008
Aldermanbury Square, EC2
Tube: St Paul's, Barbican or Bank

Office buildings are much the same: shell, core and fit-out – a peculiar 'sartorial' presentation, at best a tastefully characterfully branded design that the developer can present and promote. The principal architectural firm does the scheme design; if the practice is lucky, it also becomes the executive architect. Its interior role is restricted to the entrance lobby and common spaces (lifts, toilets, etc.); more rarely, it does some of the fit-out work. Otherwise, the interior is a private and sometimes privileged realm offered as a design potentiality to some other design wit. At Aldermanbury Square, Parry has provided a building with an elegant, even suave, character: dressed in a carefully proportioned stainless steel skin given an entasis that curves in toward the top.

On the other hand it is where the branding exercise meets with the building's urban context that things get interesting. Here, walk-through access is provided at ground level from Wood Street to Aldermanbury Square, enabling views through to the architect's reception fittings and his contribution to the woven hanging on the wall. To one side is a water feature, and the square itself is populated with young trees. It is the latter urban spaces that make an all-important contribution to others in the area (such as the former graveyard in Love Lane, the Guildhall piazza, etc.). But it is all rather soulless and less than the corporate equivalent of Postman's Park that it might have been.

The 19-storey building provides approx. 35,600 sqm and the floor plates are nominally 34.5m wide. Compare it with Farrells' building of 20 years earlier.

**Right**: a typical floor plan.
**Below**: the ground-level site plan.

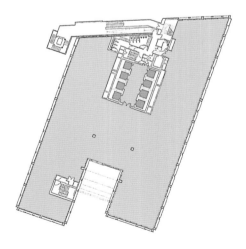

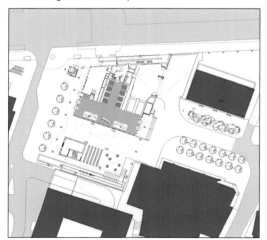

## 6. One London Wall

Foster + Partners, 2003
One London Wall, EC2
Tube: St Paul's, Barbican or Bank

Another work from the prolific Foster team and the fourth in this immediate area (sitting behind Rogers' 88 Wood Street). Two things are most interesting about this 19,000 sqm building. First, the minor oddity of the built-in Guild House that sits at ground level, adjacent to the old Roman and medieval wall. Second, the problem of the front door: is it at ground level or at first-floor level? It's on the first because the design had to accommodate itself to the Barbican deck – a left-over from a 1950s dream of a 'pedway' system that was to weave its way through the City. Here it crosses from the Barbican deck over London Wall (originally 'Route Eleven', the only dual-carriageway in the City).

## 7. Moorhouse

Foster + Partners, 2005
Moorhouse, EC2
Tube: Moorgate

There is something very clever about the Moorhouse building: dramatically curved in plan and section, with a counter-pointing flat western façade – a fascinating play on the neo-Miesian slab-blocks that once lined London Wall and a very neat way of resolving the different street interfaces in a classically diagrammatic Foster gesture. But that's it (all 21,000 sqm of it). The smart one-liner is almost all there is and, ironically, one could easily walk by and hardly give it a second glance.

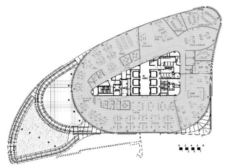

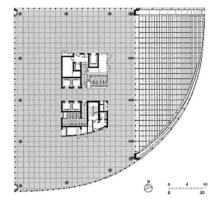

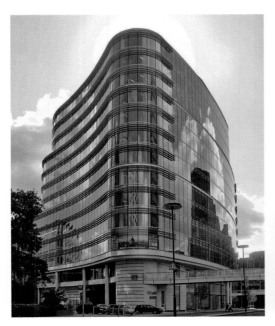

### 8. Alban Gate
Farrells, 1991
London Wall and Wood Street, EC2
Tube: St Paul's, Barbican or Bank

Sir Terry Farrell was the UK's premier Post-Modernist and remains a major name in master planning, but his work is forever fashionably unfashionable. Here, nearly 25 years ago, in a Michael Graves North American, 1980s style, Farrell shows off his skilled compositional gamesmanship three metres away from Eric Parry's building (which is about the same size: 36500 sqm). This includes a demonstration that Po-Mo can also be structurally acrobatic (here, in the manner the building spans across London Wall). Otherwise, the building suffers the same

problem as Foster's One London Wall in having to interface between the street and the Barbican deck, thus an inability to properly serve as a gateway up onto the Barbican in the manner Farrell originally intended (the fault of the planners, we're told). Compare with Embankment Place and MI6, as well as 25 Gresham Street.

### 9. 35 Basinghall Street
Bennett Associates, 2006
35 Basinghall Street, EC2
Tube: St Paul's, Barbican or Bank

This 18,500 sqm building from the eminent firm of Bennett Associates stands opposite Aldermanbury Square. It is a worthy enough work, but fascinating to compare with One Coleman just further along Basinghall Avenue, constructed at the same time.

### 10. Two Wren churches
Sir Christopher Wren, 1677–80
Gresham Street, EC2
Tube: St Paul's

While you are in the area, take a look at St Lawrence Jewry (1677, bottom right (10A)), bounding the Guildhall piazza in Gresham Street, totally restored after WWII, and St Anne & St Agnes (1680, bottom left (10B)), next to the Grimshaw building. The latter is relatively distressed, but thus has rather more character. The black oval within the Guildhall piazza indicates the location of the Roman arena.

## 11. One Coleman Street
David Walker Architects, 2007
One Coleman Street, EC2
Tube: Moorgate

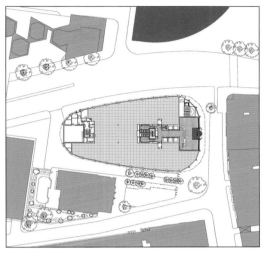

This is an upbeat and clever (17,000 sqm) building, sitting comfortably on a corner of London Wall, opposite Foster's Moorhouse building and, like that building, sporting curves that, here, do a lot to accommodate a pavilion block to its disparate neighbours. Much is made of restoring the street-line on London Wall and of providing a green space on the south side. Meanwhile, the striking geometric cladding panels are reminiscent of Seifert at Centre Point, in the West End – except that there, Seifert made the panels load bearing. The top-level breaks out into polished stainless steel and is similarly 1960s, reminding one of polished chrome car trimmings. In Walker's words:

> The fenestration is set at an angle to the edge of the floor plate, enhancing tangential views from the building while creating a robustly modelled surface to the external building face. This arrangement runs around the building to resolve the curvature of the floor plate while creating a directional movement to the façade with alternate floors arranged in the opposite direction.

**Above**: ground-floor site plan. The curved building at the top is Foster's Moorhouse building, on the edge of the Barbican. **Below**: general view and close-up of the pre-cast concrete cladding panels.

There is a daring originality about the building and a characteristic crispness of detailing from Walker.

## 12. Barbican and Golden Lane
Chamberlin Powell and Bon, 1952–79
Tube: Barbican

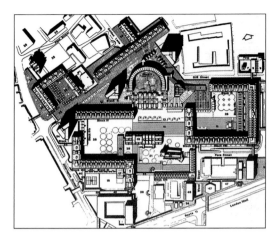

Don't miss these two (very different) estates designed by the same firm of architects The Barbican (2000 flats of 164 different types and about 4000 residents (12A)), in particular, will never be repeated and is rather popular (go there in the spring and take note of all the flowers on balconies – an important sign of contentment). To a large extent the pedestrian deck does work, possibly because of its scale, although it does isolate the development from the surrounding city (well, that's why it is a 'barbican') and parts (e.g. along London Wall) are currently being demolished. The preceding Golden

Lane estate (to the north, comprising 557 flats and maisonettes (12B is very different: more in an English 1950s version of Californian Case Study houses reinvented as terraces and a tower block sporting an exuberant roof-top feature. Both estates are (quite rightly) listed. The three Barbican towers are 42s high (approx. the same as recent tall office buildings).

## 13. City Police Station
McMorran & Whitby, 1965
Wood Street, EC2
Tube: St Paul's, Barbican or Bank

This is a totally idiosyncratic building which seems to refer itself to the stripped Classicism of 1935 rather than to the Swinging Sixties of 1965; however, if you look closely you might notice that this is not just a palazzo centred around a courtyard (for police horses and dogs), but also a clever exercise in the then-fashionable podium+tower typology first explored by SOM in New York (see, for example, Millbank House). Here, the tower is residential, the palazzo-cum-podium block's chimneys are vents, and its rustication is

peculiarly abstract. Also see this practice's extension to the Old Bailey and a building in Pall Mall, on the west side of Barry's Reform Club. Po-Mo well before its time.

## 14. The Guildhall West Wing
Richard Gilbert Scott, 1969–75
Albermanbury, EC2
Tube: St. Paul's, Barbican or Bank

The West Wing of the Guildhall was completed in 1974, by Richard Gilbert Scott, son of Giles Gilbert Scott (d.1960). It is redolent of the late 1960s, yet complete with medieval constructional tropes (the overhangs, or jettying). As RGS remarks: "At this time – the

early 1970s – concrete held sway in architecture and my aim with this building was to echo the arch forms of the Gothic in this material, in an effort to unite the old Guildhall with the new." RGS's office also worked on the Guildhall Yard (featuring the outlines of an amphitheatre, set in black, within the paving).

## 15. Guildhall Art Gallery
Peter Gilbert Scott + D.Y. Davies, 2000
Guildhall Yard, EC2
Tube: St Paul's, Barbican or Bank

## 16. One Wood Street
Fletcher Priest Architects, 2007
One Wood Street, EC2
Tube: St Paul's or Bank

The Gilbert Scotts have kept returning to the City Corporation and this area. Here, Richard Gilbert Scott (b.1923) has given us an idiosyncratic Po-Mo work: an art gallery that also serves as a cloakroom and reception area for events in the old Guildhall. It is made more peculiar by adjacency with the 18th century Guildhall entrance, the 15th century Guildhall itself, the 1960s Guildhall extensions, Wren's St Lawrence Jewry and the outline of the Roman amphitheatre set into the pavement of the piazza (Guildhall Yard). (A one metre, 700-tonne 'transfer raft' beneath the gallery protects Roman remains.)

It used to be that GMW probably had more modern City buildings than anyone else. Now it looks as if Fletcher Priest have taken over. This is one of the better examples.

Peter Gilbert Scott remarks:

> The specification called for the building to last indefinitely and to be totally bomb-proof. The City Surveyor required the building to pay for itself by providing sufficient rentable office space above the Art Gallery. The Remembrancer needed the Art Gallery spaces to be used for ceremonial purposes with a floor to ceiling height in the main gallery sufficient to allow the Pikemen to do their drill; also to provide cloakroom accommodation for 1200 people attending Civic Banquets. The Art Curator naturally required the space to hang, conserve and store the Corporation's collection, which had survived the war in storage. [...] In addition, provision had to be made for the Manuscript Store, then currently under the Old Library and Print Room.

It was, in other words, a problematic undertaking that produced a very odd building. (In addition, during the project D.Y. Davies went bust.)

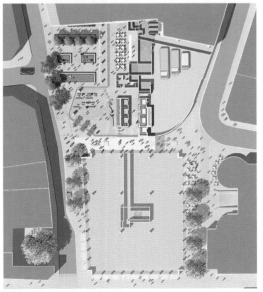

Bank to
the River
Thames

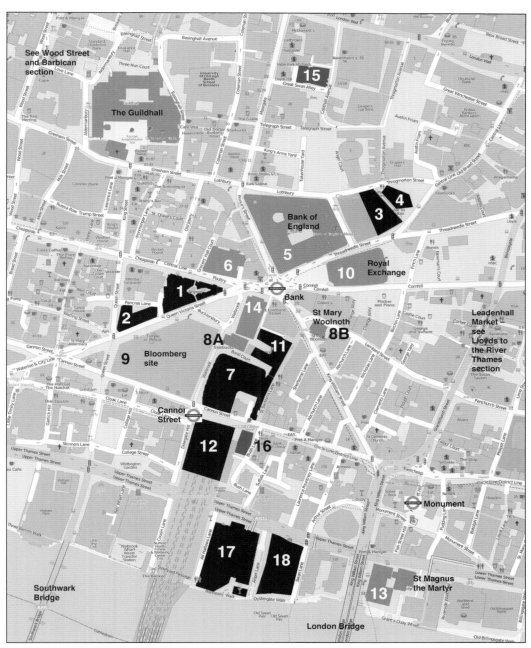

Bank is a junction of six roads and has the Bank of England as its principal building, followed by the Royal Exchange. The junction is defined by a series of notable buildings by famous architects: Curtis Green, Edwin Cooper, Jim Stirling and Michael Wilford, Wren and Nicholas Hawksmoor. The ceremonial house of the City of London Mayor (the Mansion House, 1758) is here. You can branch off from Bank down alley-ways that are often neglected, but sometimes offer surprises and enables one to be in touch with the underlying medieval street pattern that defines the conservation area in the heart of the City.

**Opposite page**: OMA's New Court; photo courtesy of Allies and Morrison (Hufton+Crow)

# The City: Bank to the River Thames

## 1. One Poultry
Stirling & Wilford, 1998
Poultry, EC2
Tube: Bank

One Poultry was already incongruously at least ten years out of fashion when completed, after a long period in gestation. A key reference to that contentious background is the corner feature onto Bank, but unless you have a mental photograph of the notable Victorian buildings (designed by John Belcher, 1870) that were previously on the site, it might appear arbitrary to you (such is the problem with narrative architecture). The central drum is pure Wilford rather than Stirling. Go up to the Conran restaurant and terrace bar at the top – it's worth it; here you can reflect upon how quickly architectural fashions can change – and perhaps how that may be utterly irrelevant to the quality of a work and the games-manship it exhibits.

## 2. 60 Queen Victoria Street
Foggo Associates, 1999
Queen Victoria Street, EC4
Tube: Bank

This building was completed about the same time as One Poultry and was designed by the firm set up by Peter Foggo, after his work on Broadgate apparently left him feeling that was not the way he wanted to prac-tise architecture. Sadly, Foggo died not much later, but his firm continued. Here they appear to be taking some inspiration from Jean Nouvel and his Arab Institute in Paris, perhaps also from Hopkins on the nearby Bracken House. Certainly, this is an unusual façade, both in its detail and its finish (pre-patinated copper, which has hardly changed since construction). (See Cannon Place.)

### 3. 60 Threadneedle Street
Eric Parry Architects, 2009
60 Threadneedle Street, EC2
Tube: Bank

Parry's idiosyncratic chrome and black building provides nine storeys of office accommodation totalling 19,900 sqm with its floor plates organised around two internal atria. The design is completely different to his buildings in Finsbury Square (2002), Paternoster (2001) and at Aldermanbury Square (2008) – somewhat Gotham City in tone.

### 4. 125 Old Broad Street
Grimshaw with Sheppard Robson, 2008
125 Old Broad Street, EC2
Tube: Bank

This 26-storey building used to be the Stock Exchange, designed by Llewelwyn Davies Weeks in 1972 as a Brutalist concrete work. Then the Exchange moved out to Paternoster Square (into a Parry building) and this building was stripped down to its structure and – this is the clever part – a 2m floor extension strip was ranged around each level. Simple, clever. And then the new structure was re-serviced and reclad in *moderne* guise.

### 5. Bank of England
Sir John Soane/Herbert Baker, 1833 and 1942
Threadneedle Street, EC2
Tube: Bank

All that is left of John Soane's original work (1788–1833) is the screen wall that wraps and encloses the Bank. One has to imagine what once lay behind it (where Herbert Baker's work (1921–42) now stands): a series of rooms, courts, domes once lit by lamp and daylight, within which Baker attempted to embody the tradition of the private house and communicate trust.

### 6. Midland Bank (former)
Edwin Lutyens (with Gotch & Saunders), 1924
27 Poultry, EC2
Tube: Bank

This HQ for the Midland Bank is a refined exercise in the 'grand manner' and full of Lutyens' irrepressible masterfulness mixed with humour. It closed a few years ago and still awaits reopening as an upmarket hotel (designed by EPR).

## 7. The Walbrook Building
Foster + Partners, 2011
Walbrook, EC4
Tube: Cannon Street

Like Cannon Place, the Walbrook offers 36,500 sqm of accommodation, with floor plates of approx. 4,700 sqm. (There appears to be a developer's conventional wisdom in different areas of the City; for example, compare with the Wood Street area – push and shove a bit, and dress the building differently and, remarkably, they are all much the same.) Here the Semper-ian dressing is very different: a sort of Michelin-man building, pneumatically pumped up, swelling in strange places. Oddly, this determined aesthetic is most effective at the rear, where the service entrance is (wrapping around St Swithin's Church Garden – a church rebuilt after the Great Fire, but damaged in WWII).

**Financial Layout**

On the more public street side the bulbous swelling and canting is perhaps less successful. Having said that, the smooth integration of horizontal fins and vertical structure is quite refined. Certainly, the building communicates a strong branding character and, like Cannon Place, directly across the road, it can also be characterised as 'bloody-minded'. As for the hidden-away interface between New Court and the Walbrook (photo left), it is surely ideal for dead cats.

## 8. Two churches at Bank
St Mary Woolnoth – Nicholas Hawksmoor, 1727
St Stephen Walbrook – Wren, 1679
Tube: Bank

St Stephen Walbrook (Walbrook, EC2, **8A**) is possibly Wren's finest City church – a building whose lackadaisical exterior does little to prepare you for the gamesmanship going on inside. The current central altar is by Henry Moore (1972) and the pulpit is original. There are, of course, many remaining Wren churches in the City (see Wikipedia and similar websites).

St Mary Woolnoth (Lombard Street, EC3, **8B**) is rather neglected, but you can get in during the week and have an opportunity to see how Hawksmoor's turbulent baroque exterior resolves itself into a calm cubic geometry on the inside. The galleries were removed long ago and possibly would have added to the geometrical subtleties. There was once a narrow street in front, making the robustness of the overall architectonic all the more remarkable. Hawksmoor's other churches in London are also worth visiting, especially St George's Bloomsbury.

## 9. Bloomberg Place
Foster + Partners (expected 2016)
Walbrook, EC2
Tube: Bank

This is one to watch out for. Foster designed an extension for Bloomberg to Giles Gilbert Scott's 1920s building in Finsbury Square (Citygate House, 2001). Now his practice has designed an entirely new London HQ opposite Wren's St Stephen Walbrook, OMA's Rothschild building and his own Walbrook office building. It comprises two 10s buildings for 2500 people (totalling 100300 sqm) and a retail content to rival that of One New Change (4400 sqm). Foster is quoted as saying: "It's not a timid building, It will leave a large impression on London." Watch it arrive.

## 10. The Royal Exchange
Sir William Tite, 1844
Cornhill, EC3
Tube: Bank

The third Royal Exchange on this site – a building modelled on a Dutch example of an arcaded courtyard where people would gather to trade. This version sports a grand portico and is surrounded on the long outsides by small shops, as if a version of lean-to buildings against a cathedral. At its heart is a central galleried atrium (now roofed over) with shops, café, bar, etc. It is a fine typology, one that should be repeated in a modern guise (but hasn't been). This third design was completed by the City Architect William Tite (also responsible for Leadenhall Market). It went through a difficult history in the 1980s and 1990s before being altered to essentially what we see now in 2001 (the café came later). Soak it up, but be beware that the jewellery shops are expensive – for bankers with a bonus burning a hole in their wallets.

## 11. New Court (Rothschild Bank)
OMA, 2011
St. Swithin's Lane, EC2
Tube: Bank

Although this is simply another trading house for an exclusive banking house, Koolhaas – with Allies and Morrison as executive architects – has produced a well-crafted work that carefully insinuates itself into an aged urban fabric, especially respecting relations to Wren's St Stephen Walbrook. Surprisingly, this degree of contextual aspiration is relatively rare in the City.

Also, as a habit of mind, one expects a building from Koolhaas to deliberately neglect detailing. But this is not the attitude of his practice, or of Allies and Morrison. In fact, there are some rather fine details, including the look-no-hands stone soffit to the entrance area, and the fit-out of the archive area that sits to one side of the central courtyard. (Some interior parts are also rather sumptuous, but you are unlikely to see them.)

From a medium distance one can see that the building is actually three parts with slightly different claddings – except that behind the façade it is one floor plate. From further away (something like the terrace at the top of One Poultry) you can see a fourth part hidden when one stands on the street: the daring 'TV-box' that serves as a client reception and entertainment suite on top of the building, giving onto a formally landscaped roof terrace.

Rather strangely, the design occasionally leans toward being mannered. For example, there are some curious diagonals to the façades that are excused as necessary structural elements. They aren't. And the lean on the TV-box is somewhat disturbing on the inside. Nevertheless, this is a fine building worthy of close attention.

The security guards expect your curiosity and, if you are polite, they are usually polite in return. But ask about what you can photograph. Usually this excludes the building itself unless you are outside its property boundary.(!)

**Above**: New Court in context: the Mansion House (left), St Stephen Walbrook (centre) and the Walbrook building (right). **Below**: the entrance and accommodational parts of the scheme.

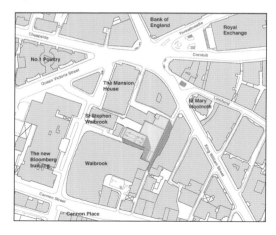

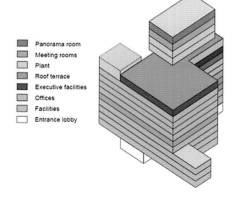

- Panorama room
- Meeting rooms
- Plant
- Roof terrace
- Executive facilities
- Offices
- Facilities
- Entrance lobby

(Photo courtesy of OMA)

The architects of the New Court scheme tell us that:

[The scheme] reinstates a visual connection between St Swithin's Lane and St Stephen Walbrook. Instead of competing as accidental neighbours, the church and New Court now form a twinned urban ensemble, an affinity reinforced by the proportional similarity of their towers [!]. New Court is comprises a simple extrusion transformed through a series of volumetric permutations into a hybrid of cube and annexes: a 'cube' of open office space and appendices of shared spaces and private work areas. The central cube of the building consists of ten efficient and flexible open-plan office floors which facilitate views over St Stephen and the surrounding City. This cube is surrounded by four adjoining volumes – annexes – with support facilities to the Bank's operations such as meeting rooms, vertical circulation, reception areas, and a staff café and gym. The fourth annexe, a Sky Pavilion, sits at the top of this central cube. The Sky Pavilion [...] affords a clear view of Wren's most famous London Church, St Paul's Cathedral, and the rest of the City, and provides an appropriately unique space for high level functions. At street level, the entire cube is lifted to create generous pedestrian access to the tall glass lobby and a covered forecourt that opens a visual passage to St Stephen Walbrook and its churchyard – creating a surprising moment of transparency in the otherwise constrained opacity of the medieval streetscape. Reconnected, the two establish a continuity that radically transforms St Swithin's Lane and the setting of the Church.

A & M more simply tell us that:

The building comprises several distinct components. The principal and largest of these is the central cube, which contains eight regular floors for the general business operations of the bank and two floors linked by a generous accommodation staircase which are occupied by the executive offices, meeting rooms and dining rooms. To three sides of the cube are annexes which contain the support spaces: the archive, the vertical circulation, restrooms and ancillary kitchen and storage accommodation.

**Top**: view down on Bank.
**Left:** building section.

## 12. Cannon Place
Foggo Associates, 2012
Cannon Street Station, EC4
Tube: Cannon Street

This is a megastructural 36,000 sqm office building with individual floor plates up to 4,660 sqm in size and was constructed over a busy, functioning commuter rail station. It looks simple, but the design and construction was seething with difficulty, and it is remarkable that Foggo Associates have distilled the site and project constraints down to such simplicity: a height control because of the nearness to St Paul's (meaning there can be no plant on the roof; note a plant tower on the eastern side); a lower level zone for Cannon Street Station; the requirement that the station should function throughout the building works; Underground lines running right across the northern end of the site (hence the enormous cantilever over the whole of the frontage); a requirement to reconstruct the Cannon Street. Underground station; and Roman remains over the southern half of the site which called for reuse of the foundations belonging to the building formerly on the site.

That the design manages to squeeze an eight-floor 'sandwich' into such an equation is quite an achievement. Imagine what you can't see and look carefully at what you can. (The contractors found the RSH Leadenhall building relatively easy after their completion of Cannon Place.)

If there is an Achilles' heel to the project it lies in the problematics of addressing human issues of 'intimacy' – a difficult word for anyone addressing such project challenges that have, at their heart, a factory-office intended to be filled with money-making traders. Instrumentalism (as a machine paradigm) and humanity continue to make somewhat discomforted bedfellows.

**Opposite page**: the interior: very large and designed as a trading floor or similar large-scale corporate work-space, awaiting a fit-out that will introduce layers of reassuring comforts into otherwise generic space.

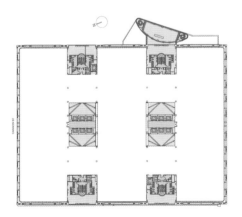

## 14. The Mansion House
George Dance the Elder, 1752
Bank, EC4
Tube: Bank

The 'house' of the Lord Mayor of the City, now used for ceremonial occasions such as the Chancellor of the Exchequer giving us bad news. The loggia beneath the pediment is peculiarly squashed but probably adequate for an address by some figure of power to a crowd packing the road junction – which, of course, never happens.

## 15. Chartered Accountants Hall
Belcher & Partners, 1893, 1931; William Whitfield, 1970
Moorgate Place, EC2
Tube: Bank or Moorgate

A good example of architecture that is to a large extent mute and must be examined, even read about: three phases of this building's history, extending the original character, completing it and then – once around the corner – leaping into a contemporary mode.

## 13. Adelaide House
John Burnet, Son & Dick, 1925
London Bridge, EC3
Tube: Monument

It may look vaguely Egyptian, but there is a distinctive neo-American robustness to this early steel-framed building. Other innovations included an internal mail system, central ventilation and a miniature golf course on the roof. Also see the same architect's **Kodak Building** on upper Kingsway (1911), which was similarly steel-framed.

The adjacent church is Wren's St Magnus-the-Martyr (1676) – one of the least altered of all the Wren churches. It houses a model of the old London Bridge, as inhabited.

## 16. 80 Cannon Street (Bush House)
Arup Associates, 1976
Bush Lane, EC4
Tube: Cannon Street

This Arup Associates building (to the left in the photo below, located immediately east of Cannon Place) employs an exoskeleton which leaves a column-free interior: a stainless steel (somewhat redundant) structure, water-filled for fire protection (suggesting a bizarre boiling kettle if a fire ever takes place!). The base level was originally intended as a rail station – which was never realised and, unfortunately, someone later had the bright idea of infilling the lower parts with retailing. A degree of imaginative effort is needed to locate its image back as it was, but this remains an unusual design.

## Dissimilar neighbours:

### 17. One Angel Lane
Fletcher Priest Architects, 2010
90–94 Upper Thames Street, EC4
Tube: Cannon Street

### 18. Riverbank House
David Walker Architects, 2010
2 Swan Lane, EC4
Tube: Cannon Street

This pair make interesting neighbours. **One Angel Lane** provides 49,000 sqm and **Riverbank House** just over 42,000 sqm, but the embodied site challenges and the disparate approaches to making architecture are significant. Angel was constrained by the foundations of the British Telecom building formerly on the site (it reuses some 30% of Mondial House's basement, its foundations, etc.) and its architects adopt a concern with narrative. In essence, Riverbank is more akin to Cannon Place: a tough, almost diagrammatic scheme, although now more crisp and elegant.

Similarity comes with three shared concerns: the riverside frontage; maximising the amount of corporate office accommodation; and providing the building with a branded character that articulates the exterior and penetrates through to the internal common areas. Both buildings make a contribution to an enhanced river frontage with public access and Angel makes great play of the *de rigueur* feature of most new office buildings: roof terraces for entertaining clients. In turn, Riverbank provides the branding gesture of dramatic balconies with yellow underbellies. But a deeper difference should be noted. Coleridge once remarked: "An allegory is but a translation of abstract notions into picture-language. [...] On the other hand [...] a symbol partakes of the reality that it renders intelligible." Malraux similarly remarked that: "the distinguishing feature of modern art is that it never tells a story [...] Modern art is rather the annexation of forms by means of an inner pattern or schema." Certainly, the narrative concerns of Fletcher Priest are hardly evident to anyone experiencing the building (as opposed to the client and planners presented with proposals): a justificatory spin that makes much of the history of this aged Thames site but is not obvious to anyone without the historical knowledge that the large timber sections along the river frontage are a re-membrance to timber wharfs that were once here. Similarly, the fully glazed office accommodation is wrapped in literary stories about the artful-

Photo courtesy of OMA

ness of the 'pixelated' patterning on the glass that offers a mixed palette of river water and mud colours. It works well, but perhaps in spite of the narrative. Walker, on the other hand, is more concerned with the direct experience of the thing-in-itself – no doubt arguing that the aesthetic of a building either 'works' or it does not: one shouldn't need to rely upon the mediation of narrative guidance. His scheme takes its inspiration directly from the site geometry and deftly turns this into a simple and bold articulation. The literary chatter of One Angel Lane is here a simple architectonic gesture: mute, but with a smiling face. Like Cannon Place, the scheme is almost 'diagrammatic' – which either works and hits the Aristotlian mark or entirely misses the target. This one hits the mark. On the other hand, the balconies are as baroquely theatrical

as the Fletcher Priest timbers – not entirely intentionally: the design suffered 'value engineering' compromising the structural integrity of the original design (they are steel add-ons to the main concrete frame). Overall, that both buildings are satisfactory perhaps suggests that it is theory that misses the mark. Nevertheless, there is an important issue of intentionality at issue.

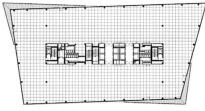

**Lloyds
to the
River
Thames**

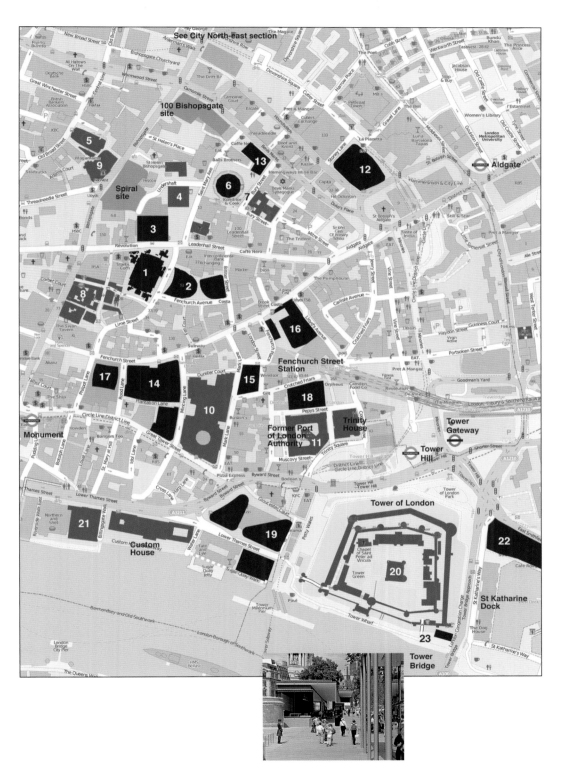

# The City: Lloyds to the River Thames

## 1. Lloyds '86 Building
Rogers Stirk Harbour+Partners, 1986
Cornhill, EC3
Tube: Liverpool Street, Tower Hill or Bank

The historic listing of Lloyds (as Grade I) tells us that this is "a seminal late 20th-century building by one of Britain's most significant modern architects. It exemplifies the High Tech style in Britain, with its boldly expressed services and flexibility of plan throughout the impressive exterior and interior." Well, yes, but this is a description telling us little about the third custom-designed building for Lloyds, designed to last 125 years rather than 25 (by adapting to change rather than having to be replaced), authored by an architectural practice about to close up the shop when it won this job. The client – an age-old, blue-chip City organisation tracing its history back to 1689 – gave a huge budget for a one-off design, but then subsequently (during a period of financial scandal) had to sell the building on to a German bank eight years after completion – a classic instance of hubris. (Etc. It's a long story and worth investigating; mute appearances tell you little.) Oddly, the project outcome appears to have been a surprise to many of the underwriters and even the Lloyds Board. A design redolent with left-wing values was not entirely appropriate to an organisation that lived in terms of symbols of hierarchy. For example, the first thing the Chairman did on moving in was to appoint a French interior designer to alter everything he could. Does Lloyds any longer have relevance, or is the listing telling us that 1986 may as well be 1774 when the Lloyds insurance market moved into the Royal Exchange? Certainly, this is a seminal work, but the current interior fit-out is a dim version of what it originally was, even though the building itself has, ironically, hardly changed (they can't afford to alter anything).

Photo Graham Challifour

**Top right:** at night (photo courtesy of Lloyds).
**Right:** floor plan at a gallery level. Note the retained portico (top left) from the 1927 building that was also on this site. The 1958 building was opposite, on the site now occupied by Foster's Willis Building. When completed, the '86 building and the '58 building worked as one complex.
**Below**: view to the Lloyds '86 building from inside the Gherkin.

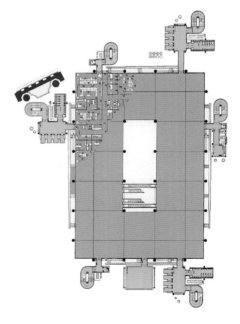

## 2. Willis Building
Foster + Partners, 2008
15 Lime Street, EC2
Tube: Liverpool Street, Tower Hill or Bank

The parallels between the careers of Rogers and Foster will one day make a rich academic history. Meanwhile, we can marvel at the coincidences that locate the works of these architects adjacent to one another. Here, the Willis Building (yes, of Willis Faber fame, one of Foster's more notable early works) replaces the Lloyds '58 Building and graciously acknowledges the importance of Lloyds in the manner it also enhances this upper part of Lime Street with a façade that curves back. But then it towers above the Rogers building.

Overall, the ground level allows for generous open spaces and the towers themselves are stepped back in order to provide the roof entertainment terraces that have become a compulsory feature of City buildings. Together, we have a grouping of two Rogers and two Foster designs, interplayed like some poker game in which the stakes keep rising (with Rogers' new Leadenhall building currently way out in front).

The site is that of the Lloyds 1958 building by Sir Edwin Cooper. Sculptural panels from its roof have been retained on Lime Street.

**Below**: view from the top of the Gherkin, toward the Willis Building, with the 'Walkie-talkie' and the Shard beyond.
**Middle right**: the ground plan of the Willis Building.
**Bottom right**: the reflection of the Lloyds '86 Building in the curved glazing of the Willis Building.

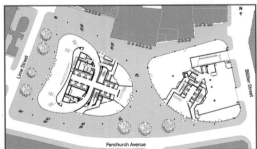

## 3. The Leadenhall Building
Rogers Stirk Harbour+Partners, 2014
122 Leadenhall, EC3
Tube: Bank

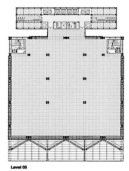
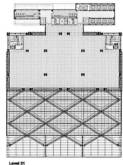

Level 05          Level 31

Statistics are usually rather silly, but the Leadenhall Building invites them. It sits opposite the Lloyds '86 Building of 48,000 sqm (15 floors and about 88m high), the Willis building of over 44,000 sqm (125m high), and the Gherkin of 76,600 sqm (and 195m high), but the Leadenhall Building has less than 57,000 sqm lettable over 47 floors and tops out at 225m high. So it has 77% of the accommodation in the Gherkin, but higher. (Agents are notoriously casual about gross and lettable, so take such figures as approximate.)

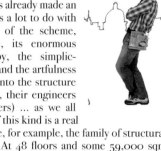

At the time of writing Leadenhall is just about ready for occupation, but has already made an impression that has a lot to do with the shear bravura of the scheme, its gigantic scale, its enormous ground-floor lobby, the simplicity of the schema, and the artfulness that has been put into the structure by RSH and Arup, their engineers (and by the builders) ... as we all know: simplicity of this kind is a real achievement. (Note, for example, the family of structural 'knuckle' details.) At 48 floors and some 59,000 sqm lettable this is a large building exhibiting an equally large gestural lean backward in order not to block a long view to St Paul's. We suggest you take a look at the family of structural junctions and, when looking at the north side, remember that this is made up of prefabricated units installed with primary services parts already in place. Will it get the love/hate reaction that the Gherkin received? Perhaps, but unlike the variable output from the Foster office, RSH manage to provide a family of solutions that are yet, each one, very different and unique to their site and project challenges. If there is a doubt it is over the uncomfortable junction between the lobby area of this stand-alone structure and the few remaining older buildings to the west – which include a listed Edwin Lutyens Midland Bank building of 1929 – one doubts that it will ever be removed and replaced by another tall 'pavilion' ... but never say never. And that rear, north facade: it doesn't quite live up to the south, street presence.

CGI image courtesy of RSH

**Top right**: typical lower and upper level floor plans
**Centre**: CGI to the seven-storey lobby area
**Top Right opposite page**: CGI view from the east (CGI images and plans courtesy of Rogers Stirk Harbour+Partners).
**Right**: 122 Leadenhall in construction.

CGI image courtesy of RSH

### 4. Commercial Union Building (former)
GMW, 1969
Cornhill, EC3
Tube: Liverpool Street, Tower Hill or Bank

The tall pavilion plus piazza of what is now the Helen's Building remains a resilient typology. This is London's exemplary tower+piazza typology, now some 40 years old and in competition with Lloyds, the Willis building, the Gherkin and the Leadenhall building. But what a marvellous grouping, complete with two medieval churches, H.P. Berlage's Holland House and some Post-Modernism.

(Also see GMW's former Banque Belge building at 147 Leadenhall (1975), just west of a Lutyens bank and, in turn, west of the Leadenhall building.)

### 5. Tower 42
Richard Seifert, 1970–1981
Old Broad Street, EC2
Tube: Bank

This used to be the HQ of the newly merged Natwest Bank (National Provincial and Westminster banks, 1968) – and so Seifert gave them a plan matching the logo of the bank. Neat: Po-Mo well before its time! The core is large and solid, with only a thin perimeter of offices. It should have been demolished but was instead converted: the lower area is by GMW; the Wagamama next door is Fletcher Priest, as is the upper-level fit-out (where there is a restaurant). Go around to the rear and you will see remnants of the pedway system still in place. Ironically, Seifert was a detested figure in architectural circles throughout his life. Now he is a hero!

## 6. 30 St Mary Axe

Foster+Partners, 2003
30 St Mary Axe, EC3
Tube: Liverpool Street, Tower Hill or Bank

What can we tell you? We have had problems with the Irish; they turned up in 1993 in a large truck loaded with explosives and parked it outside the historic Baltic Exchange; there was a massive bang and extensive damage over a wide area; and people were killed. The building had to be demolished; the conservation lobby wanted a new building put there which included the historic parts; the City planners and most developers were more horrified by that intention than by the Irish: that is not how the City of London responds to market needs. And so Foster was given a brief to design a unique building that could not reasonably include the historic elements. Hence the Gherkin. The building's is relatively simple: a series of rectangular floor plates set around a structural core, with floors spanning to an exoskeleton. As one moves from floor to floor the plan shifts around by 4 degrees ... hence the twisting. The triangular gaps between floors were meant to wrap all the way up the building until (one presumes) someone woke up to the fact that this would make an excellent chimney – hence it is cut off at intervals that vary depending upon the floor depth. The uppermost part is really a glass-house with superb views (and with a bar; a restaurant is below). The overall shape was made possible by Mark Burry, brought in as a consultant from Melbourne. Otherwise it's a tower + piazza model, like its neighbour, GMW's former Commercial Union building.

**Right**, from the top: in the restaurant; looking down a triangular light well; and a view from St Helen's church (dating from the 13th century).

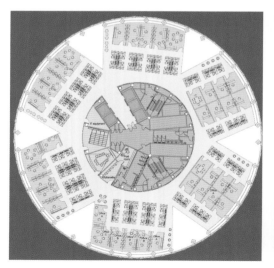

## 7. Holland House
H.P. Berlage, 1914
Bury Street, EC3
Tube: Liverpool Street

The Gherkin ruined the street impression this build-ing was meant to make, so we have to call upon your imagination: approach the building obliquely and slowly walk by, ignoring the Gherkin piazza and watch-ing the green glazed façade open up to you. It takes a few seconds. It's simple, but no one does this kind of thing anymore ... such a simple joy. The lobby is about all that remains of the origi-nal interior, complete with Claude Bragdon 'projec-tive' geometric light fittings. (Bragdon, a New Yorker, was caught up in Theosophy and the Gurd-jieff movement during the 1920s.) The fine sculp-ture of a ship ploughing the ocean on the south-west corner is by Joseph Mendes de Costa.

## 8. Leadenhall Market
Sir William Tite, 1881
Bank, EC2
Tube: Liverpool Street, Tower Hill or Bank

This inner-block complex – once a medieval poultry market, rebuilt in 1881 , now mostly cafés, restau-rants and bars – is important: a fine example of how the inner-block areas and medieval alley-ways should have been dealt with. It remains a scandalously lost potential that was being denied decades ago and especially after WWII when the City planners instituted the 'pedway' system (give the streets to the cars and get the people

up onto a deck). You can walk rear alleys from Bank up to here, at Leadenhall. They start off poorly: areas of white glazed tiling (to reflect daylight) and signs lamenting the fact that: 'There was once on this site a notable tavern'. But things get better as one progresses eastward, ending up at Leadenhall. And then it all evaporates again. Melbourne can do it; why can't the City?

## 9. Gibson Hall
Richard Seifert, 1970–81
13 Bishopsgate, EC2
Tube: Bank

This building has the reputation of being the first 'branch bank', owned by the National provincial Bank (which became the NatWest) and designed by John Gibson (1865). Now, like so many other such places, it has been converted – here into a conference hall etc. It has a very fine façade and a marvellous sense of scale.

## 10. Minster Court
GMW, 1991
Mincing Lane, EC3
Tube: Tower Hill

It's difficult to think of another Po-Mo neo-Gothic work – they're all vaguely neo-Classical. In truth, after more than 20 years, this example's historic isolation and idiosyncratic character makes it more interesting. Certainly, that character could not be more different from earlier City works such as the former Commercial Union building. (Silver-haired GMW partners still can't quite understand why their younger employees enthuse about

the pre-Po-Mo stuff.) Apart from all that, the building is a fine example of a 'ground-scraper' instead of a sky-scraper'. (On that note, also see Merrill Lynch.)

## 11. 10 Trinity Square
Sir Edwin Cooper, 1912
10 Trinity Square, EC3
Tube: Aldgate

The former offices of the Port of London Authority, topped by a large statue of Neptune, looking as if it belongs in Chicago and looking toward the eastern docks the Authority managed (or tried to). The building next door is Trinity House, designed by Samuel Wyatt in 1794: home of the organisation that provides light ships and lighthouses around Britain's coasts.

### 12. St Botolph Building
Grimshaw, 2010
138 Houndsditch, EC3
Tube: Aldgate

There is not a lot to say about the 51,000 sqm St Botolph except that it looks somewhat like an updated and larger version of the block of flats at 125 Park Road that Grimshaw designed with Terry Farrell (1970), now blue glass instead of grey aluminium. The architects tell us: "The upper 11 floors house high specification offices, while the first and second levels provide more flexible office space with the potential to become dealing floors. The lower ground floors accommodate multi-functional space and retail outlets." Banks of office space surround a central atrium. It's a very efficient plan. As with all City office buildings there are lots of bicycle places in the basement (together with showers, etc.) but no car provision is made.

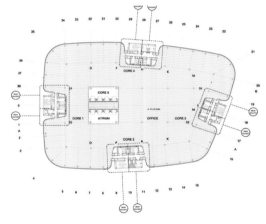

### 13. 6 Bevis Marks
Fletcher Priest Architects, 2014
6 Bevis Marks, EC3
Tube: Liverpool Street

The fashion for roof terraces we witnessed on Merrill Lynch, the Willis Building, One New Change and the like later went on to enclosed roof-rooms at places such as the Gherkin, Rothschilds and 20 Fenchurch Street. Bankers want to party, as Peter Rees (the City's long-standing chief planner) has noted. This has now reached an apotheosis at 6 Bevis Marks: a 16s building of about 15,000 sqm with a top-floor 'garden square'. The building sets up an interesting relationship with the Gherkin (where this game of sky-rooms arguably began) and mimics its diagrid structure.

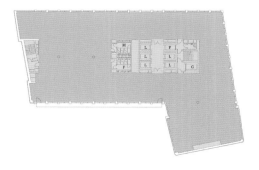

## 14. Plantation Place
Arup Associates, 2004
Fenchurch Street, EC3
Tube: Monument or Bank

The north part, on Fenchurch Street (bottom photo), rises to eight storeys with overworked stone fins and aluminium glazing panels, and then (after allowing a roof terrace) breaks out into double-walled glass. Note the differentiation between podium and fully glazed superstructure. Plantation Place South (upper photo) is about one-third the size (16,000 sqm as against 50,200 sqm), but enjoys a more successful façade treatment. (See McAslan's Wellington House.) Between the developments is a large art work (*Time and Tide*, by Simon Patterson).

## 15. Mark Lane
Bennett Associates, 2014
Fenchurch Street, EC3
Tube: Monument or Bank

A 23,000 sqm office building adjacent to Minster Court and adding itself to the public square in front of Fenchurch Street Station. It steps down from 15 to 7 storeys with a series of enclosed terraces, thus proffering a variation to terraces and/or a roof-top room that is here described as "winter garden break-out spaces with panoramic views".

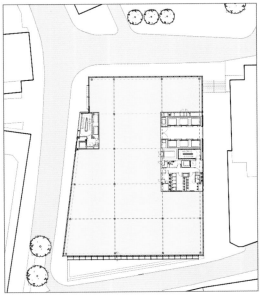

### 16. Lloyds Register of Shipping
Rogers Stirk Harbour+Partners, 2000
Fenchurch Street, EC3
Tube: Tower Hill

Don't confuse this with the other Lloyds building. While not as radical, it is, in its way, equally impressive, this time as a design insinuating itself into a tiny site and incorporating a very fine 1900 T.E. Collcutt building (for the Board to meet, as one might expect). The building is hidden away, through a gateway, beyond a former churchyard – until, that is, one looks up and sees it towering above the Collcut and other older buildings. With 15 floors it provides 34000 sqm of net space in a building with a tiny (but tall) central atrium and low floor-to-ceiling heights. It is a fine building that shows off all the usual Rogers Stirk Harbour tropes.

**Above**: the ground floor of Lloyds Registry, indicating the low coffered concrete ceiling.
**Below**: section through the atrium. The former churchyard is on the right, where older buildings front the street.
**Right**: the site plan of Lloyds Register of Shipping. The new parts are squeezed into a tiny site surrounded by older buildings, including that by Collcutt and also the Fenchurch Street railway station. The entry court is an old churchyard and is accessible Monday to Friday.

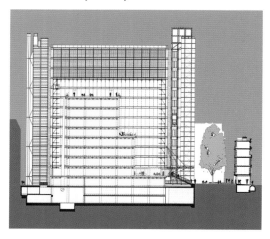

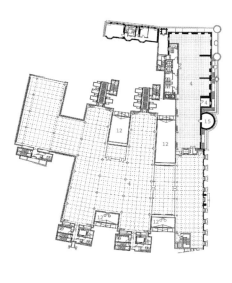

## 17. 20 Fenchurch Street
Rafael Viñoly, 2014
20 Fenchurch Street, EC3
Tube: Bank or Monument

This 55,000 sqm (36 storeys and 177m high) design quickly became nicknamed the 'Walkie-Talkie'. It could have been 'retro-brick', as Martin Cooper's 1980s Motorola cell-phone has been nicknamed... Or perhaps the autumn 2013 fuss over its focused sun rays melting a car will mean that the 'Walkie-Scorchie' moniker will stick.

The rationale for the shape is structurally and commercially beneficial, but the rationale is simple: people like to be at the top of tall buildings. Usually (as at the Shard), the largest floor plates are at the bottom. Reverse this convention and one has an eminently saleable format, especially if it includes a publicly accessible top floor which fractures the hermetic qualities of most tall office buildings. (Viñoly is keen on commercial–public interchanges and enthusiastic about his 'sky-garden'.)

The design was first proposed in 2004, when it was criticised by both English Heritage and Unesco as an oppressive and overwhelming form: a "brutally dominant expression of commercial floor space" that threatened to add the Tower of London to a 'World Heritage in Danger' listing. It was subject to a public inquiry over these heritage concerns and also bitterly contested by neighbours who felt their rights to light were being threatened – a complaint the City planners overrode, with its chief

Planner, Peter Rees, quoted as saying: "We came to think of it as the figurehead at the prow of our ship" and "A viewing platform where you could look back to the vibrancy of the City's engine room behind you." In fact Rees is keen on the idea of the City as the heart of swinging commercial London: "The secret of the City's success is having places to gossip," he has quipped. "We are taking every opportunity to create the party city in the sky. [...] It's very important to our business offer that people can party as close to their desks as possible."

Public opinion appears to be divided – as it usually is with tall buildings and is with the Shard. However, there is a certain elegance as well as novelty about the Walkie-Talkie.

The building will be complete in about April 2014. Enjoy the party (if you are invited) and fine views that can be added to those available from the Gherkin, the Shard, London Eye, etc.

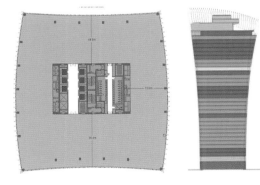

Images courtesy of Land Securities

### 18. Doubletree Mint Hotel
Bennett Associates, 2010
7 Pepys Street, EC3
Tube: Tower Hill

There has been a minor rash of City hotels in recent years and two in the City Doubletree are notable: Allies and Morrison's building near Liverpool Street Station, and this one, of 583 rooms, near Tower Hill. Bennetts have done a good job and the hotel features a roof terrace bar (which, in truth, should have been more generous). (Compare with Foster's ME Hotel.)

Photo courtesy of Bennetts (Edmund Sumner / View)

### 19. Tower Place
Foster + Partners, 2002
Tower Place, EC2
Tube: Tower Hill

This 59,000 sqm gross complex comprises two office buildings lent greater unity and presence by a semi-outdoor glazed-over space featuring a large 'curtain' of suspended glass that is very much: 'Look Ma: no hands!' (The glass compression struts are an impressive touch.) It invites photographs, but the roaming security guards like to discourage you to the point of threatening legal action. Actually there are rights of way through the area, so technically they can't stop you if you walk between a double row of stainless steel studs to be found in the ground (leading to the bus parking area below). On the other hand, just stand further back, outside the property line and they can't do anything. Terrorism is serious; however, this kind of tourist hassle negates what the exterior space is all about.

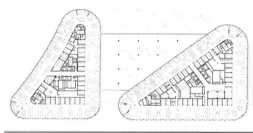

Photo courtesy of Foster + Partners)

## 20. Tower Hill Environs
Stanton Williams Architects, 2004
Tower Hill, EC3
Tube: Tower Hill

There are more than a few annual visitors to the Tower of London: 2,500,000 in fact. They not only want tickets, but souvenirs, toilets and fish'n'chips. Stanton Williams Architects were an admirable choice for such a project. The work is certainly a contrast to the now-demolished Po-Mo restaurant pavilion designed for this site by Farrells (although it is somewhat regrettable that his better Po-Mo work has been disappearing, one by one). Even Barcelona in the 1980s and 1990s would have been proud of Stanton Williams' urban design work. (Also see the Kings Cross front concourse area.)

Tower Hill is a fascinating place. Stand at its heart and look around. You will see 2000 years of London history: a medieval wall upon Roman foundations east of the Tower Hill Station; beyond that, St Katharine's Dock, from the 1820s, now with a Rogers office building; in front, the Tower of London from the 1066 invasion; on

the north-east corner, the former Port of London Authority building topped by Neptune, overlooking the docks (designed by Edwin Cooper in 1912); next to that, on its east side, is Trinity House (Samuel Wyatt, 1794); in front, Edwin Lutyens' memorial to sailors lost in WWI; over the river, London's house of its Mayor: City Hall (designed by Foster); all around, a group of City buildings which include Foster's Tower Place (2002). Meanwhile, it is difficult to persuade anyone that there is architectural merit in the Tower of London, a World Heritage Site. However, there is. One has to ignore the history and other tourists in order to cut through to the thing–in–itself and to approach the architectonics of a whole which, urbanistically, includes a peculiar 'village' set into the north-east corner for long-term workers.

**Right**: view to the Tower Bridge and the Tower of London from the Gherkin.

## 21. Billingsgate
Horace Jones, 1875; Rogers Stirk Harbour+Partners, 1988
Lower Thames Street, EC3
Tube: Tower Hill or Monument

This was London's principal fish market (by Horace Jones, 1875) until it was replaced by a new building just north of Canary Wharf. It was converted by Rogers into quite fine office spaces (albeit much of this underground, within impressive brick-vaulted spaces), just after the 1986 'Big Bang', but the tenants never occupied it and the building has been looking for a permanent role in life ever since.

Photo courtesy of RSH

## 22. Tower Bridge House
Rogers Stirk Harbour+Partners, 2005
St Katharine's Way, E1
Tube: Tower Hill

The comparison to make here is with Rogers' Channel Four building in Victoria. Both have relatively simple plans of twinned rectangular office areas, the whole given a dramatic front end in which an architectural branding statement is concentrated as an acrobatic display of steel and glass. In both instances, in different ways, this works very well. At Tower Bridge House (formerly K2) it works best at night, when its singular modernity stands out against all that surrounds it – especially against the Tower of London, but also the neo-warehouse office building built at St Katharine's Dock after the originals suffered mysterious fires at a period when no one was quite sure what to do with such redundant buildings.

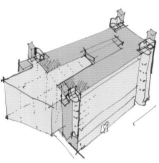

## 23. Tower Bridge Wharf Café
Tony Fretton Architects, 2012
The Wharf at The Tower of London, EC3
Tube: Tower Hill

This is a somewhat odd building in an unusual location – beneath Tower Bridge, legitimated by formal references to the crenellations of the Tower – but now upside down. And it's in timber instead of stone, although both are grey. Having said that, it is a pleasant enough work whose architectural treatment mixes a talent for the understated with the politics of what one does in such a place of revered heritage (the Tower is a World Heritage site).

The architects say: "The new four-part arrangement enters into a dialogue with the adjacent Tower of London outer wall, itself an assembly of towers and curtain walls of differing height and form. The choice of cladding material – rough sawn English sweet chestnut vertical cladding – is chosen to blend closely with the hues and tones of the Kentish Ragstone of which both the Tower walls and Tower Bridge are largely made. The stained sawn timber is like that used to build the utilitarian buildings that have historically occupied this site on the Wharf."

No doubt some visitors would prefer something less respectful and rather more like the Make pavilion at St Paul's (which possibly gives Fretton sleepless nights).

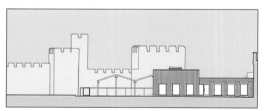

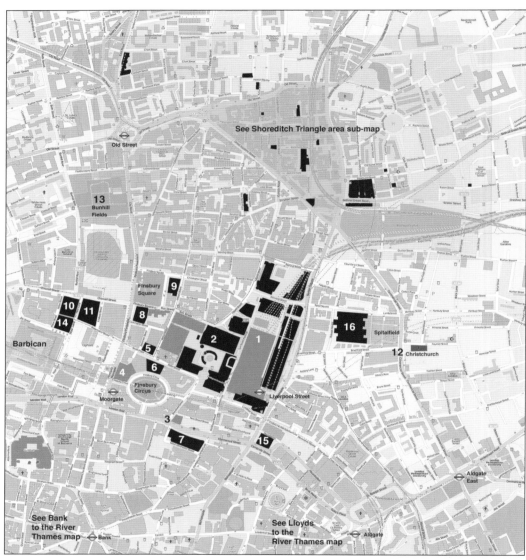

The north-eastern edges and fringe to the City of London are centred around Liverpool Street Station and the Broadgate development that envelopes it. This was completed in the late 1980s but some parts were soon being modified and buildings radically adapted and added to. The Broadgate Tower is the most significant example of the latter. Currently, a central part of the development is being redeveloped by Make Architects.

The next major area is immediately to the east: Spitalfields – where bankers meet with market entrepreneurs and then the immigrants of Brick Lane (increasingly an outreach of Hoxton and Shoreditch).

On the west of Liverpool Street is a group around Finsbury Circus and Finsbury Square. Further west are the Barbican and Golden Lane estates.

Shoreditch and Hoxton were, until relatively recently, simply parts of the East End (like Spitalfields). However, the expansion that followed the deregulatory 'big bang' of the mid-1980s reversed the City's historically introverted character, prompting an expansion in every direction (including upward). In part, this was to the north and east, particularly by means of a joint development project of the railway lands around Liverpool Street Station – which then encouraged further development across the road, around Spitalfield market.

For a while there was a strange planning hiatus over the Spitalfields area and, as at Borough, the vacuum was filled by entrepreneurs – here, quite unlike the bankers they serviced. Now supplemented by the Foster development, it has all been very successful.

Simultaneously, during the mid-1990s, the Shoreditch/Hoxton area was discovered by artists looking for cheap studios. Developers, restaurants, bars and a 'night area' designation quickly followed. What still looks like a derelict area is London's own version of grunge-city where media people meet fashion people meet the inhabitants of Brick Lane and Spitalfields. The TEA building (converted by AHMM) is an especially good example of how risk-taking developers can make the most of what is going on (and tenants make characterful use of the space available to them). However, the area has become somewhat touristy and the government has (perhaps with misguided good intentions) decided to capitalise upon the area's popularity by designating the Old Street roundabout as a global 'Tech City' – which, of course, means they risk killing it off).

**Top right**: view to the Broadgate Tower, from Curtain Street, in Hoxton.
**Right**: view into Broadgate.

## 1. Broadgate

Various architects, 1984–2014
Bishopsgate, EC2
Tube: Liverpool Street

The original buildings (on this site No.1 Finsbury Avenue and its two neighbours, 2 and 3 Finsbury Avenue) were designed by Arup Associates (under Peter Foggo, completed 1984) and constituted their first ever speculative office building – and they are still impressive (1). Following this, they were appointed for the master-plan of a scheme wrapping Liverpool Street Station, refurbishing that station and providing half of the office buildings on the site (2A). The remainder (2B–D) were designed by SOM's Chicago office in a new, trendy Po–Mo style. The complex was completed in 1992. One of the SOM designs (2D; 10 Exchange Square) was soon radically altered and its façade remodelled. Another (2C) has remained as a rather acrobatic and rather Chicago-looking building. Broadgate Tower and 201 Bishopsgate (3) date from 2008. Thirty years has seen a lot of change in this development.

At the time, Broadgate was pushing the boundary of the City northward, into another borough. Something similar was simultaneously happening on the east side, in Spitalfields. However, we here bump into the traditional immigrant area around Brick Lane and a peculiar inter-mediate period resulted in a new Foster building, rede-velopment of the market (with new restaurants, etc.) and a general change in the character of the area that matched general changes in Hoxton and Shoreditch.

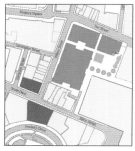

**Above**: plan of the original building on the site: No.1 Finsbury Avenue, by Arup As-sociates, under Peter Foggo. This was the first speculative office building the practice had designed (everything previous to this was custom-designed for specific users) and it is indicative of how times have changed since then that we now look back on this 'anti-commercial' attitude as distinctly peculiar.
**Below right**: winter ice skat-ing in the Broadgate Circle.

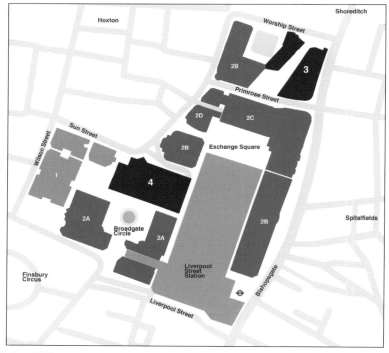

No.1 Finsbury Ave.

Exchange House

Broadgate Circle

## Broadgate: what to look for:

• How the masterplan wraps Liverpool Street Station and provides three squares in the London tradition.

• The first buildings on the site (No.1 Finsbury Avenue, on Wilson Street) are in the American tradition of post-war SOM, Saarinen, etc. (Photo top left.)

• How the Bishopsgate buildings by SOM and the other buildings by Arup Associates (e.g. around Broadgate Circle) constitute two opposing ideas of what architecture is all about, and yet both were forced by the developer (Stuart Lipton) to use lots of the same granite). Arup were attempting to continue with the values of Finsbury Avenue; SOM, meanwhile, were being distinctly Post-Modern.

• How SOM's Exchange House strives to be a Po-Mo version of Hi-Tech, straddling the railway tracks beneath the building. Two of the four arches penetrate the interior.

• How Arup's Broadgate Circle ironically strives to be like a Roman ruin. This character has more recently been submerged under the added retail content (particularly the upper-level bars, etc.) that we now see.

• How one of the SOM buildings was quickly updated to current fashions (2D). Similarly, the entire site was soon brought into line with current disability legislation (note ramps, lifts, etc.).

• How little retail content there is in the development. This was originally about 5% of the floorspace and was subsequently supplemented around Broadgate Circle.

• How Liverpool Street Station (designed by British Rail Architects) is an eclectic sleight-of-hand exercise in the old, the new, and the new pretending it is old.

• How Broadgate Tower, at the northern end of the site (3), is witness to SOM being more contemporary, but its acrobatic structure includes numerous phoney elements placed there for narrative and aesthetic effect.

• How the Make building (Broadgate 5) has replaced some of the Arup accommodation on a much larger scale and again in another style.

• Lots of art! (Flanagan. Serra, Dine, Segal, Lipchitz, Botero, etc.) Go to the Welcome Centre, just west of Make's new building).

## 2. Broadgate 5
Make Architects, 2015
Broadgate, EC2
Tube: Liverpool Street

This replacement building in the heart of the Broadgate development is 13-storeys and 105,000 sqm – much larger than its predecessor on this site for the past twenty-two years. It is for UBS and some floor plates can accommodate up to 3000 trading desks and 750 traders. The familiar total glass façade has been avoided and only 35% is glass (the remainder being stainless steel panels, providing a thermally high-performing envelope). At the time of writing (completion is expected in early 2015) the frame of the building provides an interesting contrast in scale and character with No.1 Finsbury Avenue (1994) and the first Arup Associates building in the Broadgate complex.

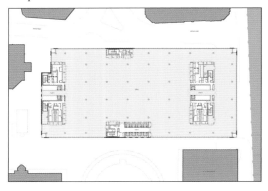

Images courtesy of Make

## 3. 85 London Wall
Casson Condor, 1990
85 London Wall, EC2
Tube: Liverpool Street

Buildings like this aren't constructed in the City any more: smaller, designed for professional firms that once comprised comparatively few employees requiring complexes of cosy offices and meeting spaces – quite unlike today's giant law firms inhabiting the City. The deeply recessed mullioned window panels and semi-projecting bays are designed to solve the problems of turning the corner at the prominent acute angle of the site.

## 4. Britannic House
Edwin Lutyens, 1920
Moorgate, EC2
Tube: Moorgate

This building (which has façades on Moorgate and Finsbury Circus) and Lutyens' other principal City building – the former head office of the Midland Bank, at Bank – are worth browsing. They are artful and idiosyncratic, but you have to look closely and make comparisons in order to acknowledge these qualities. Such notable 'grand manner' works in the City are now few and far between. (The building is adjacent to Fletcher Priest's Finsbury Circus House.)

## 5. Southplace Hotel

Allies and Morrison, 2012
3 South Place, EC2
Tube: Liverpool Street or Moorgate

This 80-bedroom hotel bears familiar A&M tropes, but feels like a large house that has been converted and dressed up, i.e., somehow underscaled and out of place, This probably results from its position on the wrong side of a boundary between the City and the borough of Islington. Other than this – an issue compounded by Fletcher Priest's new building across the road – it's a finely put together 'house'. Try the roof-top restaurant.

Photos courtesy of Allies and Morrison (Guy Montagu-Pollock)

## 6. Finsbury Circus House

Fletcher Priest Architects, 2013
South Place, EC2
Tube: Liverpool Street or Moorgate

The first thing striking one about this 11-storey refurbished building of about 13,000 sqm (net; 18,600 sqm gross) is the differences in scale between it and A&M's hotel across the road (and in the borough of Islington, not the City). There is an elegance and strength about this façade – which, of course, is all about the simplicity of window treatment and the materials employed. The façade on Finsbury Circus is an older, Po-Mo exercise, so look at the north façade (below).

Photo courtesy of FPA (Nick Worley)

### 7. Winchester House (Deutsche Bank)
David Walker Architects, with Swanke Hayden Connell, 1999
1 Great Winchester Street, EC2
Tube: Liverpool Street

There is a rather 1930s feel to Walker's streaming façade along London Wall, but inside this 2800 sqm building is an early example of a 'dealing factory'. This was 1999 and it now feels like a long time ago. Inside this urbane and finely detailed street frontage the fit-out is both office building *and* art gallery. The art is impressive and, of course, valuable, but unfortunately the same cannot be said for the Pringle Brandon fit-out which showcases it. (Apart from in the lobby, the notion that grand art should be in suitable settings seems to have eluded the wit of the fit-out designers).

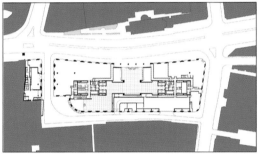

## 8. Citygate House
Foster + Partners, 2001; fit-out by Julian Powell-Tuck
39–45 Finsbury Square, EC2
Tube: Moorgate

Bloomberg's is rather like Reuters on steroids and this extension to a gentleman's club (designed by Giles Gilbert Scott in the 1920s) received an admirable fit-out by Julian Powell-Tuck (since, inevitably, altered somewhat). The Foster extension is idiosyncratic: rather like something by SOM in the 1960s. Foster has another Bloomberg building going up at Bank, opposite his Walbrook building (completion late 2014 or, if the site archaeologists have their way, later). Note the disturbingly similar building opposite, on the west side of Finsbury Square.

## 9. 30 Finsbury Square
Eric Parry Architects, 2002
30 Finsbury Square, EC2
Tube: Moorgate

This notable limestone façade makes a significant contribution to the uplifting of a rather dreary and neglected square just over the boundary from the City to Islington. It has inspired many a copy of off-set gridded frontages. Internally, there is a clear span from perimeter to central core and also a small central atrium. Also see Parry's buildings in Paternoster Square, 60 Threadneedle Street, etc.

The building just opposite, to the north (26 Finsbury Square), is by ORMS (2012).

Photo courtesy of Foster + Partners (Nigel Young)

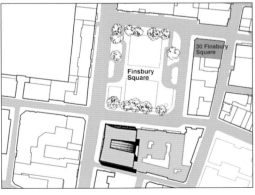

### 10. Ropemaker Place
Arup Associates, 2009
25 Ropemaker Street, EC2
Tube: Moorgate

This 21-storey building provides approx. 1,400 sqm of retail space and 55,000 sqm of net lettable office space. The developer (British Land) considers they have successfully delivered "a great range of floor-plates and a high level of specification to meet operational needs." These have been organised by Arup as "six large-scale interlocking cubic forms that rise up as a series of garden terraces." While the latter have become *de rigueur* for such developments, one presumes rights of light were a primary aspect of the design challenge and engendered these stepped forms. To assist them, Arup "collaborated with light sculptors and artists right from the beginning of the project too, helping to shape what would become a unique space in the City of London, on the inside and out." While this provides the aesthetic validity now deemed to be important for most contemporary schemes, the internal spaces are necessarily an open and uniform body ready for fit-out by other designers and the six interlocking cubic forms hardly show themselves as such either on the exterior or the interior. In other words, the rationale given in the diagram at bottom right (below) bears little relation to a habitable reality. On the other hand, such issues underscore the essential branding challenge of any office building. The detailing of reflective cladding, 'eye-shades', etc. is rather clever.

Photo courtesy of Arup Associates

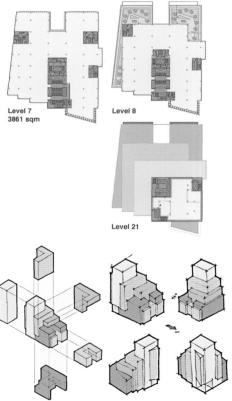

Level 7
3861 sqm

Level 8

Level 21

## 11. Milton Gate

Sir Denys Lasdun with Peter Softely & Partners, 1991
1 Moor Lane, EC2
Tube: Moorgate or Barbican

This peculiar all-glass, block-filling, 15,000 sqm, 9-storey office building lays claim to the hand of Sir Denys Lasdun, assisted by Peter Softely. It manifests Lasdun's fascination with castles and comes complete with corner towers and oriel windows. There is (of course, as one expects from Lasdun) a diagonal entry route (originally intended as a retail court). The building also has a double-façade, but was designed in the days when there was little alternative to coloured glass in order to cope with solar-gain. It is very green, literally.

Strangely, it is ageing rather well. The building enjoyed a major internal refurbishment completed in 2007 (by Squire and Partners).

Also see Arup Associates' Plantation Place and Ropemaker Place.

## 13. Bunhill Fields Burial Ground

Between City Road and Bunhill Row, just north of Finsbury Square.
Tube: Liverpool Street, Old Street or Moorgate

A burial ground? Well, yes, especially if you are interested in urbanism, open spaces and the like. You can find maps dotted around the City indicating the location of a whole series of such valued spaces, including St Dunstan's-in-the-east (near to the Tower), Postman's Park (photo bottom right, just north of Paternoster) and the churchyard of St Peter's, Cornhill (to the rear). See the City of London website for details or go to one of the 'gardens', where you will find a map. John Wesley's chapel (1778) is across the road.

## 12. Christ Church

Nicholas Hawksmoor, 1715
Commercial Street, E1
Overground: Shoreditch; Tube: Liverpool Street

Hawksmoor has six remarkable churches in London (Christchurch; St Anne's, Limehouse; St George, Bloomsbury; St Mary Woolnoth, Bank; St George-in-the-East, Wapping; and St Alfrege, Greenwich). In each case

the vigorously expressive external detailing reduces itself to a more calm internal geometry (notably at St Mary Woolnoth, where everything comes down into a cube).

Christchurch was recently restored. Whatever merits this may have, like many such restorations it has introduced a note of disjuncture between a distressed edifice redolent with the character of history and the pristine quality of a restoration (although less so at St George, Bloomsbury, perhaps the best of the surviving churches by Hawksmoor).

Whilst here, take a look around the corner, to the east, in Fournier Street – a group of post-Great Fire 17th-century (now gentrified) terrace houses which retain many of the original features.

## 14. The Heron
David Walker Architects (with RHWL), 2012
Moor Lane, EC2
Tube: Moorgate

This 36-storey podium+block development (Guildhall School of Music below, residential tower above) sits adjacent to the Barbican but could not be more different. The tower comprises a good mix of apartment sizes, many of them one-bedroom studios. Upon completion a three-bedroom apartment (175 sqm) was priced at about £5.5m (plan below, top). The building is mostly glazed (photo bottom right). This is the architect's description of the scheme:

> The redevelopment proposals provide a new world-class performance facility for the Guildhall School of Music & Drama – including a new 625 seat concert hall, 225 seat theatre, 120 seat studio theatre, and associated rehearsal, administrative and teaching spaces, which are located between Basement 2 and Floor 6. A 28s private residential tower sits above the School at the eastern end of the site. The scheme is arranged into two distinct elements: The School, which occupies the entire footprint of the site and is formed into a 6 storey block and the residential tower, which sits at the eastern end of the school block. The tower has been positioned to minimise any detrimental loss of daylight to the residential units of the Barbican. The massing of the tower has been carefully composed with due consideration to long distance views, particularly those from the Thames.

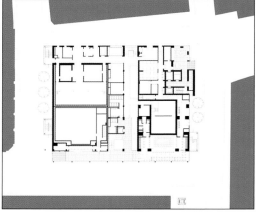

## 15. Heron Tower

Kohn Pedersen Fox Associates, 2008
110 Bishopsgate, EC3
Tube: Liverpool Street

One of a cluster of towers in this area, outside of viewing corridors to the dome of St Paul's Cathedral. The key novelty of this 46-storey design (providing 41,150 sqm of office space) is a series of 3-storey internal 'villages' set around an atrium, with floor plates of between 1200 and 1000 sqm. (Something similar is used on the HOK building for Barclays at Canary Wharf, and on an SOM building also there.) The core is set on the south face and is clad with photovoltaics (engendering an odd, disorienting experience when riding the glass lifts).

Overall, the Heron is impressive but strangely devoid of presence other than bulk. The architects claim that "Our aim for Heron Tower was to break-out of the box of the commercial high rise development and to challenge its basic assumptions." However, the 'thing' remains very much 'a box' that seems rather divorced from both its inner life and, especially at ground level, from City life. Little is given away apart from a correlation between the strident diagonal struts and the three-floor increments.

At the top there is a publicly accessible bar and restaurant. And the lobby shows off an impressively large aquarium (12 x 4 x 2m).

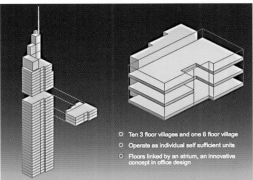

○ Ten 3 floor villages and one 6 floor village
○ Operate as individual self sufficient units
○ Floors linked by an atrium, an innovative concept in office design

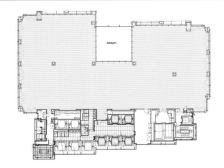

Atrium

### 16. 1 Bishops Square
Foster + Partners, 2006
1–10 Bishop's Square, E1
Tube: Liverpool Street

This is a typical Foster project: a sound scheme, but something again seems to have gone wrong in the detailed handling – a serious issue when the scheme is meant to be coping with the distinct 'otherness' of life in Spitalfields market. There is a brave attempt at an interface between street-life seeping over from Brick Lane into banker-life seeping over from Broadgate, etc., but the interaction only works because the former has some vitality to it. Nevertheless, the fundamental strategy is sound, providing an early example of the trend toward the provision of party-terraces (well, this was 2006). Have a look at Nicholas Hawksmoor's remarkable Christchurch and wander over to Fournier Street, just beyond, then through to another strange interface in Brick Lane between the Bangladeshi restaurants and the grungy white middle-class stuff at the northern end. It is the incongruous intermix that makes this area so interesting.

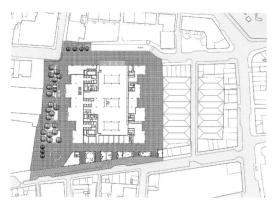

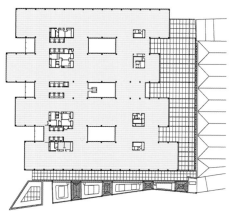

**Top**: view to 10 Bishops Square.
Left: ground floor and a typical office floor of 1-10 Bishop's Square.
**Above**: view into the market shed.
**Right**: Hawksmoor's Christchurch, which has been totally refurbished inside (as has St George, Bloomsbury).
**Bottom**: Fournier Street. These houses date from the late 17th century. You can play architective, roughly dating such buildings, simply by looking at the windows. After the Great Fire of London (1666) the building regulations progressively removed all woodwork from the façades, pushed the windows back and reduced the amount of frame showing. (There are, of course, other indications. If you are interested, also go to the Bloomsbury area.)

FREEHOUSE

# The City:
# Shoreditch
# and Hoxton

BARLEY MOW

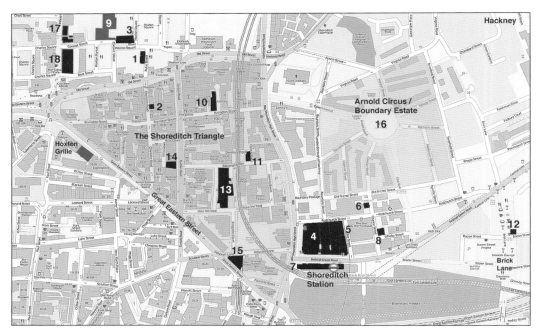

There are a number of focal points in the area around about the so-called 'Shoreditch Triangle'. The west is being taken over by City tenants; the east is spreading toward Brick Lane and inner Hackney (an area of gentrification).

The point about Shoreditch has been its distressed 'edgy' qualities representing everything that sanitised City areas are not. This has been what has attracted media people to the area (notably into the Tea building) – as well as its bars, restaurants and weekend night life in general. The government's recent attempt to promote the area as some kind of 'media city' misses the point of the values informing a district that was once home to the infamous Kray twins. Gentrification continues in areas to the north and north-east (De Beauvoir Town and Hackney).

### 1. White Cube Hoxton
Mike Rundell Associates, 2002
Hoxton Square, N1
Overground: Shoreditch; Tube: Old Street

A two-storey addition to an existing building, epitomising the arty basis to Hoxton's original popularity as an 'edgy' location (the artists have now moved on to places such as Fish Island in Stratford, with developers in hot pursuit). The old print works was converted in 2000 and then the roof addition was provided using 18 prefabricated modules. Rundell was also responsible for the Mason's Yard version of White Cube in St James' (2006).

## 2. 66 Charlotte Street
Stephen Taylor Architects, 2008
66 Charlotte Street, EC2
Overground: Shoreditch; Tube: Old Street

This building and another similar one at 10 Chance Street (next to Adjaye's Dirty House) are a pair to see together, but this is the superior one. A key reference for both is the dark engineering brick used by Maccreanor Lavington Architects' Lux building in Hoxton Square (1998). As with the Lux, the general impression is not far removed from that of some Georgian houses: walls of brickwork punctuated by large windows (see the photo bottom right), now emphasising a degree of structural ambiguity enhanced by laser-cut metallic details (also used by Maccreanor Lavington on some of their housing schemes). The general aesthetic has become fashionable in recent years, often with offset window openings and dark-coloured bricks which, ironically, mimics the pollution found on genuine Georgian buildings.

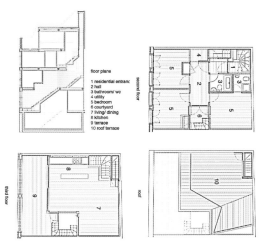

floor plans

1 residential entrance
2 hall
3 bathroom/ wc
4 utility
5 bedroom
6 courtyard
7 living/ dining
8 kitchen
9 terrace
10 roof terrace

## 3. Lux
Maccreanor Lavington Architects, 1998
2–4 Hoxton Square, N1
Overground: Shoreditch; Tube: Old Street

This in-situ concrete building was designed as the architects' shell-and-core development, later with a small cinema and art gallery. It didn't work out and the building has been subsequently converted to other office and café uses ... but it still looks good and set a trend. (See the note above regarding a recent return to brickwork, etc., as in the Georgian example on the far right, whose alarming lack of brickwork almost suggests the presence of a concrete frame.)

## 4. Tea Building

Allford Hall Monaghan Morris, 2000-12
Shoreditch High Street / Bethnal Green Road, E1
Overground: Shoreditch; Tube: Old Street or Liverpool Street

The Tea building epitomises and exemplifies the Shoreditch media success story. It was formerly an 1890 tea distribution and bacon smoking factory and Derwent took a punt on it, staring off tentatively and improving the building as it proved to be a success and the general character of the area changed (including a new Shoreditch station across the road). The architects say:

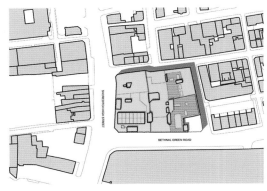

Encapsulating a new solution to the evolving demands of contemporary working life and avoiding an over-designed and sterile approach, Tea Building establishes a set of low-cost spaces that can be continuously reconfigured by tenants with the help of architect and landlord to form an intelligent and constantly evolving whole. The design strategy – robust and straight-forward – has focussed on the provision of inherently flexible unit sizes and configurations to attract a diverse mix of tenants.

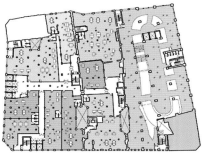

Left: entrance area, with container-reception box.

Left centre: typical corridor space: simple, bare, large graphics.

Above: Site plan and typical floors. In the top site plan and the lower plan (a typical upper floor) the large area to the right is the offices of Mother, the advertising agency (note the giant concrete desk that wraps the room). This west end is the 'biscuit building.' The middle floor plan is the ground floor.

Left: inside the Mother agency, with its over-sized concrete desk that winds through the room.

## 5. Shoreditch House + Rooms
Archer Architects, 2012
Ebor Street, E1
Overground: Shoreditch; Tube: Old Street or Liverpool Street

Shoreditch Rooms (a hotel) and Shoreditch House (a private club for 'creatives' accessed through the hotel lobby) form the south-eastern corner of the urban block AHMM have managed as a whole. The hotel – designed by Archer Architects, with Tom Dixon among the interior designers – is a club that likes to think of itself as the edgiest in London (complete with roof-top swimming pool, photo top right). Certainly, it knocks spots off the likes of Pall Mall clubs for gentlefolk, the bankers' club at the Gherkin, etc. But it is equally theatrical.

## 7. BoxPark
Roger Wade, 2012
Bethnal Green Road, E1
Overground: Shoreditch

## 6. 10 Chance Street
Stephen Taylor, 2007
10 Chance Street, E1
Overground: Shoreditch

Another work by Stephen Taylor (see Charlotte Street) Chance Street was once lined with lower-grade silk weavers' houses. Here, Taylor manages to squeeze three small units onto an equally constrained site. Chance Street also has Adjaye's Dirty House and Shoreditch House Rooms.

Developed by Roger Wade, BoxPark is an attempt to do a number of things. Above all it aims to be a mini 'brand-city' "filled with a mix of fashion and life-

style brands, galleries, cafés and restaurants" placing "local and global brands side-by-side, creating a unique shopping and dining destination". It is veritably "a living, fertile community of brands packed with talent, innovation and attitude that puts creativity and fashion back where they belong: on the street". BoxPark aims to exploit that curious Shoreditch phenomenon called 'the more grungy/edgy it seems, then the more everything costs.' The fundamental equation is simple: take the notion of a 'pop-up' retail environment made of containers, add 'cool' brands tied into the thriving potential of this end of Brick Lane, add 'attitude', capitalise on the new links provided by the Overground station and cash-in on the Olympics (it was opened around that time). It has, admittedly, been done quite well, although the rapidity with which this whole area has become a hollowed-out tourist destination is alarming. (Go, for example, to Colombia Street Flower Market on a Sunday morning.)

## 8. Dirty House

Adjaye Associates, 2002
Chance Street, E1
Overground: Shoreditch; Tube: Old Street or Liverpool Street

An enigmatic house conversion for two artists (Tim Noble and Sue Webster), externally painted in anti-graffiti paint: sombre, private, with reflective glass windows but transformed at night when the top storey is lit up. Behind the retained brick walls are two studios topped by a sleeping and living space. An inner steel frame keeps the whole thing in place; deep window reveals indicate the internal; insulation added to the existing brickwork. Like the INIVA building, the exterior is designed to obfuscate but not deny what is going on in the interior. Again, as at INIVA, games are played with recessed and flush glazing.

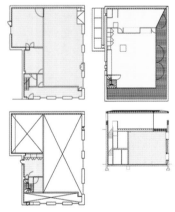

The planning of Dirty House is somewhat less enigmatic than the exterior.
In essence, there are two high studios (see section at bottom) and an upper residential floor.

## 9. Circus space

Tim Ronalds Architects, 2007
Coronet Street, N1
Overground: Shoreditch; Tube: Old Street or Liverpool Street

An unusual project off Hoxton Square: the UK's premier circus training school, and one of the top three such schools in Europe, occupying the former refuse-fired electricity generating station, built in 1895-97. It was originally converted to a circus training school by Philip Lancashire between 1993–96, providing a gymnasium and training space. Ronalds Architects later built a Creation Studio and Acrobatic Studio, several artists' start-up workspaces and a new link building. See the Ironworks baths in Clerkenwell, also by Ronalds.

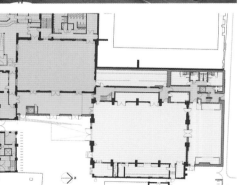

Photo courtesy of TRA (Morley von Sternberg)

## 10. Iniva
Adjaye Associates, 2008
Rivington Place, EC2
Overground: Shoreditch; Tube: Old Street or Liverpool Street

The Institute of International Visual Arts is as enigmatic as any of Adjaye's other designs of this period and certainly bears an affinity to Dirty House. There are some interesting details in a building whose façade establishes a unified presence that defies easy interpretation and correlation to what is inside. Look down one side and then walk down to the opposite end – and then note how perspective has been played with. It's rather clever, although hardly obvious.

There is not a lot to the interior of INIVA, despite the promise of the exterior: reception, a gallery and a café on the ground floor; with a library, seminar rooms and, at the top, an administrative floor. However, the detailing is well considered as well as economic.

## 11. Bateman's Row
Theis & Khan Architects, 2010
24 Bateman's Row, EC2
Overground: Shoreditch; Tube: Old Street or Liverpool Street

A tight site adjacent to the railway lines, converted into studios for the architect and a residence for the family above (except that they quickly sold on and moved out). It's an admirable and well-proportioned piece of infill (look carefully).

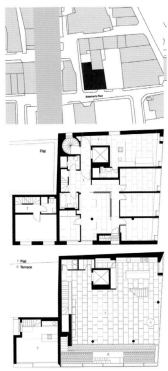

**12.** 23 Bacon Street
William Russell, 2002
23 Bacon Street, E1
Overground: Shoreditch; Tube: Old Street or Liverpool Street

An early example of gentrification in the Brick Lane area, done about the same time as Adjaye's Dirty House (who, incidentally was once the partner of Russell, and is now a partner at Pentagram). The entry area is now a bit more defended than originally intended (as in this photo). Also see Russell's work in south-west London.

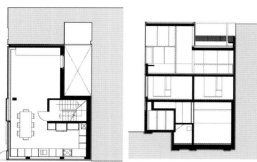

**13.** Amnesty International
Witherford Watson Mann Architects, 2005
17–25 New Inn Yard, EC2
Overground: Shoreditch; Tube: Old Street or Liverpool Street

A work that put this young firm on the map (they were the Stirling Prize winners in 2013). In theirs words:

the complete re-working of two furniture factories and a new extension, brought Amnesty International UK's 170 staff together in a single 'home'. Carefully judged relationships between the 250 seat auditorium, teaching, exhibition and working spaces with the surrounding urban context, have enabled staff integration and provided new opportunities to engage with their members and the public.

Also see the Whitechapel Art Gallery.

## 14. Curtain Road
Duggan Morris Architects, 2014
141–145 Curtain Street, EC2
Overground: Shoreditch; Tube: Old Street

A welcome refurbishment and extension to this old building by a firm with a refreshing take on matters: four storeys (inc. basement) of studios and three of apartments. The scheme has enjoyed an extensive examination of context and neighbourly relations, together with a series of more subtle architectonic moves that establish its presence.

**Top**: the context of the new upper-floor extension (141–145 is on the left).

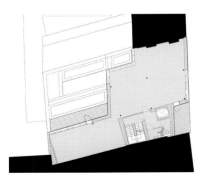

## 15. Village Underground
Foxcroft & Laurent, 2006
Great Eastern Street, EC2
Overground: Shoreditch; Tube: Old Street or Liverpool Street

Old containers and Tube carriages on top of a warehouse – what Shoreditch used to be all about (they are offices). It's bizarre, incongruous, wonderful and is unlikely to be repeated – not in this area, anyway.

## 16. The Boundary Estate
LCC, 1900
Arnold Circus, E2
Overground: Shoreditch

A replacement for some of the worst slums in London and a monument to late Victorian endeavours to house the working class in better housing (well, the 'industrious' sector of that class). It is the conclusion of charitable housing schemes and the beginning of local borough programmes that continued through to the 1970s, when Thatcher brought it all pretty much to a close.

## 17. Urbanest Student Accommodation
Feilden Clegg Bradley Studios, 2009
East Road, N1
Tube: Old Street

A scheme described as "134 student units, 36 single rooms in 6 bed cluster flat configurations and 50 twin room which share a shower room and kitchenette between two bedrooms". You might be more interested in the playfulness of the street façade. The ground level is retail and workshops.

## 18. 10 East Road and Linen Court, etc.
Lifschutz Davidson Sandilands, 2012
20 East Road, N1
Tube: Old Street

A large scheme of 673 more student rooms and 300 hotel rooms on a site adjacent to so-called 'Silicon Roundabout' (Old Street), together with an office building (Linen Court) of 3800 sqm net. In effect, the overall scheme bridges between the City, Hoxton and residential areas to the north.

**Left**: a typical room at Urbanest.

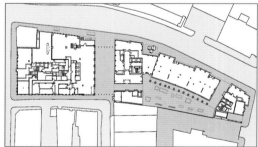

**Above**: the site plan for 10 East Road and Linen Court.

**Left**: Linen Court – the building in the East Road group that is nearest to the Old Street roundabout – manages to achieve a dramatic presence (top left of the plan above).

# The City:
# North-West side
# to the
# River Thames

# The City: North-West side to the River Thames

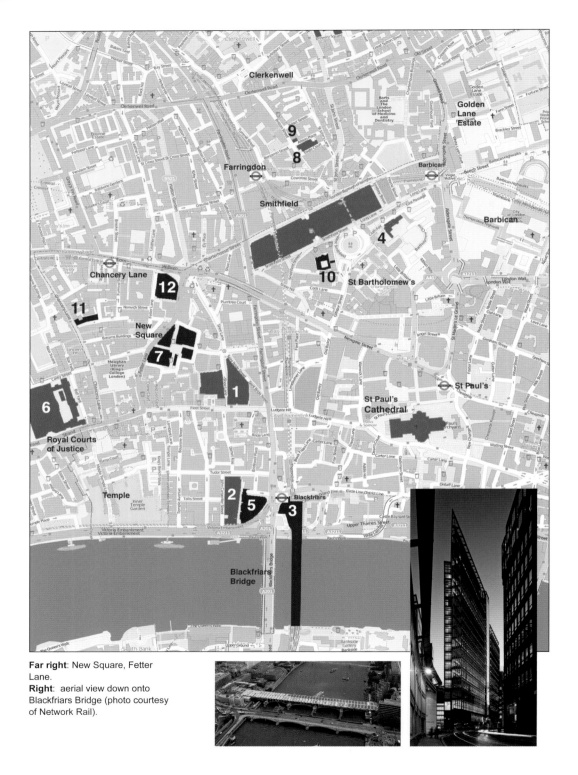

**Far right**: New Square, Fetter Lane.
**Right**: aerial view down onto Blackfriars Bridge (photo courtesy of Network Rail).

Although the political boundary of the City is as far west as the Royal Courts of Justice, its true geographical boundary is Farringdon Road, beneath which lies the Fleet River. Until relatively recently, the area to the west of this river was dominated by Fleet Street and its newspaper industry.

The City's spill in this direction took place in the late 1980s when the newspapers moved out, not only leaving major sites in Fleet Street ripe for redevelopment, but also an area of support firms in buildings to the north, in Clerkenwell — an area taken over by architects and designers, quickly followed by furniture companies.

Examples in Fleet Street include the new investment office buildings erected where the Daily Express and the Daily Telegraph (1930) had been. Both frontages still remain and the Daily Express at 120 Fleet Street, EC4 is a splendid example of Art Deco (Sir William Owens and Robert Atkinson, 1930–32).

Another example is the building designed for J.P. Morgan by BDP (1992): a massive Hi-Tech/Po-Mo neo-palazzo. This sits behind the rather fine Davis & Emmanuel school of 1880 which, as one might expect (as at Lloyds Register), is used for executive meeting rooms.

Immediately beyond that, further west, is a more significant barrier to expansion westward: the Inns of Court – a district of lawyers since the Middle Ages that has its focus at George Street's Royal Courts of Justice. The Inns are worth perambulating (the gates close about 5 p.m.).

To the north of St Paul's the Smithfield Meat Market (attributed to the City architect, Horace Jones, completed in 1868) serves as a barrier between City developments and Clerkenwell: architect-city. It is near here that Hopkins' Haberdasher's Hall is hidden away.

In general, this north-western and western fringe area has no large-scale developments such as Broadgate, except for the notable development of New Square, Fetter Lane. However, larger (and controversial) developments are beginning at the west end of old Smithfield market. (A scheme from John McAslan+Partners obtained planning permission in July 2013.)

## 1. 120–9 Fleet Street
Sir Owen Williams, Ellis & Clarke, and Robert Atkinson, 1933
120-9 Fleet Street, EC4
Tube: St Paul's, Chancery Lane

The former Daily Express at 120 Fleet Street, EC4 is unmissable, especially during Open House London (in September). All you now see is the Vitrolite façade (London's first curtain wall) and the original lobby, but the latter (by Robert Atkinson) is by far the best example of Art Deco in London. Next door, at 135–41, is the former Daily Telegraph building (by Elcock and Sutcliffe with Thomas Tait and Owen Williams as consulting engineers (1931)). The former printing building behind is now the Goldman Sachs Building by Kohn Pedersen Fox (1991).

## 2. J.P. Morgan building
BDP, 1998
John Carpenter Street, EC4
Tube: Blackfriars

A classic Po-Mo building that should be compared with GMW's neo-Gothic Minster Court (at Fenchurch Street). This neo-Renaissance palazzo for trading comes in at over 66,000 sqm, with two trading floors of some 4645 sqm each. The riverside building is the old City of London School (1882), by Davis & Emmanuel.

### 3. Blackfriars Station
Jacobs Architecture, 2013
Tube: Blackfriars

A Will Alsop concept for the extension and cover to the tracks on the bridge, executed by Jacobs Architecture, who boast it is the "largest solar panel-covered bridge in the world", providing 50% of the station's needs (900,000 kWh per annum).

### 4. St Bartholomew-the-Great
Cloth Fair, EC1
Tube: Farringdon

Described by Pevsner as "the most important 12th century monument in London" this is a marvellous place of layered attendances, some of them very negative. Every architectural enthusiast will surely wallow in its strange juxtapositions and even clashes of features, details and styles. The building has Norman parts supplemented by centuries of further work that Henry VIII attempted to demolish. Aston Webb was responsible for the early 20th-century restoration (until 1928). Like the Soane Museum, one shouldn't miss this place. Ignore the history and simply soak up the architectural dispositions, collisions and the rest (which are worth comparing with All Saints, at Margaret Street, in the West End, completed hundreds of years later).

### 5. Unilever Building
Lomax Simpson with Burnet & Tait, 1932; KPF, 2008
Victoria Embankment, EC4
Tube: Blackfriars

You need to go inside, to the atrium, of this 1932 building that has been gutted and reconfigured. The original was designed by a Unilever Board member with the notable architects John Tait and an ageing John James Burnet. The public can access the atrium, where they will find a cafe.

### 6. Royal Courts of Justice
George E. Street, 1882
The Strand, WC2
Tube: Farringdon

Street's court building even houses a memorial to the architect within its grand central hall (scene of many a TV drama). It is quite an artful and picturesque pile, but actually has a very rational classical plan and, in that sense, is rather like the Houses of Parliament building. Like that other building this one was a problematic project undertaking. (Often open during Open House London.)

## 7. New Square, Fetter Lane

Bennett Associates, 2008
Fetter Lane, EC4
Tube: Chancery Lane

A superior and urbane development of five buildings, all designed by Bennetts, rising from 2 (the management building) to 19 storeys, providing about 65,000 sqm of offices and another 25,000 sqm of retail space. The masterplan is excellent and well scaled and Bennett Associates have, remarkably, lent a different character to each building. Each is more 'green' than the current Building Regulations require. Now if only estate agents would desist from calling this area 'mid-town', as if it were in Manhattan.

Images courtesy of Bennett Associates (Peter Cook)

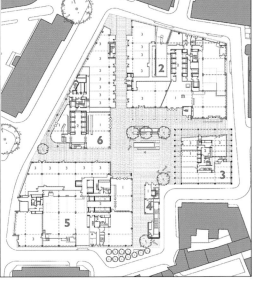

Images courtesy of Bennett Associates (Peter Cook)

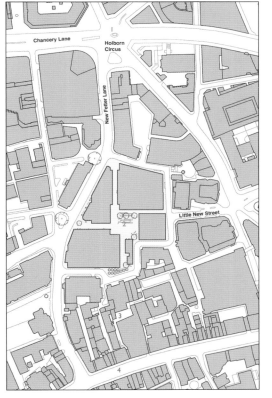

## 8. Goldsmiths Centre
Lyall, Bills & Young, 2012
Eagle Court, 42 Britton Street, EC1
Tube: Farringdon

In the architects' words: "The development comprises a new building and an adapted Grade Listed II Victorian School linked by a glazed atrium. As well as the core educational facilities, the centre provides commercial workshop space, a large exhibition area, seminar space, a café and offices." This simple *parti* works well, creating an interesting top-lit entrance area, with the new wing to one side. "The primary function of the Centre," we're told, "is to provide post-graduate education, business start-up studio space, business skills tuition and support for young goldsmiths, plus craft skills training to pre-

apprentice silversmiths close to Hatton Garden, the traditional home of the trade in London." The place describes itself as "a hub for members of the Jewellery, Silversmithing and Allied Trades, the local community and the general public." It's a pleasant development.

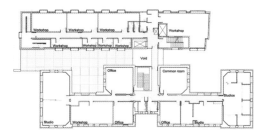

Photos courtesy of LBY (Morley von Sternberg)

## 9. 44 Britton Street
CZWG ,1988
18 West Smithfield, EC1
Tube: Farringdon

A rather joyful, quirky, eclectic and slightly mad design with (perhaps) vague references to Ledoux, etc.

(note the concrete 'logs' as window lintels), intrinsically putting up two fingers to po-faced architectural values in its celebration of architecture as fun (frozen jokes rather than frozen music). Designed for the journalist Janet Street-Porter, this is typical Piers Gough and gets better as it ages and retains its uniqueness.

### 10. Haberdasher's Hall
Hopkins Architects, 2002
18 West Smithfield, EC1
Tube: Farringdon

This building designed for the Worshipful Company of Haberdashers sits opposite Smithfield market and St Bartholomew church, but it is hidden within the urban block. It has been designed as a cloistered courtyard and is very much about scale, proportion, brickwork, lots of oak, leaded roofs and large ventilating chimneys – all very Hopkins, manifesting a body of concerns first made evident at Bracken House.

### 11. 40 Chancery Lane
Bennett Associates, 2014
40 Chancery Lane, WC2
Tube: Chancery Lane

Another from the Bennetts office (9500 sqm), not far from New Square, incorporating two small 19th-century buildings into the scheme, forming an inner court and described as being "carefully designed to replace or incorporate existing buildings on the site with a premium development that respects adjacent listed buildings, acknowledges surrounding scale and materiality, and responds to key views".

CGI courtesy of Bennett Associates

### 12. Sainsbury Business Centre
Foster + Partners, 2002
33 Holborn Circus, EC1
Tube: Chancery Lane

A simple enough 38,400 sqm office building. It's all about the atrium and a base reminiscent of Tower Place, but is rather less dramatically impressive than one suspects was intended.

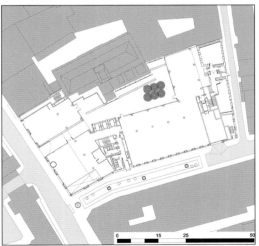

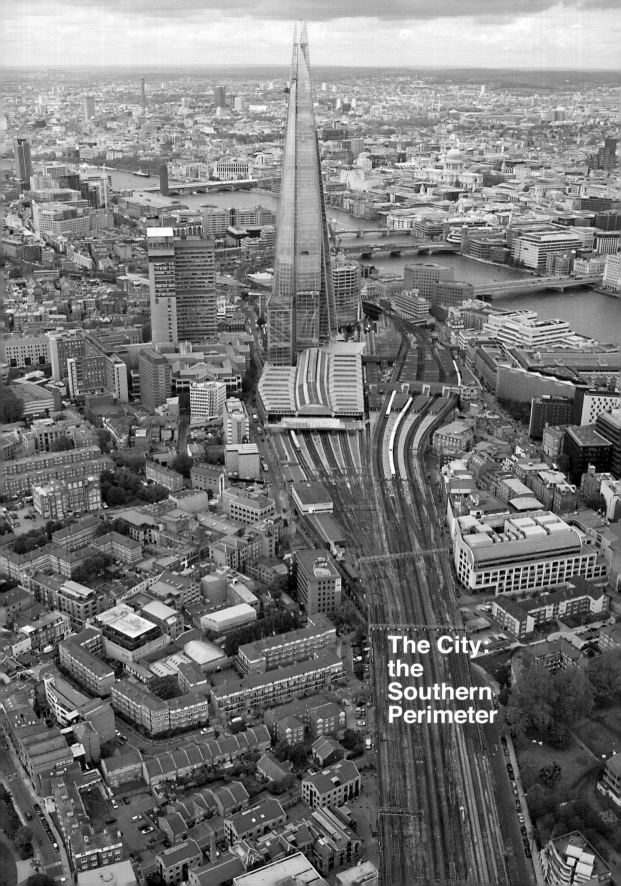

The City:
the
Southern
Perimeter

## The City: a leap across the River Thames ...

A settlement in the place of 'south-work' has existed since the Romans arrived and constructed London Bridge. Two of their roads met here and the place later became a market-town, with a church constructed on the foundations of a Roman building (now Southwark Cathedral). As an arrival point into the City of London, Southwark became owned and controlled by the City as the 'Bridge Ward Without '– a place of inns, prisons, prelates and places of pleasure and notoriety (including theatres such as the Globe) and, later, of warehouses, docks and the like.

London Bridge Station accepted its first trains in 1836 and was subsequently expanded and redeveloped on a massive scale. For example, the railway lines into the station sit upon a vast area of brick vaults that slice through the area up to where the Shard is now located.

In the post-war period Southwark was a relatively isolated area lost to the attentions of people in the City and West End, despite the flows of commuters to and from London Bridge Station; however, matters dramatically changed in two stages. The first was in the mid-1980s, with deregulation in the City that prompted massive expansion in every direction, including upward and across the river to Hays Galleria, the area around, and then into the riverside strip we now know as More London. The latter reached a first stage of completion (including City Hall) in 2000 – the same year that the Tate Modern opened – and there was a desirable riverside embankment walkway all the way from the London Eye through to Butlers Wharf. This newness included the (at first) wobbling Millennium Bridge, taking people directly between the Tate and St Paul's Cathedral.

Since that time the area has undergone accelerating change. Southwark Street, for example, was a dreary area until Bankside 123 was constructed, together with a reconstructed Globe Theatre, the Jerwood Space, Palestra, etc., although much of this redevelopment is along the Thames rather than more deeply into Southwark. On the other hand, the demand for new housing has prompted redevelopment all over the borough. Meanwhile, the stretch of riverside development is continuing westward around the Nine Elms and Battersea Power Station area.

At the heart of all this still sits the railway station. The arrival of the Shard, extensive works at ground level and the popularity of Borough Market across the road are currently transforming this location.

One of the more significant instances of urbanity within this area is More London – a development planned and designed in detail by Foster. Here, Tower Bridge and Butlers Wharf mark a termination to an embankment walkway that runs westward to Vauxhall Bridge (it actually extends further in each direction, but less easily and comfortably). At the heart of More London is the 'globe' of City Hall – the house of the Greater London Assembly and London's Mayor, designed by Foster's former employee, Ken Shuttleworth, who later founded Make Architects.

**Photo opposite**: looking west, above railway lines leading into London bridge Station, over which the Shard towers.

Photos courtesy of Foster+Partners (Nigel Young)

The southern side of the river, across from the City of London, separates into western and eastern parts (respectively, between Blackfriars and Southwark Bridge, and between London Bridge and Tower Bridge). These are linked by an embankment walkway and the area around Southwark Cathedral (Borough Market).

This entire area was, until relatively recently, a poor and neglected relation of the City lying across the River Thames. In the late 1980s boom years the City suddenly expanded over the river to Hays Galleria, then More London and later to an area near the Tate Modern (Bankside 123, Palestra and a new building on Blackfriars Road by AHMM).

It was also during the 1980s that Butlers Wharf was redeveloped as a mixed area of residences and smaller offices. However, the most significant change in the area was the arrival of the Tate Modern in 2000, together with a new riverside walkway that transformed this once lost

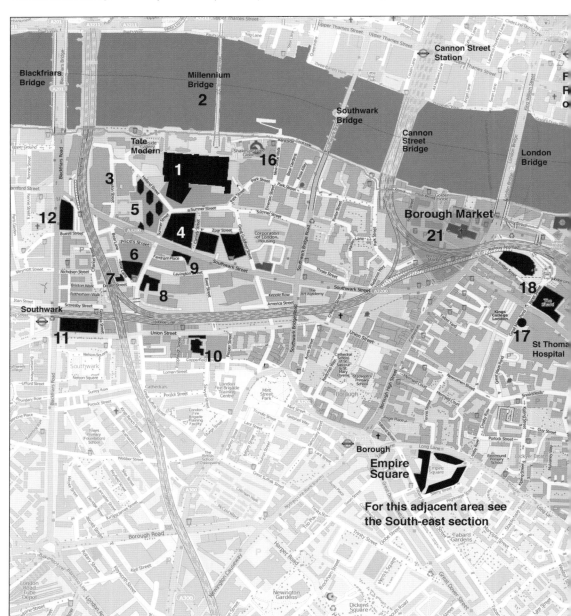

part of London and opened up a link from Westminster, along the river, to Tower Bridge.

The more intense developments are to the north of the east–west rail lines that slice through this area (e.g. More London, the Shard, the Tate Modern and Bankside 123). The area to the south side of London Bridge Station is more mixed, with many older residential buildings as well as new buildings such as the Fashion Museum, White Cube, the Jerwood Gallery, etc.

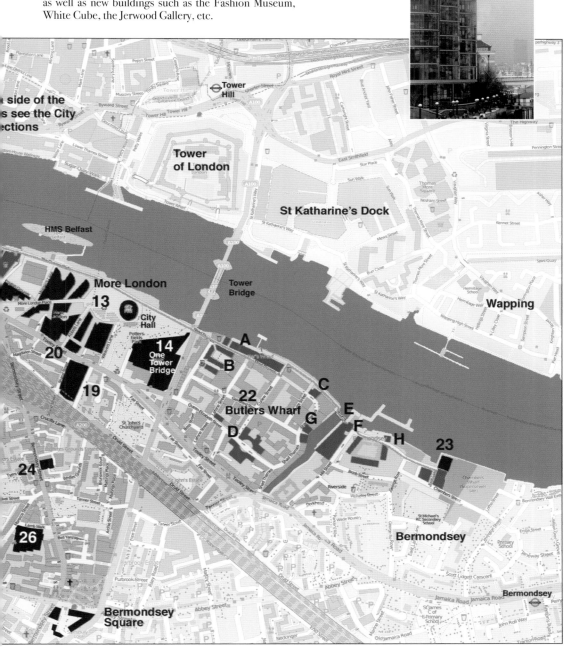

## 1. The Tate Modern

Herzog & de Meuron, 2000–2015
Bankside, SE1
Tube: Southwark or St Paul's

Herzog & de Meuron's transformation of Giles Gilbert Scott's oil-fired power station, completed in 1963 and closed in 1981 after the 1974 economic crisis when oil prices shot up, is a strange mixture of exhilaration and disappointment. The Turbine Hall can be impressive (photo below: Anish Kapoor installation), but the gallery spaces, the cafés and the like are under whelming. Even the hall is less impressive since the 'light-boxes' that were a clever way to illuminate it have been switched off (photo bottom right, before this economy cut).

The Tanks (over thirty metres across and seven metres high) were also converted by H & deM and opened in 2012 as a facility "dedicated to exhibiting live art, performance, installation and film works". They are described by the architects as raw industrial spaces that should be seen not merely as an annexe, "but as the roots of [...] something really fundamental to Tate's vision." By this they mean their design nearing completion at the time of writing: "a new dramatic eleven-levels tower housing new gallery spaces, rooms for the Friends, etc."

This extension is described in the CGI and drawings on the opposite page. It is 64.5 m high and its new gallery spaces are linked to the fourth floor of the Gilbert Scott building by a new bridge that crosses the Turbine Hall. It will be open in 2016.

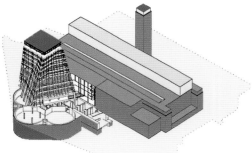

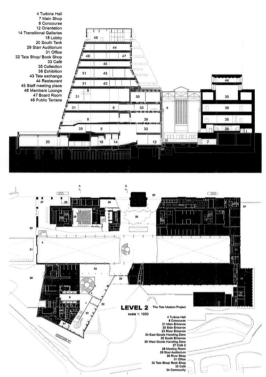

4 Turbine Hall
7 Main Shop
8 Concourse
12 Orientation
14 Transitional Galleries
18 Lobby
20 South Tank
29 Starr Auditorium
31 Office
32 Tate Shop/ Book Shop
33 Café
35 Collection
36 Exhibition
43 Tate exchange
44 Restaurant
45 Staff meeting place
46 Members Lounge
47 Board Room
48 Public Terrace

**Above and right**: the new, brick-clad extension to the Tate Modern is essentially above the 'Tanks' and described as a 'root' part of their development. To achieve this shaping has necessitated a quite complicated steel and concrete structure behind the brick facing. (Compare with the much smaller LSE Student building by O'Donnell & Tuomey.) We are told that a direct passage will take visitors directly from the Tate's principal riverside entrance, through the turbine hall and out onto a new public plaza at the rear of the site, thus linking the embankment more strongly to Southwark Street.

**LEVEL 2** The Tate Modern Project
scale 1: 1000

4 Turbine Hall
8 Concourse
21 Main Entrance
22 Side Entrance
23 River Entrance
24 East Goods Handling Zone
25 South Entrance
26 West Goods Handling Zone
27 Colli 2
28 Meeting Room
29 Starr Auditorium
30 River Shop
31 Office
32 Tate Shop/ Book Shop
33 Café
34 Community

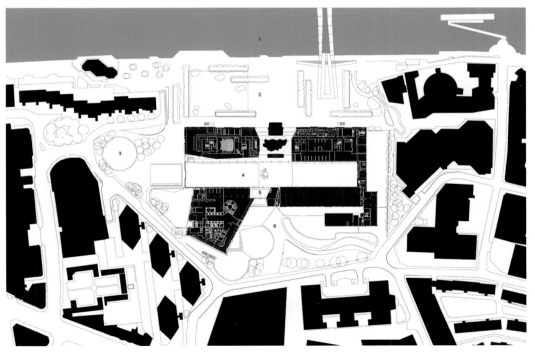

## 2. Millennium Bridge

Arup, with Foster+Partners, 2001
Bankside, SE1
Tube: Southwark or St Paul's

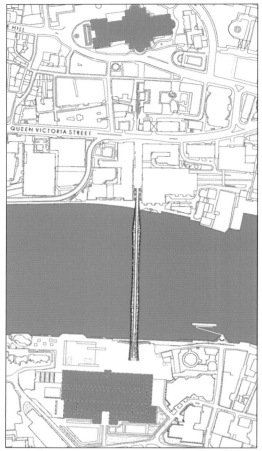

Yes, it did wobble – seriously and, some people assure us, dangerously: the natural outcome of trying to design such a flat suspension geometry (Foster's notion of 'a blade of light'). The answer was simple: dampeners, as found on a car's suspension, but it took some clever engineers to discover the causes. Otherwise the Millennium Bridge is very impressive but arguably makes a poor comparison with the likes of Hungerford Bridge, where the flat and wider walkways invite buskers to linger and entertain us. Urbanistically, the principal feature of the bridge is its direct connection between St Paul's and the Tate Modern on the south side of the river. However, both ends are necessary quite different. The St Paul's end is the most successful; the Tate end is a bit manifests the inability of Foster and the Swiss architects to agree on how the issue of a restricted termination should be handled. At the north end, the bridge more easily leads onto a pedestrian formal route up to St Paul's; however, at the southern end the bridge is brought to an abrupt termination and users have to turn around upon themselves in order to access the embankment.

## 3. Bankside Lofts
CZWG, 1998
Hopton Street, SE1
Tube: Southwark or St Paul's

CZWG have turned out a large number of forgetta-ble projects and one or two more memorable ones: Bankside Lofts is in the latter category. Adjacent to the Tate Modern, it comprises 130 apartments above retail spaces. There are some interesting flourishes, such as the timbered car parking area. As the authors say: "The Bankside Lofts development is a combination of convert-ed and new buildings set around a new raised garden. A red-brick Italianate ex-cocoa mill is at the centre of the group." A rich and successful mix.

**Below**: another nearby (and rather less successful) CZWG project, in Southwark Street: Bankside Studios (2001), about which the authors say: the design "unifies three existing buildings over a continuous stone base, with its main design

feature being the canting out of the two upper floors over the street in increas-ing degrees. This mega cornice creates a sense of enclosure over Southwark Street."

## 4. Bankside 123
Allies and Morrison, 2007
Southwark Street, SE1
Tube: Southwark

These three buildings by A&M (directly opposite the architects' studios) were the principal project that transformed this previously dreary and forgotten street. They're large, each with an atrium and ostensibly linked from reception area to reception area, as if on a skewer – a nice concept that security issues dismantle. The geom-etry of the overall site plan relates to the Tate and seeks to provide 'fingers' that enable passage from Southwark Street toward the Tate. Together, these 10–12-storey buildings deliver some 85,000 sqm of space. The anti-solar-gain fins (200 of them on the largest block) are said to be randomly arrayed (set by dice throws!, presumably within parameters set by engineers.) It's a good-quality development. (Compare the site plan with the same archi-tects' St Andrews housing scheme.)

## 5. NEO housing

Rogers Stirk Harbour+Partners, 2012
Southwark Street, SE1
Tube: Southwark

The Rogers manner of handling projects has become a recognisable stylistic brand – which is not to say that project issues are constrained into a formulaic approach, but rather that their way of thinking and handling issues seems to work. Here, a set of five carefully planned and arranged steel-framed apartment towers deliver the right kind of developer's mix adjacent to the prestigious Tate Modern. If there is a problem, it is that no one is quite sure if the structure is redundantly theatrical or authentically so; and that the occupants appear as if goldfish in a bowl, i.e., on show. Also see Riverlight, in Nine Elms (where, interestingly, EPR are the executive architects).

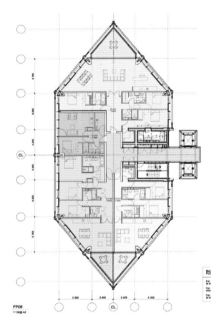

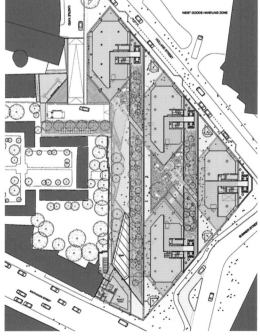

## 6. Bear Lane housing
Panter Hudspith Architects, 2009
Bear Lane, SE1
Tube: Southwark

Bear Lane is an admirable and rather 'crusty' effort to deal with a developer's brief for 89 flats above retail on the ground floor, local planners and the usual design & build form of contract in order to deliver something worthy. It's not all the architects intended (the plan has a central corridor instead of the dual-aspect layout originally intended, for example) and so they settled for what they could – which was to get away from a monolithic block and fragment the appearance of the whole: "by breaking down the mass of the building using smaller stacked elements the scheme is viewed as something other than a typical apartment building." Every flat façade is different, in order to find a way to move toward an interplay of individuality and collectivity (inevitably, the underlying model being Italian historic towns). It makes quite a contrast with the expressivity of Rogers' NEO scheme. Also see this practice's Royal Road project.

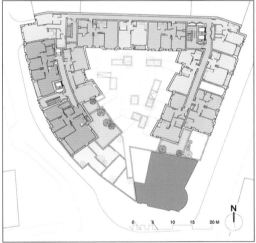

**Above**: plan of the overall scheme around a first-floor courtyard.
**Below left**: a typical flat plan.

## 7. Dolben Street housing
Associates of Ideas, 2010
Dolben Street, SE1
Tube: Southwark

This small housing project of five apartments immediately attracts one's attention: it has verve; it has a strident curve; it flashes glazed bricks, there's something relaxed about it ... and it's not a bad plan for such a peculiar site. It sets a good standard for inner-city blocks that are rarely this satisfactory.

## 8. Great Suffolk Street student housing
Allies and Morrison, 2010
17 Great Suffolk Street, SE1
Tube: Southwark

Student housing has become big business: secure hotels for affluent students, usually foreign, watched over by mum and dad's hoteliers. Many are very large; most are hardly interesting. This is an exception: on a budget, but loaded with typical Allies and Morrison tropes.

Photos courtesy of AOI

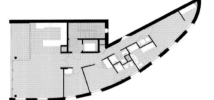

**Above**: window treatment on the student housing.
**Below left**: general view. The Dolben Street scheme is just to the left, out of camera. The beige brickwork adjacent to the pub belongs to the Bear Lane housing.

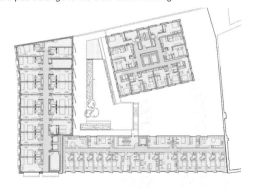

## 9. Allies and Morrison Studios

Allies and Morrison, 2004
Southwark Street, SE1
Tube: Southwark

A neat insertion into a line of buildings opposite 123 Bankside – now extended into the adjacent historic building to the west. Models fill the window space; the café next door is their own; and the interior is ever-so vaguely Tadao Ando. The extension (Farnham Place; on the right, below) is, if anything, an even nicer work, showing off A&M's skills at adapting and extending existing buildings with exhilarating touches of detail.

## 10. Jerwood Space

Paxton Locher, 1998; Munkenbeck+Partners, 2008
Union Street, SE1
Tube: Southwark or London Bridge

Refurbished Victorian school buildings converted into rehearsal spaces for dance, offices, apartments and a street strip of gallery space (with café, of course). The rather fine upper rehearsal spaces faced in Corten steel are by Alf Munkenbeck.

Photos courtesy of A&M (Nick Guttridge)

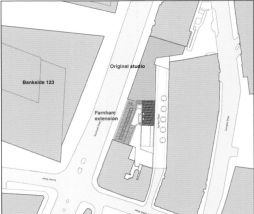

**Top:** general view to the Jerwood Gallery.
**Above**: the Munkenbeck-design upper parts.
**Right**: the ground-floor gallery space designed by Paxton Locher.

**Left**: views to the A&M studios (second phase).

119

## 11. Palestra House
Alsop Architects, 2005
Blackfriars Road, SE1
Tube: Southwark

A large beast with a few artful gestures: canted columns at the ground floor; an overhanging upper level (missing the underbelly lighting that would have made a huge difference); and offset, 'pixelated' cladding. It is similar in size to the Blue Fin building around the corner at 123 Bankside and makes an interesting comparison (28,000 sqm lettable office space). One is a characteristic Alsop poke-in-the-eye; the other is tasteful A&M (whose work Alsop dislikes: it's boring) ... and then see AHMM's nearby building (and, by 2017, Ian Simpson's tower).

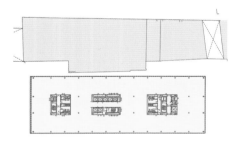

**Above**: typical floor plan of Palestra.
**Below**: typical floor plan of 240 Blackfriars Road.
Note: the plans are not to the same scale.

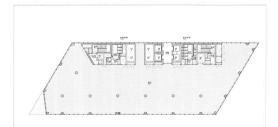

## 12. 240 Blackfriars Road
Allford Hall Monaghan Morris, 2014
240 Blackfriars Road, SE1
Tube: Southwark

Inevitably, one compares this AHMM building with its neighbours – Palestra and Bankside 123 – as well as AHMM's other output (such as its 'white-collar factory' concerns). Due for completion in March 2014, the 20-storey building provides some 21000 sqm of office space and 818 sqm of private apartments in an adjacent building. The offices present an abstract and crystalline character striving toward being iconically sculptural (somewhat like Allies and Morrison at 100 Bishopsgate). But this is not another TEA building (or an Angel building, 2010; or Biscuit Factory, 2008 – all by AHMM) and is hardly 'a white-collar factory'. It is described as "a simple extruded parallelogram [...] cut away in several planes: diagonally to the north, to orientate the building towards the river; at the base, to increase public space at street level; and across the roof, to create a dynamically-shaped sky room."

A 170m-high mixed-use building (including 271 flats) is being constructed across the road at One Blackfriars Road. (Architect: Ian Simpson; completion intended for 2017).

CGI image courtesy of AHMM

## 13. City Hall and More London
Foster + Partners, 1998-2012
Tooley Street, SE1
Tube: London Bridge

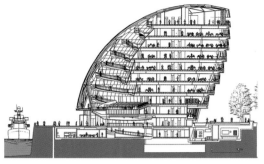

More London's masterplan strikes a diagonal from London Bridge Station through to City Hall and Tower Bridge (in the process by-passing Hays Galleria). Because the buildings shade the riverside walkway they are oriented north–south, with 'fingers' between them; however, these tend to be dead alley-ways. Overall, one is impressed, but there is a slightly diagrammatic quality to the development (the proverbial Achilles' heel of any architecture rooted in a machine paradigm). City Hall (2003; the house of London's Mayor and London Assembly; interior photo bottom right)) is a building designed for 400 people, but houses more like 700. The intention to be an open, 'democratic' building never worked – in part because of increased security arrangements after 9/11. The landscaping and 'Scoop' adjacent to the Hall has been successful as a scene of outdoor events. And the river walkway is invariably busy with tourists posing before Tower Bridge.

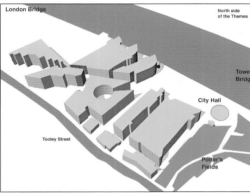

Photos courtesy of Foster + Partners (Nigel Young)

### 14. One Tower Bridge
Squire and Partners, 2014
Potter's Field, SE1
Tube: London Bridge

Potter's Field, adjacent to City Hall and to Tower Bridge, has taken a long time to reach development stage. Now, Squires (commissioned by the Berkeley Group)have designed an upmarket residential scheme that bounds the park in a manner ensuring good views to the river and to Tower Bridge – especially from the penthouses which, at 180–300 sqm, are described as 'the ultimate in urban living' (with prices to match). As at One Hyde Park, the emphasis is upon personal service. The ground floor has a considerable amount of commercial and retail content, also providing foyers into the residential blocks. The architects say:

> The buildings [...] form a new commercial street which visually and physically connects the bridge and surrounding streets. The new buildings frame the view of the Southern Tower and accommodate retail frontages with apartments above. The proposal encourages activity and pedestrian flow between Tooley Street and the riverside and helps to define the edge of the park with a new linear building connecting Shad Thames with More London.

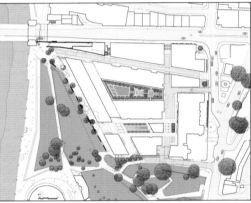

CGI courtesy of Squires

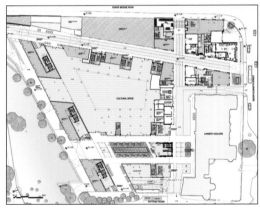

**Top left:** view from Tower Bridge, indicating the relationship to City Hall, with the Shard in the background. These apartments aren't in the same league as One Hyde Park, but that is the prevailing model forming the basis of a scheme with many access points, minimised common areas, concierge service, etc. Here, however, the complex has been opened up to public penetration at ground level.

**Above**: the Potter's Field setting; the ground-floor plan (note the central 'cultural area'.

**Left**: a mid-level apartment level plan.

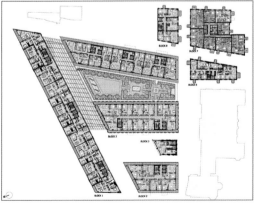

122

## 15. Hays Galleria

Michael Twigg-Brown & Partners, 1986
Battlebridge Lane, SE1
Tube: London Bridge

This warehouse was designed by William Cubitt and completed in 1856. It surrounds a dock where barges loaded and unload, infilled in preparation for the so-called 'Big Bang', with the buildings converted into office space for a bank (at the same time Billingsgate Market was being similarly converted). Despite stylistic differences, the Galleria arguably has a degree of charm absent from

the bland spaces between the Foster office buildings (the 'fingers' that bring daylight to the riverside). At a planning level, what is regrettable is that Hays and More London – as independent developments – have nothing to do with one another apart from sharing a place along the riverside walk and an entrance point on Tooley Street.

## 17. Plant wrap, Guys Hospital

Thomas Heatherwick, 2007
Great Maze Pond, SE1
Tube: London Bridge

Heatherwick here offers a characteristic sideways look at how one hides a heap of hospital air-conditioning plant and, as usual, comes up with a novel solution of complexity made from simple components. The adjacent hospital entrance area is by van Heyningen and Hayward.

## 16. The Globe

Pentagram, 1995; Allies and Morrison, 2014
21 New Globe Walk, SE1
Tube: London Bridge

The re-created Globe Theatre is a reminder that, in Shakespeare's day, this design was a bridge between medieval concerns with harmonic geometries (cf. John Dee's Preface to his translation of Euclid's Elements) and the shift from master-builders to what was soon after being provided by (equally neo-Platonic) architects such as Inigo Jones (who, incidentally, was also a theatrical masque designer), followed by a whole body of 'speculative' amateurs, prior to a creeping modernist develop-

ment called professionalism that peaked in the late 19th century. Whether Pentagram picked up on esoteric geometries and reproduced them is a moot point. This also goes for Allies and Morrison, who have supplemented the outdoor theatre with a 350-seat indoor one (the Sam Wanamaker Playhouse) based on a drawing of John Webb, 1666.

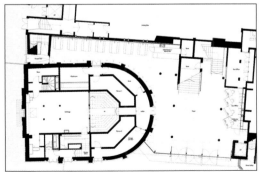

CGI courtesy of A & M

## 18. The Shard
Renzo Piano Building Workshop, 2013
St Thomas Street/London Bridge Station, SE1
Tube: London Bridge

Some love it; some detest it. On the negative side no one knows what it is doing here (spoiling the view from Parliament Hill to the dome of St Paul's), why it is so tall and why its content of layered offices (floors 2–28), restaurants (31–33), hotel (34–52) and apartments (53–65) – all topped by a public viewing gallery – is not expressed on the uniform exterior. On the positive side it is quite a building, well detailed (apart from where it hits the ground?) and a notable landmark viewable from all kinds of peculiar locations. Yes, the views out are impressive, although the London Eye is arguably better value. The building is 72 storeys high, and tops out at 310m.

**Right top**: the labyrinth of brick structures beneath the station and train lines. **Centre**: an instance of peculiar juxtapositions.

**Below right**: upper residential floor and lower office floor.

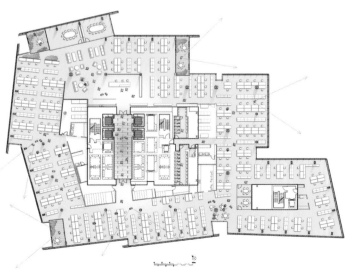

Images courtesy of RPBW

### 19. 160 Tooley Street
Allford Hall Monaghan Morris, 2008
160 Tooley Street, SE1
Tube: London Bridge

This is a refurbished and extended warehouse, providing offices, retail and five upper–level apartments. The scheme follows through the idea of 'a white-collar factory' as what AHMM call "built research into how the office building can be artistically and technically reconsidered." This is an admirable attempt to get away from familiar corporate architecture, but difficult to achieve (the new pretending it is old and characterful, and yet not distressed). In fact, the external design plays the kind of compositional gamesmanship more usually coming from Allies & Morrison.

### 21. Borough Market
Bermondsey Wall, SE1
Tube: London Bridge

Borough Market is best thought of as a successful bottom-up initiative that succeeded in establishing a spatial and social phenomenon later formally taken up by the municipality and others, and now a London  institution. It is a busy Saturday farmers' market set adjacent to Southwark Cathedral and a good place to go when you are browsing architecture in this area. Other than this phenomenon of public space, there is little of contemporary design, but see Fish (designed by Julyan Wickham) and more recent extension to Southwark Cathedral by Richard Griffiths (2002), who was also responsible for much of the work on the old hotel at St Pancras, etc.).

### 20. Unicorn Children's Theatre
Keith Williams Architects, 2005
Tooley Street, SE1
Tube: London Bridge

An elegant building providing a 350-seat auditorium. Williams was given a brief to make the theatre 'rough but beautiful'; however, while features such as the fully glazed projecting balcony above the entrance work nicely, the theatre's difficulty is an aesthetic somewhat at odds with the building's role as a children's theatre. 'Roughness' appears to have eluded the architect. While the work is quite beautiful, a touch of the distressed 'shabby-chic' one finds in many older buildings (as AHMM's Tea Building) and some restaurant interiors (e.g. Pizza east of Shoreditch House) would not have been out of place (admittedly, not an easy thing to achieve in a new work.)

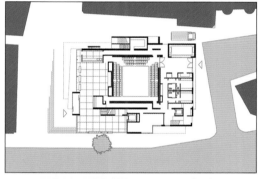

Photos courtesy of KW

## 22. Butlers Wharf
Various architects, 1988-99
Shad Thames, SE1
Tube: London Bridge or Bermondsey

Being so close to Tower Bridge and filled with potential, Butlers Wharf was quick to be redeveloped during the 1980s, after the docks had closed and everyone realised what a huge problem they had on their hands. Look around the whole area, including beyond St Saviour Dock on the eastern side.

### A. Butlers Wharf building
Conran Roche, 1990
Shad Thames, SE1
Tube: London Bridge or Bermondsey

One of the first warehouses to be converted with a committed modernist aesthetic in mind rather than something less urbane (as was the tone of that era, when optimism in the former docklands area was at a relatively low level). Shad Thames leaves us with cross-bridge reminders of what it was once like along here, not so long ago: a tight street, packed with trucks loading and unloading from the riverside and inboard warehouses. Conran was a champion of Modernism when all about him were turning to either Hi-Tech or Po-Mo. Roche used to be a key player in the development of Milton Keynes.

### B. Horselydown Square
Julyan Wickham & Associates, 1989
Shad Thames, SE1
Tube: London Bridge or Bermondsey

One of the first new-build developments – still modern, quirky, and vaguely Dutch, from an architect now practising as Wickham van Eyck Architects (he married the daughter).

## C. Design Museum
Conran Roche, 1989
28 Shad Thames, SE1
Tube: London Bridge or Bermondsey

Actually an old brick warehouse circa 1930, completely and utterly theatrically made over to look neo-Gropius *et al*, 1925, soon to be replaced by the new home of the Design Museum in West London. Po-Mo – mostly neo-classical, with one London instance of neo-Gothic – had more variations than is usually acknowledged.

### D. The Circle
CZWG, 1989
Queen Elizabeth Street, SE1
Tube: London Bridge or Bermondsey

Over three-hundred new build apartments. Amusement takes priority over other design considerations. Is that so bad? The glazed bricks are a recurring CZWG theme. However, the 'broken vase' façade profile looks more like a gigantic threatening owl – such is the fate of narrative symbolism. Note the timber log props, etc. to the balconies – all good fun (and reminiscent of what Gough did for Janet Street-Porter, in Britton Street).

### E. St Saviour Dock Bridge
Nicholas Lacey, 1997
Shad Thames, SE1
Tube: London Bridge or Bermondsey

An acrobatic pedestrian bridge meant to swing, but rarely does (boats rarely enter here), leading to China Wharf, etc. Lacey lived in a houseboat nearby and was also responsible for works such as the first parts of Container City.

## F. China Wharf

CZWG, 1988
Mill Street, SE1
Tube: London Bridge or
Bermondsey

One of the finest gestures from by CZWG – full of cheerful verve and a relaxed quirkiness. The cantilevered boat is a rare example of an architectural joke that actually works. Compare with works like Outram's pumping station on the Isle of Dogs.

## G. The Mellor Building

Hopkins Architects, 1990
Shad Thames, SE1, on St Saviour Dock
Tube: London Bridge or
Bermondsey

An outstanding work: offices with retail at ground level and an apartment designed for Terrance Conran at the top. It was about this time that Hopkins was designing Bracken House and demonstrating an idiosyncratic take on what the Hi-Tech idiom was all about.

## H. Reeds 'C' Wharf

CZWG, 1999
Shad Thames, SE1, on St Saviour Dock
Tube: London Bridge or Bermondsey

Designed in 1987 and constructed some ten years later: an oddly formal diamond plan (see the Janet Street-Porter house in Britton Street) and is unremarkable, but nevertheless a welcome novelty in this area.

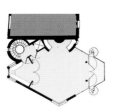

## 23. Luna Building

Glenn Howells, 2006
Bermondsey Wall, SE1
Tube: London Bridge or Bermondsey

One can easily get here from Shad Thames in Butlers Wharf, across the Lacey St Saviour Dock bridge. This simple, 47-unit apartment block contrasts with adjacent dockland warehouses and always hoped to set a modernist, positive precedent. Also see the newer housing round about. Howells has other work in London such as the Printworks at Elephant & Castle (and with Allies and Morrison at Bromley-by-Bow).

## 24. Fashion and Textile Museum

Ricardo Leoretta, 2002
Bermondsey Street, SE1
Tube: London Bridge

Zandra Rhodes' hot, Mexican figuration of her own character was designed by the notable Mexican architect, Ricardo Leoretta, and bears distinct Luis Barragán overtones. It's fun but incongruous, without much correspondence to Southwark (especially on a winter's day).

Perhaps that is a good thing. However, the project also failed in its guise as a Fashion and Textile Museum and is now operated by Newham College and, we are told, is now "a hub of learning, ideas and networking for the fashion and jewellery industry."

### 25. Monroe (jeweller's) Studio
DSDHA, 2013
37 Snowfields, SE1
Tube: London Bridge

A tiny but very nice conversion into studios described as follows: "The façade is precious, precise and carefully made; it is designed to celebrate the 'art of making' and constructed entirely from prefabricated structural timber panels."

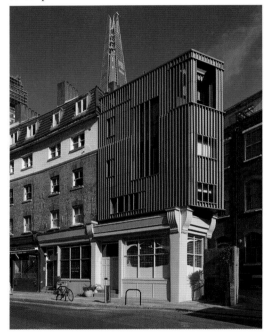

The architects of the Monroe Studio tell us:

the spacing of the vertical 'fins' on the elevation shifts selectively in front of windows to animate the façade and control views in and out of the building, introducing dynamism in the street, and de-scaling the building as a micro-tower in the company of both the Shard and Guy's Tower. The rhythm of the façade is accentuated with a double height glazed area on the south elevation, across the workshop and meeting room levels, offering unobstructed views to the surrounding area. The horizontal detail relates directly to the neighbouring terrace to reference, but not mimic, the context.

### 26. White Cube, Bermondsey
Casper Mueller Kneer, 2011
Bermondsey Street, SE1
Tube: London Bridge

O ne of a series of White Cube galleries in London – this time a set of very large spaces (totalling 5400 sqm) in Bermondsey. It's all about the interiors. Also see the White Cubes in Mason's Yard (St James) and Hoxton Square.

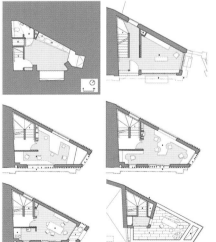

Going East
from the City

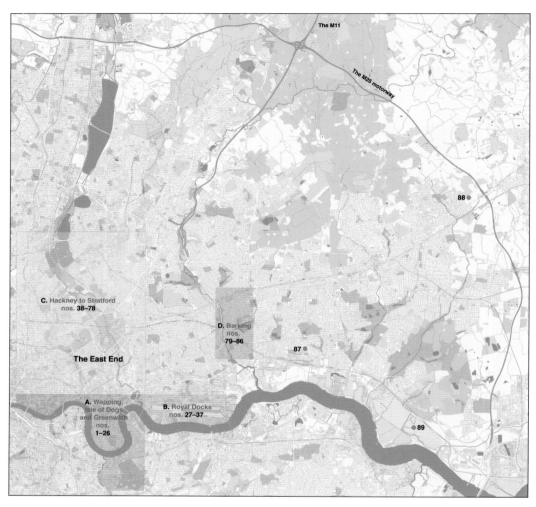

## Four key areas East of the City

A.  **Around Wapping, Isle of Dogs and Greenwich.**
    Map nos. 1–26
B.  **The Royal Docks.**
    Map nos. 27–37
C.  **Hackney to Stratford**
    Map nos. 38–78
D.  **Barking Central**
    Map nos. 79–86

Nos. 87–89 are outlying works and are indicated in the above map.

The City of London (Londinium and the commercial heartland of the metropolis) sits between what was once prime farmland to the west and poor, marshy ground to the east. The City has also been fuelled by coal since the Middle Ages and the prevailing south-west winds take pollution eastward. In addition, the River Thames flows from west to east, taking 'soil' waste from residences and industry out toward the English Channel. For all these reasons the East End became an area of docks, warehouses, industry and the houses of the many people who worked in the area. Since the docks began to close (in about 1970) the area has undergone a long period of regeneration accompanied by a clean-up of the air and the water – particularly up to the River Lea and the Lea Valley, lying just east of the Royal Docks.

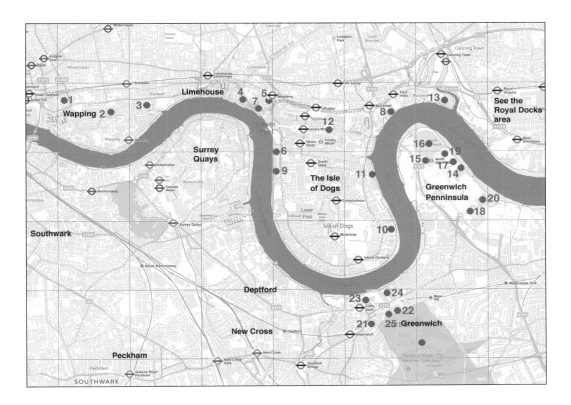

This area is accessible by the DLR and the Jubilee Line and is oriented to the River Thames. It breaks down into a number of distinct sub-districts:

### Wapping

This compact area adjacent to the City and the Tower of London is not easily accessible except from Shadwell (DLR) or Wapping stations (Overground), or simply walk from St Katharine's Dock.

### The Isle of Dogs

This is the redevelopment 'flagship': Canary Wharf. Between the Isle and Canary Wharf is Limehouse. On the opposite (east) side is Trinity Buoy Wharf (Container City) and the western end of the Royal Docks. Canary sits in the midst of the old docks and is surrounded to east, west, east and south by residential developments that are strung out around the periphery of the Isle (along the river). Use the Jubilee Line to Canary Wharf, and the Docklands Light Railway (DLR) to get to other parts.

### Greenwich and the Greenwich Peninsula

This has two distinct and contrasting parts: the older parts around Wren's hospital and to the west of Deptford Creek; and the new parts on the Peninsula (where the O2 Dome is located). Use the DLR to Greenwich and the Jubilee Line to North Greenwich.

## A: Wapping, Isle of Dogs and Greenwich

### 1. Peabody housing, Whitechapel
Niall McLaughlin Architects, 2014
John Fisher Street, E1
Tube: Tower Hill; Overground: Shadwell

A new kind of Peabody building within the midst of the old dating from the late 1900s ('Improved Model Dwellings for the Respectable Working Class'). The new building completes a set of buildings that form an inner court and replaces an original Peabody block on this site that was bombed in WWII (killing 70 people). It will provide 13 new homes (three one-bedroom, seven two-bedroom, two x three-bedroom, and one four-bedroom flats).

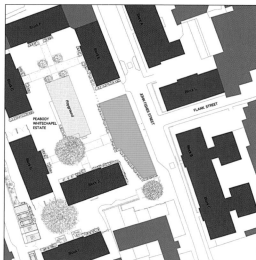

### 2. Tobacco Dock
Farrells, 1990
Pennington Street, E1
Overground: Wapping

The lost combination of a wonderful 1806 warehouse structure that impressed Schinkel and a 'fit-out' by Farrell that exhibits some ambitious cast-iron shop fronts – lost because the venture was a failure and the place is now usually closed up. Since discredited Po-Mo works are disappearing fast, it would be a shame to lose this work – one of Farrells' better endeav-

ours. Just to the north of here, on The Highway, sits Nicholas Hawksmoor's St George-in-the-East (1714–29) – one of five remaining churches this architect designed.

### 3. Shadwell Basin
MJP Architects, 1988
Shadwell Basin, E1
Overground: Wapping

One of the first attempts to break away from the nostalgia inform-ing much of Docklands' regeneration during the 1980s: still low density, but a scheme of 169 units returning to a variation on the typical London terrace house, here arrayed around a small dock basin.

### 4. Brightlingsea Place
Proctor Matthews Architects, 1996
Ropemaker Field, E14
DLR: Westferry

A terrace of 11 town-houses indicative of a change of tastes that mysteriously made itself manifest after the early 1990s recession.

## 5. Westferry Studios
CZWG, 1999
Milligan Street, E14
DLR: Westferry

An unusually and well-respected scheme from CZWG, redolent with Venturi graphic touches intermixed with a touch of mid-career Gehry and designed as a mix of 27 live-work units and nine commercial units surrounding an access courtyard. Upbeat without this firm's predilection for architectural jokes – which, for some reason, never work, except for their boat-cum-balcony at China Wharf.

## 7. Dundee Wharf
CZWG, 1998
Three Colt Street, E14
DLR: Westferry

One hundred and sixty single-aspect apartments striving to be contextual, quirky and cheerful: once rich in kerb-appeal; perhaps in readiness to be listed as a monument to Po-Mo enthusiasms. Whether you will find its features significant or trite, amusing or depressing is a moot point (see, for example, the balcony towers which parody dockside cranes), but there is usually a certain indescribable something about CZWG's work.

## 6. Cascades
CZWG, 1988
2–4 Westferry Road, E14
DLR: Westferry or Canary Wharf; Tube: Canary Wharf

Cascades was notable for manifesting a return to living in (then discredited) tall blocks – here, seeking to anticipate the scale of the projected Canary Wharf development. It now serves as a model for what everyone wants: a penthouse, in an idiosyncratic tower, located by the river. Even the brickwork is again fashionable. At the time, CZWG proclaimed: "Cascades is anti-pop, or is it? What, after all, could be more despicable than high-rise living – architects would hate it, the public would hate it. We just had to do it. It sold brilliantly." Not quite, but the scheme was daring and, urbanistically (apart from its single-aspect planning), has held up well, especially against its neighbours.

## 8. Reuters Technical Services Centre
Rogers Stirk Harbour+Partners, 1990
St Lawrence Street, E14
DLR: Blackwall

Reuters is simply a large, high-security telephonic exchange centre loaded with computers and inhabited by a handful of people. But it manifests all the usual Rogers tropes.

## Limehouse Walks

One can easily walk to or from Limehouse Basin to Stratford and to Greenwich along interesting routes.

For the latter, head east, along the river edge, to Westferry and Canary Wharf – and then down through the heart of the Isle of Dogs toward Island Gardens, then perhaps under the old Victorian pedestrian tunnel that takes you across to Greenwich. There you'll find the Cutty Sark and the Laban, as well as the new Greenwich School of Architecture. If you are feeling lively you can head up through Blackheath Park to the Royal Observatory, where Allies and Morrison have a building. Other possible diversions include areas around the edge of the Isle of Dogs, such as Seacon Wharf or, on the east side, Outram's Pumping Station and Compass Point.

Alternatively, one can walk northward: up the Limehouse Cut and the Lee Valley toward the Olympic Park site (now the Queen Elizabeth Park). At the former Olympic site there is a route to the canal and northward into more green parts of the Lee Valley. Most of the Olympic Park will be open by the spring of 2014 and you should check the Queen Elizabeth Park web-site for updates. You can also head west along the Grand Union Canal that heads to Mile End Station (where Queen Mary University campus is located).

## 9. Seacon Wharf
CZWG, 2004
Westferry Road, E14
DLR: Heron Quays or South Quay; Tube: Canary Wharf

While Cascades set out to anticipate Canary Wharf, Seacon set out to compete. Ironically, there is a lot of common sense in the scheme's urbanistic intentions – ironic because the development's indulgence in architectural entertainment belies this fact. However, it is not uninteresting ... CZWG attempts to introduce features guaranteed to upset most architects and, although we join in the groans, at least they demonstrate daring and inventiveness (but with questionable concerns and tastes, we can hear you say ...). Perhaps.

## 10. Compass Point
Dixon Jones, 1986
Sextant Avenue, off Manchester Road, E14
DLR: Mudchute or Island Gardens

Compass Point is another not uninteresting Po-Mo exercise that attempts to re-create the planning character of the larger early Victorian semi-detached neo-Tuscan villa in west London. The terrace along the river frontage, however, bears distinctly Dutch overtones, with high gables that strive to establish a riverside presence. Done again, this site would be used for apartment blocks.

## 11. Stormwater Pumping Station
John Outram, 1988
Stewart Street, E14
Tube: Canary Wharf; DLR: South Quay

This has to be by far the most admirable Po-Mo work in London. It is loaded with gamesmanship, rich in metaphor (water running down from a mountain, across hills and the plain aka a temple pediment) and also irony ('robot columns' that are service risers and ducts, together with 'blitzkrieg' prefabricated concrete elements made from redundant bricks) and simple architectural enthusiasms (Alvar Aalto). If other Po-Mo architects had been half as good as this the fashion might still be with us. Outram comments on the work as follows:

My proposal is that Architecture cannot be derived from 'dwelling' in any banal, roses-round-the-door, 'domestic' sense. [...] Architecture is the diametric opposite of such well-upholstered, 19th-century flaccidities. It is, instead, the making ourselves 'at-home' in the Kosmos. Architecture, and its only 'serious' purpose on a scale larger than the single project, is to build a general, large and civic lifespace that sets us, paltry humans, 'comfortably' situated within the Cosmos. None of this makes any sense to Architects today, as they worry about the energy-efficient hydraulic drive from the wind machine to the coffee-grinder. But if they could be troubled to discover what lies behind the buildings and cities that the Public (as opposed to the Profession) still admire, they will find my last paragraph to be true. Not that this discovery will do their 'professional' existence any good, for having come to this understanding they will also understand that they never knew it, the leaders of their Profession never knew it, their Academic Tutor never knew it, their profession does not know it, and there are no practical, up to date, handbooks on how to get up to speed on it. It is all 'in the past'. So the whole thing is best put out of mind while the mainly gratuitous, and largely self-imposed, 'hydraulic drive problem' still beckons.

Enjoy. (See: http://www.ohnoutram.com/projects-menu.html.)

## 12. Canary Wharf
Various architects, 1991 to the present
Ropemaker Field, E14
Jubilee Line and DLR: Canary Wharf

For a while Canary horrified English architects: the Americans had arrived in terms of money, project managers, architects, tastes and tenants. Their jaws dropped at the overall bravura and the robustness of the details.

In development terms Canary has experienced two distinct phases: a first phase from about 1988–91, very Po-Mo, dominated by SOM's Chicago office giving London what they thought was a London style; a second phase, after the recession, from about 1994 to today. However, it is only recently. after twenty-five years, that the development (where over 93,000 people work) has begun to mature, the owners have been seeking to diversify the tenant mix and, who knows, perhaps the surrounding residential buildings will one day creep into the midst of this banker's world. The first phase had serious access problems and this prompted the development of the Docklands Light Railway. Then the year 2000 brought the Jubilee Line to Canary and the development leapt forward again into a period when the DLR was being extended throughout east London (and into the south).

The unexpected success story of Canary was its underground retail mall – massively extended during phase two of the development. This drew out the envy of Canary's great rival, the City of London, which has more recently been striving to introduce more retail into the Square Mile (e.g. One New Change).

The architects at Canary Wharf include:
**Cesar Pelli:** One Canada Square; Cabot Place; 25 Canada Square; 25 Bank Street; 40 Bank Street; 50 Bank Street.
**Foster + Partners:** 33 Canada Square; 8 Canada Square; Jubilee Line station + the Crossrail station, in construction).
**Gensler & Associates:** 17 Columbus Courtyard.
**HOK International (UK):** One Churchill Place; 5 Churchill Place, (Barclays HQ).
**Koetter, Kim & Associates UK:** Canary Riverside; Canada Square; Columbus Courtyard; 11 Westferry Circus.
**Kohn Pedersen Fox Associates:** 30 The South Colonnade; 20 Cabot Square; 10 Upper Bank Street; 15 Canada Square; 20 Churchill Place; 30 North Colonnade.
**Pei Cobb Freed & Partners:** 1 Cabot Square.
**Will Alsop** was responsible for the **South Quay Station** and **Foster** was responsible for the **Jubilee Line station** – one of his firm's better London works.
**Ron Arad** has a fine roof-light 'lid' over a part of the shopping mall the 'Big Blue' in Canada Square (2000).
**Nicholas Lacey** was responsible for Heron Quays – what was to be a very large development before Canary arrived on the scene and took over.
**Future Systems** have a neo-military pedestrian pontoon bridge (north side). Wilkinson Eyre Architects have a pedestrian bridge on the south side.

The Foster+Partners Jubilee Line station (1999).

The Alsop dock entry control room (1990; east end of Canary).

Access escalators to the Jubilee Line station.

A contrast: Heron Quay (Nicholas Lacey, 1984–88).

**Above:** The Jubilee Station. **Right**: the Wilkinson Eyre Architects bridge (1995), moved from its original location. Note the suburban housing on the south side of the dock (from the 1980s). They are evidence of what the height of optimism was 30 years ago. **Opposite**: the impressive Future Systems footbridge (1995), which looks as if it floats on pontoons like some redundant piece of equipment from Vietnam but

actually sits on concrete pads just under the water. **Bottom right**: Ron Arad's floating blue object that serves as a roof light to the shopping mall below.

**Note**:
• There is a considerable amount of art scattered around the Canary Wharf area. (See their website.)
• The impressive Foster Crossrail station should be complete in 2015.

**Above**: Heron Quay was seen as ambitious before the Canary scheme arrived on the scene. It is worth contrasting the relationship Lacey sets up between quay, access link, building and the water – quite different to the manner in which the Canary buildings simply extend the ground plane into the dock.

### 13. Container City
Urban Space Management, 2002 on
Trinity Pier, E14
DLR: East India; Tube: Canning Town

Promoted by the London Docklands Development Corporation as an artist's ghetto of studios and live-work units, Container City comprises a set of aged warehouses on Trinity Buoy Wharf – the place where people manning lighthouses and lightships were once trained – and two complexes of stacked containers. The first was designed by Nicholas Lacey and is the most interesting, but revealed the difficulties and costs of artistic stacking arrangements (the reference being Safdie's Habitat scheme of 1967). The second is by Peter Ahrends and is a more simple stacking arrangement. You can take a boat from here across the River Thames to the O2 Dome's QEII Pier (and vice versa).

### 14. Emirates cable car
Wilkinson Eyre Architects, 2012
Cutter Lane, SE10
Tube: North Greenwich/Royal Victoria

This was an idiosyncratic project that goes from North Greenwich to the Royal Docks DLR station, completed in time for the 2012 Olympics. However, it does so in an exhilaratingly manner and one can enjoy simply riding across and then back again (with a discount if you have an Oyster card). It's a good view and complements the Shard and the London Eye (as well as a few other high points around London, such as the Mittal 'thing' in the Olympic Park). Go, of course, on a sunny and warm day rather than the usual kind of cold, grey and windswept days one finds out here in the Docklands.

### A note on Robin Hood Gardens

Located at Woolmore Street, E14 (at the north-east corner of the Isle of Dogs), RHG (1972) was designed by Peter & Alison Smithson as a notable instance of 214 'Brutalist' flats. Suffering neglect, it is due for imminent demolition. You should see it while its stands, but it is a somewhat depressing experience and we are told that most tenants will cheer when it comes down.

**Note**: for the Siemens Crystal Centre (where the cable car station is on the north side) see the Royal Docks area map.

A: Wapping, Isle of Dogs and Greenwich

## Greenwich

Greenwich is dominated by two disparate buildings: the late 17th-century Naval College (with the Queen's House), and the Millennium (now O2) Dome. Ways across the river include the Blackwall Tunnel (by car), DLR coming down from Canary Wharf, an old, Victorian pedestrian underground tunnel that leads from Island Gardens on the north side to Greenwich on the south and, more recently, the Emirates cable car that goes between the Peninsula at the Dome and the Siemens Crystal building on the north side.

## 15. North Greenwich station
Foster + Partners; Will Alsop, 2000
Tube: North Greenwich

The upper part of this Jubilee Line station (which is a Tube-to-bus transfer area set beneath a butterfly roof) is by Foster. The below-ground parts are by Will Alsop. Both were completed in 2000, as part of the major extension of the Underground system from central London out to here and beyond to Canary Wharf and Stratford. Alsop's cut-and-fill station is the part to try and linger over, even though it is underground and obviously ran out of money at some point (the ceiling, for example, was apparently meant to be more elaborate).

## 16. 02 Dome
Rogers Stirk Harbour+Partners, 2000
Drawdock Road, SE10
Tube: North Greenwich

Terrific spikey blob of a building with an exhilarating, recently installed walkway over the top. The Dome makes a remarkable landmark, but is now almost ignored. This may, in part, be because of the slow pace of redevelopment on the Greenwich Peninsula (imaginative masterplanners apply now) ... and also a less than inspiring post-Millennium celebrations internal fit-out (of which people going to gigs appear to be oblivious)

## 17. Peninsula Place
Farrells, 2008
Peninsula Place, SE10
Tube: North Greenwich

An office building as dislocated as the Ravensbourne shed, but with considerably less to say for itself. The wallpaper patterning of the façades is clever enough, but at the same time banal. One wishes that these two schemes could have worked together with the dome and begun a genuinely urbane, welcoming and sheltering that could have fed out into the surrounding area. That, of course, would have been impossible without an external leading hand (bring back William Whitfield!).These first buildings in the area give one little hope for what the developers of the Peninsula will eventually produce.

## 18. Millennium Primary School
Cullinan Studio, 2001
50 John Harrison Way, SE10
Tube: North Greenwich

This stand-alone low-energy, timber-clad primary school – with a community hall, one-stop advice and early years centres – includes many characteristic tropes from the Cullinan practice. The more private sides are open, glazed and protected by awnings; the more public sides are to the north, have smaller windows and are clad in 'wriggly timber'.

## 19. Ravensbourne School of Art
Foreign Office, 2010
6 Penrose Way, SE10
Tube: North Greenwich

Ravensbourne moved from deepest Kent so that it could connect with the vital urbanity of central London. But with nothing much to relate to and the impossibility of competing with the O2 Dome, Foreign Office gave them a concrete shed impressively wrapped in Penfold tiling. However, as a shed, it could be anywhere and the design is open to the criticism that it fails to effect an urbane solution for this windswept and usually chilly location. The underlying educational model is that of the super-generic marketplace: education off the shelf, always available for a price; intentionally ever without significant meaning in order to maintain generic qualities. The interior serving this model has been characterised as an educational car park with a *parti* dependent upon a central spatial split that engenders two atria – one of which is an impressive, port-hole window-punctuated entry space. There is a public café in the entrance, so take a look and have a coffee while thinking about education today (and apt ways to live in this area).

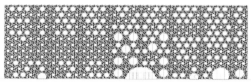

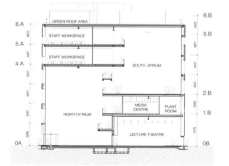

## 20. Millennium Village
Ralph Erskine; Proctor Matthews, 2000
John Harrison Way, SE10
Tube: North Greenwich

A complex of residential units at the southern end of the Peninsula is currently populated with buildings mainly from Ralph Erskine and Proctor Matthews. Erskine's units are colourful concrete assemblies; Proctor Matthews give a more complex mix of house types and a more complex architectural treatment whose exuberance becomes uncomfortably fussy and contrasts with recent housing schemes that have reverted to a more quiet, brick-clad aesthetic and simple proportionality. Hundreds of new housing units are now planned or in construction in the area. Architects include: Jestico+Whiles, Peter Barber, Studio 54, Make Architects, etc.

## 21. Greenwich School of Architecture
Heneghan Peng Architects, 2014
Greenwich High Road, SE10
DLR: Greenwich

In construction at the time of writing, this appears to be a significant project worth seeking out. The architects tell us:

The grain of narrow and wide bands structure the site, narrow bands containing courtyards, service and cores, wide bands provide the teaching and learning spaces. The grain is further drawn through to the street to create a permeable streetscape.

## 22. The Queen's House
Inigo Jones, 1616–35; enlarged by John Webb, 1662
DLR: Greenwich or Island Gardens

An odd but clever design for a small palace cut off from the river by the main road to Dover running right through its heart. The Queen would arrive by river barge, walk up to front door, up to the piano nobile, over the road and down the other side into her private grounds (now Blackheath Park). Neat and rather mad. The design is based on an Italian original but this origin was somewhat lost when John Webb extended the accommodation. The interiors are sparse but impressive and the whole has been refurbished by Allies and Morrison.

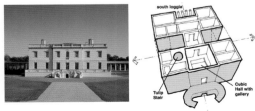

## 23. Cutty Sark
Grimshaw, 2012
Cutty Sark Gardens, SE10
DLR: Greenwich or Island Gardens

A few years ago fire seriously damaged the Cutty Sark and this new 'wrap' that develops an undercroft, beneath the ship as it sits in a dry-dock (together with the expected visitor shop, etc.) brings it back to us. The principal metaphor appears to be that of waters being pushed aside by the ship as it ploughs along: hence the glass structure around the hull. Raising the ship has enabled there to be considerably more museum space beneath the hull. Admittedly, the glass base is akin to a bulbous, over-stuffed collar, but the scheme has distinctive merits. Get there via Island Gardens and walk under the river through the Victorian tunnel. Also visit the former Naval College next door.

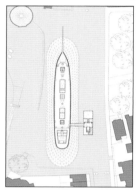

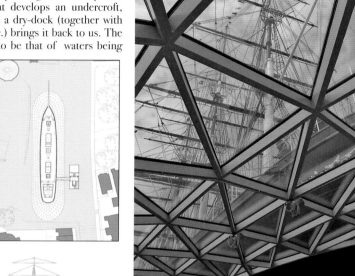

Photos courtesy of Grimshaw (except bottom right)

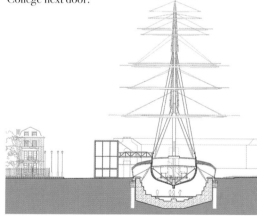

## 24. Royal Naval College
Christopher Wren, 1696–1712.
King William Walk, SE10
DLR: Greenwich

This was originally the Royal Hospital for Seamen and now houses Greenwich University and Trinity College of Music – a perfect campus for today's up-and-coming London university (branding off-the-shelf).

Besides Wren, the architects involved in the completion of the original work included Nicholas Hawksmoor, Sir John Vanburgh and Thomas Ripley. The Trinity School of Music is by John McAslan+Partners, (2001). Unusually, the campus is open to all visitors. Wander about; see the Painted Hall and the Chapel.

## 25. National Maritime Museum
Rick Mather Architects with BDP, 1999/C.F. Moller, 2010
Romney Road, SE10
DLR: Greenwich

See this together with the Inigo Jones' Queens House (22), both cut off from the River Thames by a major road heading out east, toward the Greenwich Peninsula. The key to the Mather design is the enclosure of a central courtyard with a 2500 sqm glass roof which doesn't quite achieve the simplicity of Foster's enclosure at the British Museum. The (mostly underground) Sammy Offer Wing was more recently completed by C.F. Moller, the Danish practice. In effect, it radically reorients the Museum away from Trafalgar Road to Blackheath Park.

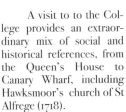

A visit to to the College provides an extraordinary mix of social and historical references, from the Queen's House to Canary Wharf, including Hawksmoor's church of St Alfrege (1718).

## 26. Peter Harris Planetarium
Allies and Morrison, 2007
Greenwich Observatory, Blackheath Park
DLR: Greenwich

Anew underground planetarium given presence in the guise of a mysterious enigmatic object at the Greenwich Royal Observatory (originally by Wren and Robert Hooke): a lopped-off concrete cone that is, we are told, tilted to align with the North Star at 51.5 degrees, its glass-filled apex canted at 90 degrees, parallel to the celestial equator. Not a lot of people know that (although there is an explanatory sign at the site). Such is narrative, but then architectural discourse is witness to a long tradition of such embodied significances.

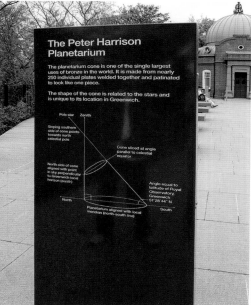

Going East B:
the Royal Docks

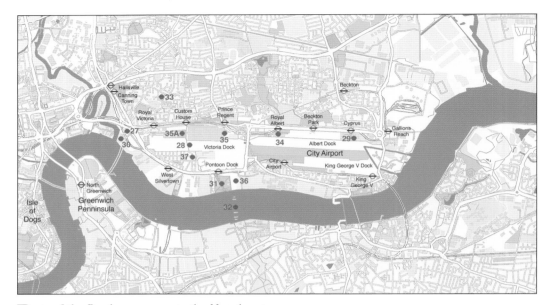

P arts of the Royals are nearer to the M25 than to central London, and so this has been the last part of the former docks to be regenerated. At the western end you will find more things of interest – up to the Barrier Park. The east end (where the City Airport is located) still remains of lesser interest, although new housing developments are going up all the time. By 2017, the first tenants should be moving into a large Chinese Business Park along the northern edge of the Royal Albert Dock (Beckton Park DLR), just west of Cullinan Studio's East London University campus. Most of the housing is on the south side of the docks, in Silvertown and around the Thames Barrier Park. A large new centre called the Halls-ville Quarter, or The Place) is being created opposite Canning Town station, with AECOM doing the master planning and Haworth Tompkins playing a major role. It is bounded by Silvertown Way, Hallsville Road, Rath-bone Street and Newham Way.

**Below**: Just south of the Hallsville Quarter is a piece of land that has more recently been used for a pop-up market called **Caravanserai**. This sits opposite Canning Town station at 100-116 Silvertown Way, E6. The market has been supported by Ash Sakula Architects as a participatory public realm de-scribed as "a place of exchange in ideas, culture and knowl-edge."

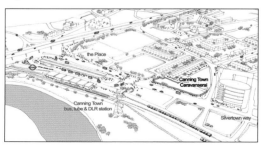

## 27. Pumping Station
Rogers Stirk Harbour+Partners, 1987
Tidal Basin Road, E16
DLR: East India; Tube: Canning Town

This pumping station was designed and constructed at the same time as the one by John Outram on the Isle of Dogs, illustrating the polarity of architectural concerns at that time. For another example see that by Allies and Morrison in Abbey Lane, just south of the Queen Elizabeth (Olympic) Park.

## 28. The Siemen's Crystal
Wilkinson Eyre Architects, 2012 (Fit-out by Pringle Brandon)
Royal Victoria Dock, west end, E16
DLR: Royal Victoria

A striking sub-Libeskind exercise in 'crystalline' shaping (a variant on lingering enthusiasms for 'stealth' geometries). The reality is a shed at the end of a windswept and often chilling dockland area and the fit-out is distinctly underwhelming. But this is a notable client employing notable London designers. Perhaps we are missing something. Take a look: entry is free and you might disagree.

## 29. Royal Victoria footbridge
Lifschutz Davidson Sandilands, 1999
Royal Dock, E16
DLR: Custom House/West Silvertown

A bridge that was designed to have a moving 'car' beneath it – which never happened. Anyway, this is still a good way to get across the dock to Silvertown.

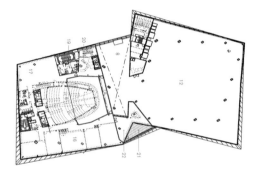

## 30. University of East London campus
Cullinan Studio, 1999
Royal Albert Dockside Road, E16
DLR: Cyprus

The part of this campus that catches one's eye is a clutch of ten housing towers providing 384 student rooms, strung along the dock edge in pairs and designed by one of London's architectural heroes: Ted Cullinan. Nice, but it gets windy and cold out here: bring back cloisters to this university campus for thousands of students. The principal university buildings (also by Cullinan) sit behind, to the north, focused around a large piazza area. Access is restricted.

## 31. Barrier Park
Groupes Signes with Patel Taylor, 2000
North Woolwich Road, E16
DLR: Pontoon Dock

A pleasant, maturing park employing abstract patterns that are (thankfully) hardly evident as one walks through the landscape. The concept is that of a 'green dock' sunken into the landscape and crossed by foot-bridges. Past problems include poor maintenance, although this seems to have been overcome. The tea pavilion (a neo-Miesian exercise, now in oak) is by Patel & Taylor, as is the memorial pavilion at the river, adjacent to the Thames Barrier.

**Above**: the café pavilion at the Barrier Park, designed by Patel Taylor, using heavy oak sections for the structure.
**Below**: the memorial pavilion to seamen who died during WWII that sits at the southern end of the Park, next to the Thames Barrier.

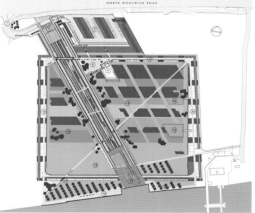

## 32. Thames Barrier

Rendel Palmer & Triton, 1984
Thames Barrier Park, E16
DLR: Pontoon Dock

This design has impressed people ever since it was constructed, but may now be obsolescent because of climate change. The gates lies on the bed of the river and swing up when needed (which is increasingly frequent). To see the Barrier you will need to traverse the Barrier Park – another good reason to make a visit on a sunny day.

## 33. Crediton Road

Sergison Bates Architects, 2013
Crediton Road, E16
Tube or DLR: Canning Town

A controversial regeneration scheme (of 14 three-storey houses in three terraces and the larger five-storey block of one and two-bedroom apartments) in one of the country's most deprived areas, therefore heavy on public space, security issues and the European home zone concept.

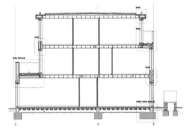

**Right**: The area just to the west of the Crediton Road scheme, opposite Canning Town Station, is being redeveloped as a new central area of shops and housing called the Hallsville Quarter. The architects of Phase One (179 residential units of private and affordable housing set around a shared garden at podium level, underground car parking, an energy centre and a supermarket of over 7,000 square metres) are Haworth Tompkins Architects. The architects for Phase Two (over 300 homes comprising private for sale units, private for rent units and intermediate units, underground car parking, retail units, restaurants, a hotel and a health centre) are John McAslan + Partners.

## 34. London Regatta Centre
Ian Ritchie Architects, 1999
Royal Albert Dockside Road, E16
DLR: Royal Albert Dock

## 35. Excel
Various architects, 2010
Royal Victoria Dock, E16
Tube: North Greenwich

A club from the respected Ian Ritchie, with an adjacent boat-house with the expected range of gym, changing rooms, bar, etc., and a unique, powered rowing tank ... plus some nice architectural touches rather let down by a poor standard of fit-out. However, it's now somewhat run-down.

It is strange to go here when nothing is on – rather like going to a stadium in between games. It is starkly vacant. The open forecourt landscaping for this exhibition/conference centre (Moxley Architects, 2000) was boldly designed by Patel Taylor (2001) in a manner that declares a low-maintenance intentionality (41A on the map; see the photo bottom left on this page).

The dramatic eastern extension of 32,500 sqm (lower photo) is by Grimshaw (2010) and takes Excel to about 100,000 sqm.

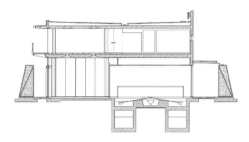

## 36. Barrier Park housing
Maccreanor Lavington Architects, 2012
Royal Albert Dockside Road, E16
DLR: Pontoon Dock

One can count on this practice turning out well-considered housing schemes and this one confirms that judgement – except that we have those double-loaded corridors again. Compare with St Andrews at Bromley-by-Bow. The white-rendered housing at the opposite (west) end of the park is Barrier Point, was designed by Goddard Manton and completed in 2001 (photo bottom right).

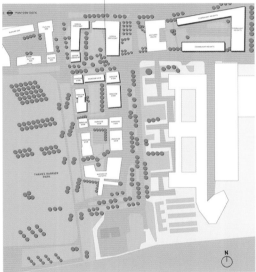

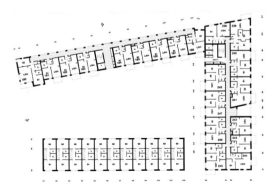

The area to the west of Barrier Park is **Royal Wharf** – a development of 3,385 homes, a new school, shops, offices and riverside restaurants, catering for a population that is estimated to reach 10,000 by completion.

### 37. Silvertown housing
Niall McLaughlin; Ash Sakula Architects, 2004
Evelyn Road and Boxley Street, E16
DLR: Custom House or West Silvertown

Two 'experimental' schemes with the same client (Peabody) and similar briefs (two-bed for McLaughlin; three-bed for Ash Sakula), but different outcomes: one exhibiting a conventional attitude to planning combined with an elegance of expression; the other trying harder to get 'under the skin', win space and seriously address family life in the home, but with a distinctly off-beat external treatment not to everyone's taste. The former is loaded with narrative references to iridescent metal-strapped timber crates that one once saw being loaded and unloaded on the docks in this area – a discourse no doubt rather irrelevant to occupiers. The attempt to make a three-storey building look four-storeys is pure architectural gamesmanship that works well; however, while the artfully flashy façade prompts admiration, it raises a question about narrative (i.e., the difference between narrativised concepts as opposed to narratives employed as concepts).

Also see Mclaughlin's more recent work for Peabody at Whitechapel and Ash Sakula's Hothouse.

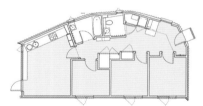

**Top Right**: the McLaughlin scheme, with the reality of normal Peabody housing behind.
**Right**: the plan and facade treatment of the McLaughlin units.
**Above:** plan of the Ash Sakula houses and the street frontage of these units.

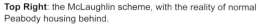

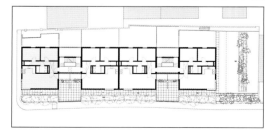

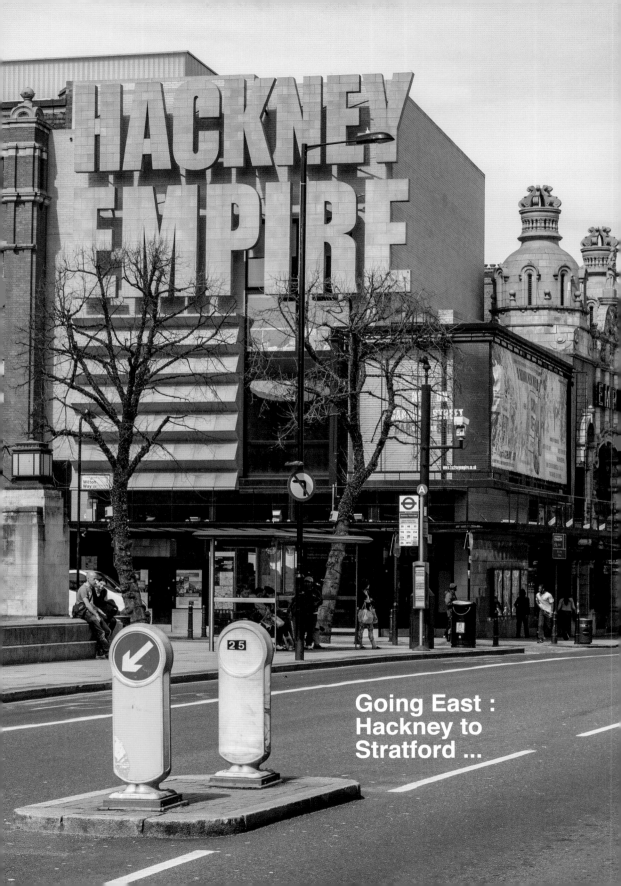

**Going East :
Hackney to
Stratford ...**

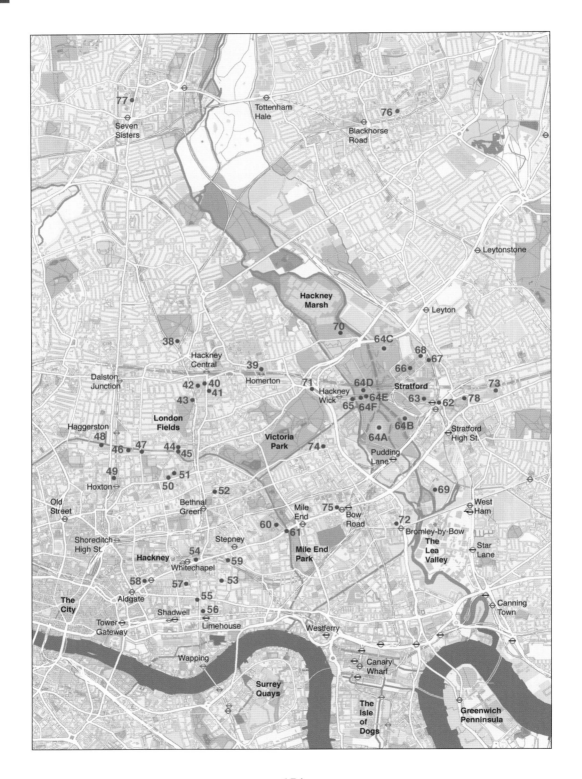

Hackney has become a major area of regeneration and 'gentrification' that has renewed an older part of the East End. Stratford has been radically transformed by the Olympic Games and continues to be a major location of urban renewal. Between themselves, and in different ways, these two areas have shifted the centre of gravity of urban renewal in eastern London away from where it has been focused for some 25 years: at Canary Wharf, in the Isle of Dogs and along the river frontages of the former docklands.

Hackney, because it is near to the City and, especially, to its north-eastern fringe around Brick Lane and Shoreditch, has a distinctly urbane character. On a Sunday it is the scene of crowds at the Colombia Road flower market. On sunny summer weekends, young families flock to London Fields, just south of Hackney Central, where the local Town Hall is located.

Stratford is changing at a different pace, with international developers pouring in money in order to capitalise upon the legacy of the Games and the continuing potential for an area that is increasingly feeling like a latter-day, high-density version of Milton Keynes (the best and most successful of the post-war new towns, constructed from the mid-1970s onward). For example, in this aerial view of the Athletes' Village (now East Village), note the difference between EV's urban grain and that of the traditional London terraces beyond. It is the former that shows us the London of the future.

Overall, development is forming a rectangle between Hackney, Stratford, Canary Wharf and the Whitechapel area fringing the City, where regeneration is taking place from St Katharine's dock in the south to Shoreditch in the north.

A useful way to travel through the area is not by Tube, but by the DLR and, especially, the Overground – what has become London's favoured mode of transport.

**Top**: on London Fields.
**Above**: aerial view of the former Athletes' Village (now East Village), at Stratford.
**Left**: the ever-popular Broadway market, by London Fields.

## 38. Mossbourne Academy
Rogers Stirk Harbour+Partners, 2004
Downs Park Road, E5
Overground: Hackney Central

A peculiar, triangular site bounded on one edge by a railway line has engendered the linear plan for this timber-framed 'academy' whose external staircase gives a nod in the direction of former Rogers projects.

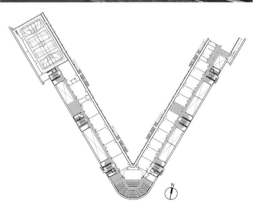

Photo courtesy of RSH (David Churchill)

## 39. Digby Road housing
Davy Smith Architects, 2011
Digby Road, E9
Overground: Homerton

A scheme from a prolific housing practice described as follows:

> The undulating form of the roof and façade of this scheme were inspired by the triangular site and the roofscape of local industrial buildings. All 97 homes in this 100% affordable scheme are dual aspect with private and shared amenity; including a green wall rising to the 14th floor – the highest living wall in Europe.

Such 'growing walls' have met with mixed success and it's interesting to see that more recent schemes from this practice are rather more quiet.

Photos courtesy of DS (Lyndon Douglas Photography)

## 40. Hackney Empire
Tim Ronalds Architects, 2005
291 Mare Street, E8
Overground: Hackney Central

Tim Ronalds is another of London's better architects – one who has a Venturi-esque enthusiasm for large signage which he puts to architectonic effect (also see Ironmonger Baths). Here, he is refurbishing and extending the old Hackney Empire – a much-loved music hall originally designed by Frank Matcham in 1901. The extension rounds the corner facing onto the open space in front of the 1930s Town Hall and lends the Empire an exciting presence that complements the original façade. It's nearing ten years old and is still fresh and uplifting.

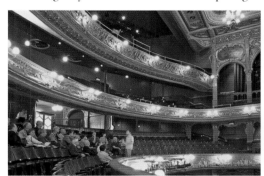

## 41. Hackney Picture House
Fletcher Priest Architects, 2011
270 Mare Street, E8
Overground: Hackney Central

The skilled conversion of an older building that nods to Ronalds' work and reinforces a theme to this central area that one would like to see extended. The new cinema complex provides four cinema screens, a café, upper-level bars and facilities for community-based organisations in this older building that was formerly two buildings combined into a club in 2001. Described as a project of reclamation and archaeology, it's interesting to see FP trying to get into a gritty Hackney mode rather than their more familiar corporate mode.

Photo courtesy of FPA

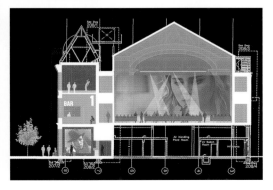

## 42. Hackney Town Hall/Service Centre
Hopkins Architects, 2009
1 Hillman Street, E8
Overground: Hackney Central

This significantly large and quite grand municipal building sits immediately behind the Town Hall. Its atrium is quite impressive, although the exterior is perhaps too muted and non-textural. Overall, it makes a major addition to the family of architectural interests in this area and is witness to the renaissance of Hackney in recent years. See a similar building at Wembley (also by Hopkins).

Photos courtesy of Hopkins (Paul Tyagi)

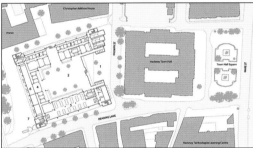

Photos courtesy of Hopkins (Sean Pollacki)

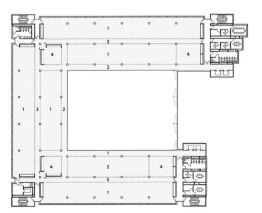

## 43. Hothouse
Ash Sakula Architects, 2007
274 Richmond Road, E8
Overground: Hackney Central. Rail: London Fields

It's inventive (by two of the best architects in London), but something went wrong ... and yet you can almost smell that talented architects were at work. The problem seems to have been over-ambition by everyone concerned followed by budget problems. Meanwhile, it makes a good setting to the northern perimeter of London Fields and has been refitted as studio spaces. Perhaps the building will one day come back to what was envisioned? In a way, it has been: the roof-top has become what Ash Sakula originally envisioned and is now the Coppa 'pop-up' café/bar above Emigre Studios, designed by Me and Sam.

## 44. Ada Street
Amin Taha Architects, 2012
2 Ada Street, E8
Overground: Hackney Central

A subtle infill project comprising two retail units with six apartments above, locating the ever-popular 'stealth' geometry into the latter-day trendiness of a street just off Broadway market. The constructional aim has a reduced palette of features, details and materials: "Look Ma: no gutters, no sills, no drains, no copings!" It's done well, although one is reminded of a now long tradition of semiotically enigmatic old pubs, painted black. Somewhere in the design background is Adjaye's Dirty House.

Photo courtesy of ASA (Paul Gooteridge)
Photo courtesy of Me and Sam

## 45. Doris' House
Peter Barber Architects, 1999
Broadway Market, E8
Overground: Hackney Central

Go around the rear of the market to see this early work from Peter Barber: a gallery/live-work conversion. The rear of the building (where one sees the extension) is opposite 2 Ada Street.

## 46. The Bridge Academy

BDP, 2008
Laburnum Street, E2 (near Haggerston Bridge)
Overground: Haggerston

One of a series of BDP schools that deal with tight sites with playgrounds on roofs (a 600 sqm site accommodates a 10,250 sqm building plus 5500 sqm of external space). This one is distinctly more Ralph Erskine-influenced than others. There is a 1150-pupil secondary school and a 240-pupil primary school. Also see Hampden Gurney school. The problem (as always) is some of the builder's detailing.

## 47. Adelaide Wharf

Allford Hall Monaghan Morris, 2007
120 Queensbridge Road, E2
Overground: Shoreditch

A fine scheme of 152 units comprising 106 private and 46 affordable that is a strong design in every sense except for its double-loaded corridor and single-aspect flats. The overall block forms a central private court – a typology that has become increasingly common. There are some admirably bold features to the design and the ground level in general has been well dealt with.

Photo courtesy of BDP
(Martine Hamilton Knight)

## 48. Orsman Road housing
PH+, 2013
Orsman Road, N1
Overground: Haggerston

Shaggy architecture by the Regent's Canal of [40 new homes (24 private, 8 shared ownership and 8 social rented apartments) above a creative office complex. The architects explain that the scheme,

> is intended to directly respond to and celebrates the character of this previously industrial landscape with a copper carapace, layered behind ivy screens, gabion walls and timber walkways, to realise a concept of 'delamination', where interstitial space creates opportunities for new natural habitats to flourish in the series of meadows, parks, gardens, balconies and apartments that are consequently created. Eventually, as the building matures, the copper skin will weather to a rich brown and the 'mole-hill' roof lights to the commercial space below will be enveloped in the tall grasses and wild flowers of the laid meadow. The building will be continually changing in response to changing site conditions and the dominant local plants of each season.

Photo courtesy of PH+

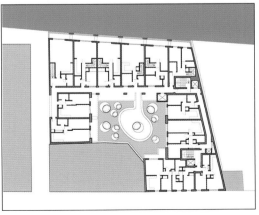

## 49. Geffrye Museum
Branson Coates, 1998
Kingsland Road, E2
Overground: Hoxton

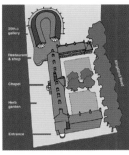

More latterly the scene of controversy over a proposed David Chipperfield extension, this very interesting museum is a rare example of work from this practice. The original building is almshouses dating back to 1715. Start at the north end and take a promenade through to the southern end through a series of historical room sets that terminate with the BC extension: a gallery, café, etc.

## 50. Blue House
FAT, 2002
Garner Street, E2
Rail: Cambridge Heath

An intriguing if incongruous Venturi-esque exercise that was formerly the home of Sean Griffiths, of the talented but now defunct practice: FAT. (See the Thornton Library, Croydon.)

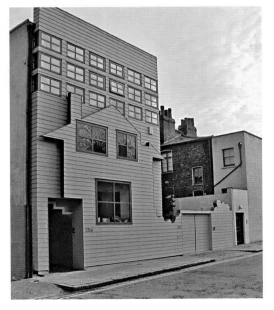

## 51. WoodBlock House
dRMM Studio, 2013
Coate Street, E2
Rail: Cambridge Heath

Engineered timber has been – at least in some sectors – enthusiastically adopted for London houses and even blocks of flats. (regarding the latter, see, for example, Fairmule House, in Waterson Street, Hackney, E2, designed by Quay 2c; see photos at the bottom of the page). WoodBlock House is a four-bedroom house with a ground-floor studio, designed for the artist Richard Wood. It bears some typical dRMM trademarks and is also next door to a Sergison Bates House of 2004 (see the photo bottom right: the rear of the two houses).

Photo courtesy of dRMM

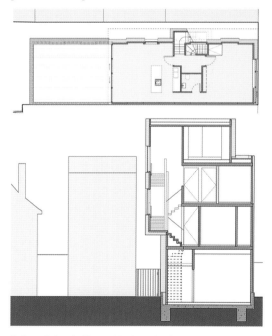

**Below**: Fairmule House, Hackney, by Quay 2c – a similar exercise in engineered-timber panels.

Photo courtesy of Quay 2c

## 52. Museum of Childhood
Caruso St John, 2008
Richmond Road, E8
Tube: Bethnal Green

Part of the V&A: a refurbished building of 1866 now fronted by a contexturalised pavilion providing entry foyer, cloakroom, etc. There's some nice detailing, although no one is too sure about the decorative treatment of the entry façade. (Also see the Tate Britain.)

## 53. Whitechapel Idea Store
Adjaye Associates, 2005
Mile End/Brady Street, E1
Tube and Overground: Whitechapel

Like Hothouse, this work has lots of good ideas that never made it to completion, leaving the visitor with gaps to infill – but there are clues. The underlying paradigm is shopping: the Idea Store (it can't be called a library) as a drop-in facility where one takes an escalator up, takes books off a shelf, and leaves. However, the budget ran out and half the escalator is missing, the installed half is usually closed or not working, and the management style has reverted to traditional library mode. It's still very much worth visiting and there is a café at the top. Note the way the frontage projects out beyond the building line, and grabs you beneath itself. Also: the striped façade whose colours are taken from the market stalls. It doesn't sing, but it could have (have a look).

See a second (smaller) Idea Store by Adjaye at Crisp Street, opposite All Saints DLR station, E14. A third Idea Store was completed by Bissett Adams at Watney Market in 2013 (see opposite page).

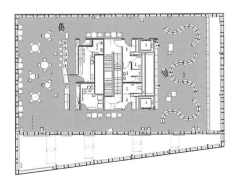

# Going East C: Hackney to Stratford

## 54. Electra House
Adjaye Associates, 2000
Ashfield Street, E1
Tube and Overground: Whitechapel

Times change quickly. In 2000 you could build anything here – including part of a terrace façade that is simply a wall of plywood. That's it. (Last seen in late 2013, it was undergoing some form of renovation).

## 56. Watney Market Idea Store
Bissett Adams, 2013
Watney Market, Commercial Road, E1
Overground: Shadwell

It looks as if there has been a managerial learning exercise informing this latest of the Idea Stores but, pleasant though it is, the design demonstrates little of the edginess of Adjaye's designs. The adjacent Watney Street Market is quite an indicator of local life in this mixed community.

## 55. Tarling East
S333, 2008
Tarling Street, E1
DLR: Shadwell

This is a deliberately 'robust' scheme , challenged by the site and the brief. It is a design that strives to give people their own front door, car parking, private open space etc., including daylight and outdoor space on a compact site adjacent to a train line. In all, there are 22 units, ranging in size from one to six bedrooms and, as the architects say, "redefining the traditional London terrace".

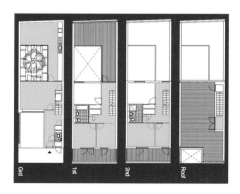

164

## 57. Blizzard Building
Alsop Architects, 2005
Stepney Way, E1 (west end)
Tube and Overground: Whitechapel

University laboratories attached to a large London hospital. They are mostly underground and pop to the surface as a glazed pavilion housing a student desk gallery and, at its heart, a trio of 'pods'. It's all very typical of this architect, non-boring-and-upbeat, guaranteed to upset some people and cheer up others. In sum: it's wonderful and slightly mad. Take the lecture hall: conceived as a place for erudite talks given in a calm forest clearing, complete with architectural features as leaves (not a narrative *of* the concept, but narrative *as* concept). However, one does smile. The real downside: much of this is behind tinted glass. Entry is usually possible during Open House London.

Waldron Road, to the south, sports a rather good terrace of neo-Georgian houses by Ettwein Bridgest. (Look at the rear.)

## 58. Whitechapel Gallery
Robbrecht en Daem, 2009
77–82 Whitechapel High Street, E2
Tube: Aldgate East

The original of this East End institution was Charles Harrison Townsend (1901). The adjacent library was incorporated into the renewed gallery in 2006. What you currently see is an wonderful neo-Viennese work on the façade by Rachel Whiteread and internal evidence of equally impressive work by the Belgian architects, Robbrecht en Daem (here together with the 2013 Stirling Prize winners Witherford Watson Mann with Richard Griffiths).

Photo courtesy of Witherford Watson Mann (David Granorge)

### 59. Beveridge Mews
Peter Barber Architects, 2012
Hannibal Road, E1
Tube: Stepney

An infill scheme that adds to an existing post-war social housing estate by adding a strip of eight houses along one edge of a green area (where garages were once located) that backs onto industrial buildings (now including some student accommodation). Unlike Donnybrook and Tanner Street (in Barking) render has been given up in lieu of cedar shingles and, overall, the detailing is much improved. There is a large potential for this kind of thing in London, and Barber (and his clients) are to be congratulated.

The units are of three, four, and six bedrooms, and are 100% 'affordable', 50% of which are socially rented. Key points emphasised include: high density, large houses created on a difficult, single-aspect site; innovative notched terrace typology, creating a variety of amenity spaces and outlooks; all courtyard houses have their own front door and a minimum of two large courtyards and roof terraces.

Also see Baden Powell Close for a not dissimilar linear scheme within an existing estate.

Photo courtesy of PB

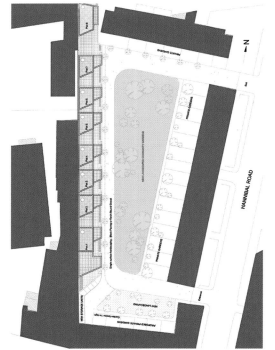

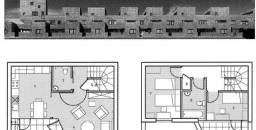

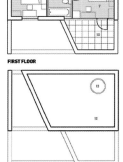

GROUND FLOOR

FIRST FLOOR

SECOND FLOOR

ROOF PLAN

## 60. Queen Mary University campus
Various architects, 1989–2013
Mile End, E1
Tube: Mile End

Queen Mary has extensively developed its campus in recent years. The first notable building on the site was a library by Colin St John Wilson (1989) – a homage to Lewerentz, with 'bagged' brickwork. Among later buildings are: a student accommodation building by MJP Architects, 1991; a Union building by Hawkins Brown in 1999 ; FCB's Westfield student accommodation building, 2004; a small, sub-Libeskind graduate building by Surface Architects, 2005; and two buildings by Wilkinson Eyre Architects: a humanities building and a maths building, both 2011. Probably the most impressive of these is Feilden Clegg Bradley's Westfield student accommodation that sits adjacent to the canal (below). You can walk from here along that canal toward Stratford.

## 61. Mile End Park road bridge
CZWG, 2002
Mile End, E3
Tube: Mile End

This kind of thing is common enough on the continent, but not in central London. Here, CZWG make the most of taking the park across a busy road and do it with panache: a bright yellow underbelly and buildings beneath that are faced in green glazed tiles. It's much admired.

Photo courtesy of CZWG

## 62. Stratford Station
Wilkinson Eyre Architects, 1999
Tube, Overground and DLR: Stratford

This rather fine Central Line station has since been extended and incorporated into transport enhancements that served the Olympic Games and now accept the Overground. It remains exemplary. People coming to the Olympic Games by Tube left this station, climbed a stair leading to a Corten steel bridge taking them over the railway lines, and to the entrance of the Westfield Mall.

## 63. Westfield Mall
Westfield, 2012
Tube, Overground and DLR: Stratford

The gateway to your getaway aeroplane these days is a shopping mall. It was the same at the Olympics. At 180,000 sqm, Westfield Stratford (original owners of tracts of land here) is not unimpressive (1m sqm of office space, the UK's largest casino, three hotels, over 50 restaurants, 5000 parking spaces, its own bus station and a 17-screen 3D cinema) and has become a huge hit among East End consumers. If nothing else, it's a good lunch stop-over for architectural tourists. You can easily walk from here into East Village (the former Athletes' Village) and even across to Hackney Wick.

Shopping malls aren't the most popular form of architecture. However, it has been noted that there is a heroic scale and ambition to the Westfield project and that, what was achieved in four years at Stratford is what would normally take a generation to accomplish. As Ike Ijeh noted in *Building* magazine:

> Stratford City therefore stands as one of the most powerful symbols of the extraordinary visionary momentum and regeneration impetus an Olympic Games can ignite. It is this and not clumsy design or critical indignation, that will prove to be Westfield Stratford City's greatest legacy.

## 64. Olympic legacies
Tube, DLR, Rail and Overground: Stratford

There is little doubt that the Games prompted the regeneration of an industrial, polluted area much in need of change. The people responsible for furthering that work after the Games are a legacy corporation (http://www.londonlegacy.co.uk). The centre-piece to this redevelopment is the Queen Elizabeth Park, adding to a whole series of London open spaces that make the city liveable. The principal content of redevelopment is Westfield, the former Athletes' Village, new offices and other homes being constructed in a manner that seeks to integrate with surrounding areas.

The principal remaining buildings include the following:

**64A** Olympic Stadium (photo left), designed by Populus (formerly HOK Sport, who had a team that included Peter Cook).
This is to become a football stadium, although the issue of the running tracks is still a major issue.

**64B** Aquatics venue (see overleaf), designed by Zaha Hadid (strutting her stuff, with S&P Architects).
Now looking more like its intended self since the temporary side-seating has been removed. This, and the Velodrome, have vied for 'most impressive' status, although the latter is a far more economic and 'green' structure. See overleaf.

**64C** The Velodrome (see overleaf), designed by Hopkins Architects. Possibly the 'greenest' and most admired of the Olympic venues.

**64D** CopperBox: Make Architects (photo left). An arena housing 7500 people during the Games. (Retained.) An imposing but simple shed that is akin to what Venturi dealt with as a 'decorated shed'.

**64E** Energy Centre at Hackney Wick, designed by John McAslan+Partners
A Big-Box-with-Chimney, in Corten steel (one of two). Big, bold and blunt without much romance to it, and all the better for that.(See overleaf.)

**64F** Primary Substation: NORD (photo left). Elegant abstract forms; even better brickwork. But the magazine photos don't tell you about the security fence, and the context.

## 64B Aquatics venue
Zaha Hadid Architects, 2012
Westfield Avenue, E15

## 64C Velodrome
Hopkins Architects, 2012
Eton Manor Walk, E15

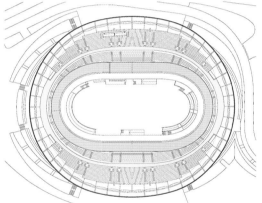

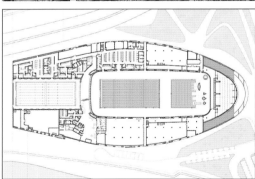

**Above**: Hopkins' Velodrome.
**Left**: Zaha Hadid's Aquatic events venue.

These two venues (if economically viable) will, together with the stadium, be symbolic memory pieces of the 2012 Games. Hadid's may be the 'sexiest' building but her work has become stylistically so branded that one suspects it is the Velodrome that will attain more lasting ('classical') appeal.

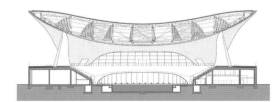

Photo courtesy of MHA (Anthony Palmer)

Photo courtesy of MHA (Edmund Sumner)

## 64E Energy Centre
John McAslan+Partners, 2012
Carpenter's Row, E15

Photos courtesy of JMP (Hufton & Crow)

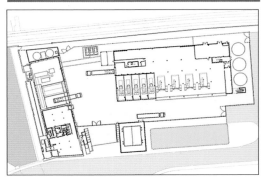

McAslan's Energy Centre – or, more properly: a Combined Cooling Heat and Power (CCHP) plant – is in the post-war tradition of such buildings, married to Saarinen's famed employment of Corten steel – which lends an instant textured and distressed appeal contrasting with the alternative of glass and slickness so favoured by other corporate clients. There is a second and similar CCHP plant just north of the entry bridge that leads into the Westfield Centre. Also see NORD's adjacent brick building.

## 65. White Building
David Kohn Architects, 2013
Queens Yard, E9
Overground: Hackney Wick

An interesting exercise in bridging between the Olympics and legacy-localism in a location (Fish Island) discovered by artists as a post-Hoxton escape to old industrial buildings by the River Lea Navigation canal. Overall, the scheme is materially 'playful, as the architect calls it – mostly meaning cheap-an'-cheerful, fitting in perfectly with the burgeoning arty scene that has taken over local warehousing, considerate and in no way corporate (and yet commissioned by the London Legacy Development Corporation). Studio spaces are provided above a piazza/bar on the ground floor. Some people like to think of this as a touch of bottom-up sanity midst capitalist speculation and hype.

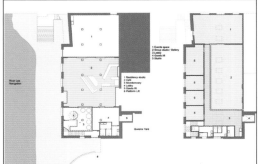

### 66. East Village
Various architects, 2012–14
Stratford, E20
Tube, DLR, Rail and Overground: Stratford

Built to house 17,000 athletes, the Athletes' Village is now East Village and provides over 2800 homes, mostly rented, but including 1379 affordable units. Many practices have been involved in the history of the Athletes' Village (and lay claim to it), but it was Patel Taylor who finally framed the masterplan and gave it design guidelines that began with a sense of place, moved to housing typologies, and then to detailed internal layouts. Sixteen different architects were then called in to designing of 'bolt-on' façades for the blocks. Unfortunately, from a distance, the overall looked effect rather East-Europe circa-1970. Since the completion of the Olympic Games some two years have passed in preparing the accommodation for a variety of tenancies.

The architects involved in the various blocks were: Denton Corker Marshall; Lifshutz Davidson Sandilands; Patel Taylor; Glenn Howells; Panter Hudspith Architects; DSDHA (photo right); Eric Parry Architects; CF Moller Architects; Haworth Tompkins; Niall McLaughlin; Piercy Conner; dRMM (photo bottom right); Studio MAD; PRP.

A polyclinic (Sir Ludwig Guttmann Health & Wellbeing Centre) was designed by Penoyre & Prasad; Chobham Manor Academy school was designed by AHMM. These original architects later became involved in transforming the interiors of the housing blocks into family homes for a redevelopment that should be complete by the summer of 2014. Meanwhile, the local village shop appears to be the Westfield shopping mall. Most of the blocks are quite high for London and most follow a typology that forms a private, inner court whose ground floor is given over to parking covered by a landscaped deck. Overall, and unexpectedly, this 'legacy village' is quite pleasant, giving the impression of being rather like a higher-density Milton Keynes, with generous pavements, wide streets and large open spaces. But it is a curious island.

Photos courtesy of dRMM

Perhaps the most inventive of the façade exercises undertaken by architects called in to add sartorial attractiveness to the athletes' accommodation was this end-block designed by Niall McLaughlin (photo left; plans below). His witty concrete cladding panels are derived from 3D laser scans taken of the Elgin Marbles at the British Museum. Not inappropriately for the Games and such a new residential area, the work gives a strong impression of belonging to the Brave New World of Mussoloni's *Esposizione Universale di Roma* (photo right). Otherwise, the block at issue is typical of most in the Village: a ten-storey surround to a private inner court whose ground floor is given over to private car parking. There were (and still are) good reasons for developing this model of urbanity, but it bears a curious undercurrent of Eastern Bloc authoritarianism.

McLaughlin also has a large and ornate block in construction at Kings Cross called Tapestry, now with aesthetic themes referencing Semper and Louis Sullivan.

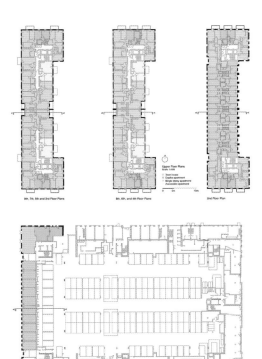

173

### 67. Health & Wellbeing Centre
Penoyre & Prasad, 2011–13
Liberty Bridge Road, E15
Tube, DLR and Overground: Stratford

The Sir Ludwig Guttmann Health & Wellbeing Centre was designed for the Olympic Games (which explains the high standards) and has now been adapted for the local community as 3800m of state-of-the-art accommodation for NHS primary care needs along with an additional 1500m of premises for the East Village Community Development Trust, all within one monolithic building, set upon a triangular site, contained on two sides by railway cuttings.

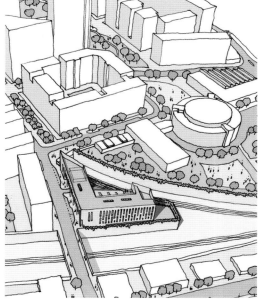

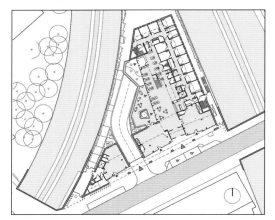

**Above and below**: Penoyre & Prasad's drawings of the Wellbeing Centre at the former Athletes' Village. Note the Chobham Manor School in the background to the above drawing (see opposite).

Photo courtesy of P&P (Anthony Coleman)

## 68. Chobham Manor Academy

Allford Hall Monaghan Morris, 2012
Cheering Lane, E15
Tube: Stratford

A large sports academy adjacent to the East Village. It first appears somewhat clunky and then one notices a variety of subtle moves and details. The Corten steel bridge over to the sports field is especially delightful. The architects tell us that the school is "designed as part of a strong new urban grain whose pattern is reflective of existing London streets," engendering "a powerful drum form" centring on three buildings. "These define space on a campus that is open, attractive, economical and sustainable."

**Below**: the Chobham Bridge giving access over a local road from the school buildings to the playing fields.
**Bottom right**: the site plan. Note the footbridge over the local road to the outer playing fields.

## 69. Abbey Mills Pumping Station E

Allies and Morrison, 1997
Abbey Lane, E15
Tube: Mile End

London's soil waste has been coming to this location just south of the Queen Elizabeth Park ever since Bazelgette instituted his famous civil engineering works and A&M's remarkable metal-clad shed is located next to the original Victorian pumping station of 1868. It is pretty much 'peakish' A&M, working on the kind of scale they appear to be best at.

The construction of this building was completed just after the early 1990s recession that neatly ended Po-Mo and Hi-Tech contentions exemplified by two other

pumping stations designed in that same period: that of John Outram on the Isle of Dogs; and that of Richard Rogers at the west end of the Royal Docks.

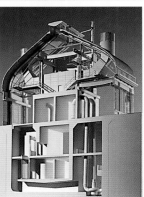

Each of these three designs maintains its own kind of stylistic integrity, although each is, functionally, very similar in purpose. One would like to say that only the A&M scheme strives to follow an unfashionable and non-dogmatic set of values that has always informed the work of this practice. However, this is true of each pumping station, even though Outram's practice no longer gets attention, whilst the other two practices continue as two of London's major practices.

## 70. Hackney Marshes Sports Centre
Stanton Williams Architects, 2011
Hackney Marshes, Homerton Road, E9
Overground: Homerton

The Hackney Marshes Centre is described by Stanton Williams as a "home of amateur Sunday League football", i.e., when lots of East Londoners turn up to play their favourite sport. It provides a new Community Hub comprising new changing rooms, a café, and an education facility. The architects say: "The Centre is embedded within the landscape, avoiding the 'tabula rasa' approach of many sports venues. Plugging a gap in the trees that surround the pitches, its massing minimises its impact on the site." Inevitably, the Centre presents itself as a defensible form and the Corten steel cladding places it in the North American/Saarinen tradition. (The plan and section are given below.)

Photo courtesy of SWA (David Grandorge)

## 71. Cadogan Terrace
Kyson, 2009
Cadogan Terrace, E9
Overground: Hackney Wick

This set of four terrace town-houses is from a firm that can't call themselves architects, because they aren't. But what they produce fractures the boundaries of professional pretensions and demonstrates that what is at issue is simply good design. (Site plan below.)

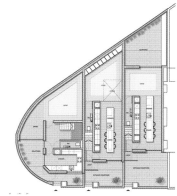

**Below**: plan and section through Sports centre.

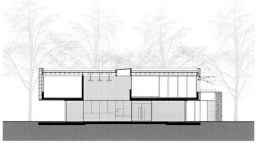

## 72. St Andrews

Allies and Morrison; Maccreanor Lavington Architects; Glenn Howells Architects, 2012
Devas Street, E3
Tube: Bromley-by-Bow

Masterplanned by A&M, this development echoes the planning on an entirely different complex of three office blocks at Bankside 123: major pedestrian routes run north–south; secondary cross routes run east–west. The reality at Bankside is that the latter run into the security within atria; the reality at St Andrews is that access to the inner courts is gated (the new norm and now conventional). The masterplan allows for 964 homes, an NHS health care facility, new community facilities and one hectare of parks and gardens. Fifty percent of the housing provided is affordable and 30% across all tenures is

family housing. Although the scheme looks admirable it does have a lot of double-loaded corridors and single-aspect apartments. One could also argue that the central courts are rather long and thin. On the more positive side, townhouses with their own entrance doors straight off the street occupy the ground and first floors. The most western block was detailed by A&M and has 194 units. The mid-block was by Maccreanor Lavington (230 units); and the eastern block was by Glenn Howells (227 units).

**Above left**: the A&M block plan.
**Above**: an upper-level plan of one of the A&M blocks.
**Below**: balconies on the Maccreanor Lavington block.

Photo courtesy of MLA (Tim Crocker)

### 73. East London University, Stratford
Richard Murphy Architects, 2008; Hopkins Architects, 2013
Water Lane, E15
Tube: Stratford

Murphy is a notable Scottish architect who has completed a number of buildings at East London University, including a Clinical Education Centre, the Cass School of Education and the Computer & Confer- ence Centre. These and other Murphy works form the body of the campus to the north of a rather fine build- ing called University House and formerly the West Ham Technical Institute (designed by Gibson and Russell, 1892). (See the numbers on the site plan below, except no. 4.)

The Hopkins-designed library (no. 4 on the plan and page opposite) fits in nicely with current predilec- tions toward brickwork and proportionality. Interest- ingly, its architecture is much calmer than that of Murphy.

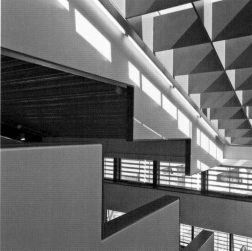

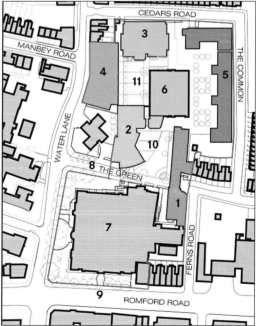

Photos courtesy of RMA

Photo courtesy of HA (Timothy Soar)

Photo courtesy of HA (Simon Kennedy)

### 74. Donnybrook

Peter Barber Architects, 2005
Parnell Road, E3
Tube: Mile End

Definitely one to see: an inventive scheme that puts on show Barber's keen commitments to basic values such as one's own front door off the street, private terraces, etc., but one ends up being witness to this architect's struggles builders somewhat indifferent to his ideals and ambitions and keen to value engineer the scheme into lower costs and higher profits. The outcome is a mix of aspiration and meanness that undermines Barber's talent and commitment. Spatially, it is rather tight. Aesthetically, one queries the transplant of North African enthusiasms. Done again, it would no doubt be in brick (see, for example, Barber's work at Camberwell).

Photo courtesy of PBA

Photo courtesy of MHA (Timothy Soar)

Photo courtesy of PBA

## 75. Phoenix School
Patel Taylor, 2013
49 Bow Road, E3
Tube: Bow

Ongoing work at two schools, including the Phoenix School for 6 to 16-year-olds with learning difficulties. Here, a new entrance has been formed for the Phoenix that makes a refreshing addition to this part of the Mile End Road (the school itself lies in the heart of the urban block).

## 77. Bernie Grant Centre
Adjaye Associates, 2008
Tottenham Green, N15
Tube: Seven Sisters

An arts centre for 'black and culturally diverse performers', i.e., a multi-arts centre providing a 300 seat auditorium and 70-seat studio/rehearsal space, plus café, bar, etc. These are formed out of a late 19th-century building that forms a reception and ticket booking area, with two buildings set behind.

## 76. St Mary's Welcome Centre
Peter Barber Architects, 2011
Church End, E17
Tube: Walthamstow Central

A backlands hostel development described by the architects as a "combination of uses including homeless accommodation, community space and counselling/vocational/life-skills training facilities all intertwined within one building". In formal terms the building is conceived as a single folding surface forming the floor, wall and ceiling of the glazed spaces; ribboning its way from the ground to the roof. The construction comprises a light weight primary steel frame with pre-cast concrete floors, together with metal stud walls stuffed with insulation and clad with an insulated acrylic render system. The roof is a warm deck single ply membrane system, also with very thick insulation. The point, however, is that it present itself as a clean and fresh building in this area.

Photos courtesy of PBA

## 78. University Square Stratford

Make, 2013
1 Salway Road, E15
Tube and Overground: Stratford

Photos courtesy of Make (Simon Kennedy)

A collaborative building serving both The University of East London and Birkbeck University. It sits in the island that was the old Stratford shopping centre, adjacent to Levitt Bernstein's Stratford Circus building of 2002 (a facility for performing arts) and Burrell Foley Fisher's Stratford Picture House of 1998. The building provides shared resources that encourage the exchange of ideas and the architects tell us:

Large windows on all sides of the ground level animate the street, with the alignment of the public space extending into the building to create the cafe, reception lobby and atrium foyer. These qualities create an accessible building that has a strong relationship with the urban, cultural and public character of the area. The cladding varies around the building; the projecting faces are clad in glossy, polished ceramic granite arranged in a vertical grid pattern, while the sides of the projecting volumes are lined with gold-coloured panels.

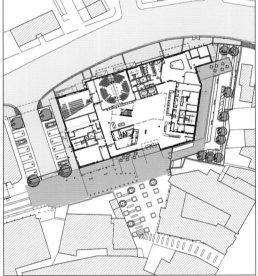

East  Central D:
Barking Central

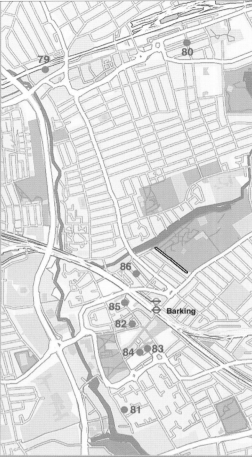

Barking is possibly as far east as you will be inclined to go from central London, but it is readily accessible. It was formerly an area whose identity was linked to the Ford plant at Dagenham, but Barking long ago entered another phase of its history and economically declined. More recently it has been undergoing major regeneration in and around the central area.

With responsibility for the central area adjacent to the Town Hall, AHMM have a major presence. They describe their central area contribution in terms of: "A cluster of new buildings – a diverse mix of forms, heights, tones and textures – positioned around the existing Barking Town Hall to capture a civic square and reintroduce historical routes." In addition, there is also housing by Maccreanor Lavington and Peter Barber, a new Skills Centre from the late Rick Mather, and other buildings of interest.

## 79. Jason Lee House

Peter Barber Architects, 2011
16 York Road, Ilford, IG1
Rail: Ilford

A dramatic reorganisation and extension of an existing property as a homeless hostel, with a central court to the rear. (It's all somewhat in the tradition of Farrell-Grimshaw adding 'service pods' to old terraces in the 1960s.) The architects tell us:

> The garden façade of the existing house is opened up and extended with a glass roof and uninterrupted views of the garden. The new building also incorporates measures to minimise its carbon footprint with ground source heat pumps, solar water heating, super insulation and daylight harvesting.

## 80. Isaac Newton Academy

Feilden Clegg Bradley Studios, 2013
Cricklefield Place, Ilford, IG1
Rail: Seven Kings; Tube: Newbury Park

A 1250-place suburban academy school with an emphasis on music and maths, and some striking architecture. The architects tell us:

> The concepts of levity and gravity have been used to define the two distinct elements of the building. The sports accomodation is located within a dramatic sports beam supported on two storey columns which intersects with a three and four storey main volume which contains the teaching accomodation. Courtyards are carved from the teaching accomodation to bring daylight and delight to the circulation spaces.

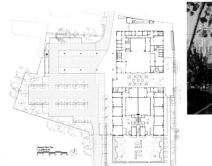

Photos courtesy of PBA

Photos courtesy of FCBS (Timothy Soar)

## 81. The Granary

Schmidt Hammer Lassen with PTE, 2012
80 Abbey Road, Barking, IG11
Tube: Barking

A restored complex that employs a new atrium as the central feature to an interplay of old and new. As PTEa comment:

> Clad in striking bronze panels, the new accommodation is attached to the existing via the vertical circulation core and a high level bridge link. A new atrium garden makes previously obscured elevations visible again. The new complex also forms the setting for a new public square as part of the regeneration of the area as a new quarter for the creative industries.

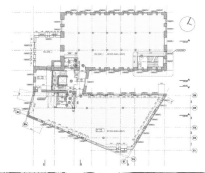

Photo courtesy of PTE

## 82. Barking Skills Centre

Rick Mather Architects, 2013
London Road, Barking, 1G11
Tube: Barking

The late Rick Mather has provided Barking with a building that defines two sides to the new market square whilst addressing the historic Magistrates Court, providing vocational training for 14 to 19-year-olds. The well-considered landscaping is by Patel Taylor.

Photo courtesy of RMA (Richard Chivers)

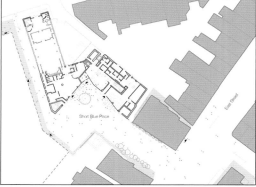

## 83. Barking Central Library
Allford Hall Monaghan Morris, 2008
Axe Street, Barking, IG11
Tube: Barking

AHMM's central area planning, its library topped by housing and MUF's rather good landscaping make central Barking worth a visit. The striking balconies may be less useful than they could have been, but there has obviously been a demand to make a statement with a strongly branded building. Similarly, the library/One-Stop Centre may have more DVDs than books, but it's an upbeat place for community members to visit. The upper-level housing might be a single-aspected+corridor arrangement, and the arcade may be strident but, again, there are lots of virtues here. The architects comment that: "the overall colour scheme not only binds together the cluster of buildings but emphasises the protruding balconies and recessed loggias." Overall, "The project [...] stands as a lived-in symbol of the wider-scale regeneration of the area." The general area has seen many changes in recent years and this dynamic continues.

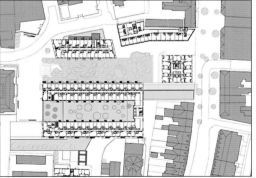

## 84. Barking Central Square
MUF, 2008
Axe Street, Barking, IG11
Tube: Barking

MUF's landscaping in the central area is exemplary. It is epitomised by an artful folly that looks as if it has

been there for generations (or imported from Venice, now with ram instead of lion). But, if one pops around to the rear (photo below), it becomes revealed as a splendid piece of self-declared scenography. The AHMM work is admirably complemented. London needs more of this.

## 85. Anne's Mews, Barking
Allford Hall Monaghan Morris; Maccreanor Lavington Architects, 2011
Linton Road, Barking, 1G11
Tube: Barking

An ongoing housing scheme (the former Lintons Estate, now the William Street Quarter, providing 470 new homes) that began with two terraces: one by AHMM and the other (photo below) by Maccreanor Lavington Architects. This first stage comprised: 14 four-bedroom houses; 15 three-bedroom houses; and 2 two-bedroom houses. Apart from the presence of cars it looks good, illustrating the preference for brickwork and simple proportionality that characterises current housing fashions. By the time you read this the development will have been much expanded. (**Below**: the masterplan.)

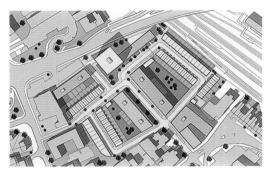

Photo courtesy of MLA (Tim Crocker)

## 86. Tanner Street, Barking

Peter Barber Architects, 2005
Tanner Street, Barking, 1G11
Tube: Barking

It is interesting to compare this scheme with two others by Barber: Donnybrook (also 2005) and Hannibal Road (2013). Barber is the rare example of a talented architect who endeavours to instantiate basic house design beliefs and, in all three of these otherwise quite different schemes, he has striven to give every dwelling its own front door off the street, together with private outside space. Tanner and Donnybrook have won admiration (we couldn't keep Neils Torp away), but there are problems: the render-on-insulation weathers badly (it has been avoided at Hannibal) and looks incongruous in a London setting (either exotically North African or a Bauhaus leftover) and the threshold experience is mean. Perhaps one carps: Barber has, against the odds of low budgets, mean space standards and avaricious builders, proven that there is an alternative in London housing. Here, at Tanner, the scheme suffers the same problem of Anne Mews: the obtrusion of cars.

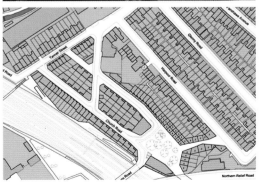

## 87. Baden Powell Close

Peter Barber Architects, 2009
Baden Powell Close, Dagenham, RM9
Tube: Becontree

Another from Pete Barber: 14 terrace units (12 two-bed and two three-bed houses, with social rent and shared ownership sale tenures) in the inimitable Barber style and set of concerns. Compare with Tanner Street and Hannibal Road in Stepney.

Photo courtesy of PBA

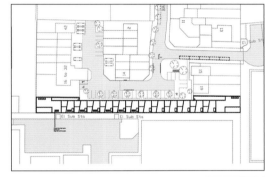

Photo courtesy of PBA

The following two buildings are quite far eastward, out toward the M25; however, we include them as indication that not everything is within Transport for London's Zones One and Two.

## 88. Drapers Academy

Feilden Clegg Bradley Studio, 2013
Settle Rd., Romford, RM3
Rail: Harold Wood

This interesting maths and science biased academy school sits on top of a hill with countryside views and adopts the form of a brick, courtyard building self-consciously recalling traditional English country houses. The architects say:

> The design responds to the practical need to improve levels of science and maths achievement and also addresses the aesthetic need for a building of beauty to reflect the surrounding countryside. [...] The design includes enhanced science and maths facilities that face each other across a central courtyard. One side of the courtyard is formed by an internal street, which provides access to principle spaces such as the library, main hall and glazed ground floor café. A colonnade wraps around the remaining three sides and allows sheltered access and circulation to the general teaching spaces. The science department extends over two stories and includes an outdoor glass biodome. The design for the science department evolved out of our collaborative work in developing more accessible science facilities.

## 89. RSPB Rainham

van Heyningen & Haward, 2007
Rainham Marshes
Rail: Purfleet

This is as far east as you are likely to go, and only then as a bird lover (or someone who likes watching bird-watchers). It is worth a visit: the Villa Savoye is adapted and reinvented as a bird watching house, place of information, café, etc.

**Below**: ground floor plan of Drapers Academy.

Photos courtesy of FCB (Timothy Soar)

The West End

# The West End

## The West End as two maps

In essence the **West End** is everything the City, as a mono-cultural trading area, is not. Here one not only finds the Monarch, Parliament and houses of government, but also places of shopping and entertainment that have their roots in the character of 18th-century London. While overseas trade was centred in the City, the West End developed as a terraced suburb focused upon the importance of the monarch, the royal court, land ownership in the hands of a few great estates, aristocrats coming up from the country, provided for by a massive population of servants and crafts people, surrounded by market gardens and brick kilns and the like. It hasn't changed that much – central London is still controlled by five great estates (diagram right): Grosvenor, Cadogan, Howard de Walden, Portman and Bedford, with the Crown Estate and the City of London as additional major stakeholders.

We have divided the overall area into two map areas, **A** and **B**. Note that the building numbering continues from one map to the other.

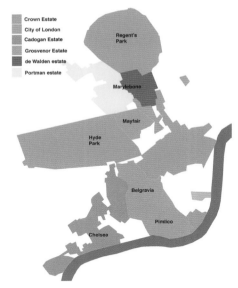

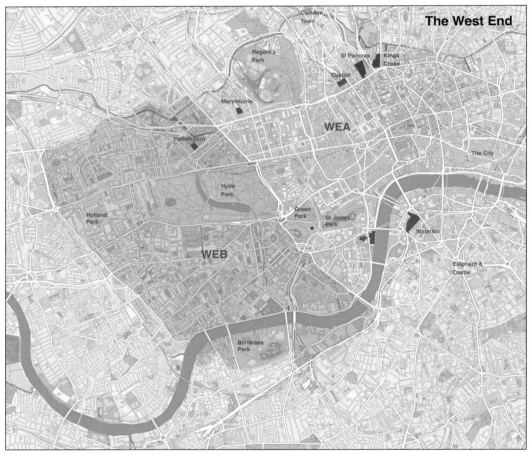

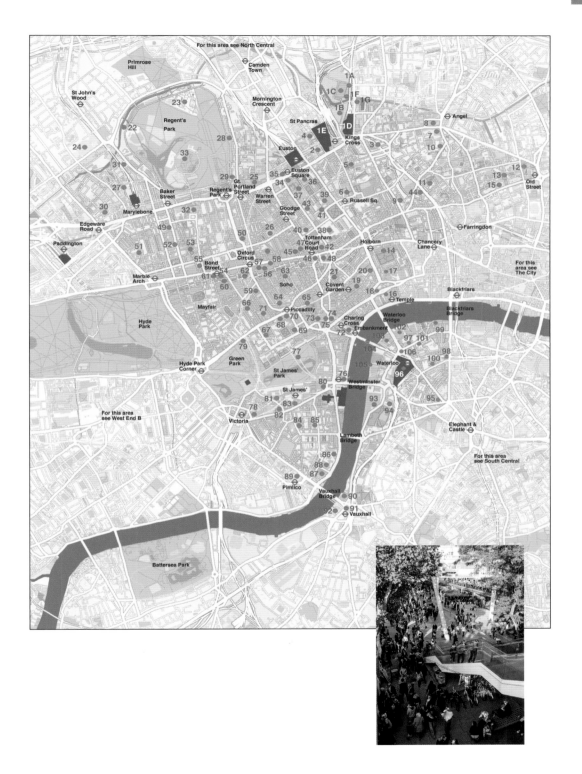

For this area see North Central

Primrose
Hill

St John's
Wood

Camden
Town

1A

1C  1F
1B  1G

23

Mornington
Crescent

Regent's
Park

St Pancras

1E  1D

22

28

4  Euston

St John's

Kings
Cross

8  Angel

7

33

2

3

10

31

29  25  35  Euston
Square

5

12

27  Baker
Street

Gt
Portland
Street

34  36

13

15

Old
Street

30

Regent's
Park

Warren
Street

6

1

44

Marylebone

32

49

37

43

39

9

41

Edgeware
Road

26

40  38

Russell Sq.

Paddington

51  52  53

50

47  Tottenham
Court
Road

Goodge
Street

42

Holborn

14

Farringdon

Chancery
Lane

For this
area see
The City

Marble
Arch

55  Bond
Street

54

61

Oxford
Circus

57  58
62  56

45  46

63

48

21

20

19

17

Blackfriars

60

59

Soho

64

Covent
Garden

18

16  Temple

Blackfriars
Bridge

Mayfair

66

71

65

Piccadilly

74

Charing
Cross

Waterloo
Bridge

Blackfriars
Bridge

Hyde
Park

70  73

75

Embankment

103

102

99

67  68

69

72

105

97  101

79

77

104

106

98

Hyde Park
Corner

Green
Park

105

Waterloo

100

St James'
Park

76

96

For this area
see West End B

78

81

St James'

80

Westminster
Bridge

95

82  83

93

Victoria

84  85

94

Elephant &
Castle

Lambeth
Bridge

For this area
see South Central

86

88  87

89  Pimlico

Vauxhall
Bridge

90

92  91  Vauxhall

Battersea Park

## 1. Kings Cross

Developers; Argent and St George
Architects: various (see below)
Tube: Kings Cross

The publicity for KX tells us that "King's Cross is the largest mixed use development (27ha) in single ownership to be master planned and developed in central London for over 150 years". It certainly has taken a long time in gestation (since the mid-1980s), been highly controversial, but makes an enormous amount of sense. The issue has always been *how* should these railway lands and historic buildings be developed? – an issue prompting endless debate, contention and negotiation between developers, stakeholders and neighbouring local authorities (Camden and Islington). The core to the rationale for development is that KX is a major national railway station adjacent to another, St Pancras – and is a logical place for dense commercial development. However, the location is also one of transition between the West End and local residential areas.

The outcome is overlaid by endless statistics (e.g. "50 new and restored buildings and structures, 20 new streets and 10 new public spaces are being created"), but what we're all concerned about is whether or not the outcome is to be one of quality – one that leans toward participation rather than overt private ownership of a kind that has become so controversial.

Foster's late 1980s scheme simply dropped a whole series of office buildings all over the railway lands as an island of commerciality. The Argent St George scheme has, instead, been described as a "perfect mix of grittiness and shininess" and "simultaneously a symbol of London's industrial and engineering past and the creative present" (Edwin Heathcote, FT architectural correspondent).

A key part of this promise has been a negotiation of mutual benefit between Argent, as developers, and Central St Martins (CSM), one of London's premier art schools eager to come together into one building and expand – hence a reuse for the central historic Granary building and railway sheds. The move was not dissimilar to having the City Hall at More London and is undoubtedly hugely important as a symbol and fact of cultural content that (ostensibly, at least) is other than a polarisation of office and housing.

CSM (with its 5000 students inhabiting a building designed by Stanton Williams Architects) has already been a success and the rest of the development should be equally so. The masterplan is by Allies and Morrison.

The KX forecourt is by Stanton Williams Architects (2013), but the canopy is by John McAslan+Partners.

### Kings Cross fundamentals

• The busy heart of the development is Kings Cross Station and its neighbour, St Pancras, where the Eurostar trains terminate.
• Between these is a group of office buildings that form a first-phase commercial heartland penetrated by a route leading from the stations toward the Regents Canal and the CSM Granary building. The architects include Allies and Morrison and David Chipperfield Architects. On the east side will be a large Google building (designed by AHMM).
• At this point the character of the development shifts and we begin to engage cultural institutions and residential developments that seek to knit into the adjacent urban fabric (not an easy task). On the west side of CSM will be a street of shops, cafés, etc. Beyond that development is mixed and will, no doubt, be amended as it unfolds.

**2008**      **2013**      **2016**      **2020+**

## 1A. Kings Cross housing

Various architects, ongoing
York Way, N1
Tube: St Pancras, Kings Cross

Key names designing housing include: dRMM, Glenn Howells, Maccreanor Lavington Architects and Niall Mclaughlin, PRP Architects. DRMM have a prominent site just to the east of CSM; however, some of the other architects have prominent buildings further north. For example, on York Way MLA have a tall, urbane building complex (R5 /Saxon Court, bearing references to the Economist group); PRP have an equally tall building (R4/Rubicon Court); and Glenn Howells has a 27 storey student housing block.

**Left**: PRP Architects. **Below left**: Glenn Howells' student building (669 units).
**Above and below**: MLA's 'embedded tower' Saxon Court scheme. The blue is social rented units (to 8 storeys; above that is shared ownership); the green is for care of the elderly; and the pink is Phase Two of market sale and shared ownership units.

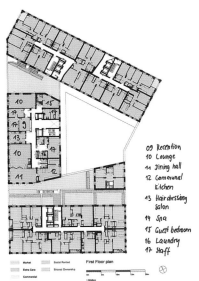

09 Reception
10 Lounge
11 Dining hall
12 Communal kitchen
13 Hairdressing salon
14 Spa
15 Guest bedroom
16 Laundry
17 Staff

First Floor plan

Market | Social Rented
Extra Care | Shared Ownership
Commercial

**Below and right**: dRMM's Arthouse housing project: 143 apartments, 29 of them affordable, arranged in four clusters with access in between). In the architects' words: "The building's façade comprises glazed terracotta tiles with the face of the towers finished in polished stainless steel, reflecting the contextual colours of the site. Responding to residents' needs for shade and privacy, sliding louvred screens animate the face of the building and allow residents the ability to control their environment with shading." The west side includes some very pleasant landscaping (by the Dan Pearson Studio).

**Note**: also see dRMM's housing schemes at **Wansey Street** and **Harper Square**. Also their housing being constructed at **Battersea Power Station** and another scheme in Southwark called **Trafalgar Square**, SE1 (in advanced construction during early 2014; Rodney Road, SE1, behind the old Heygate Estate at Elephant & Castle; to be completion expected in early 2015.)

**Below**: Another KX scheme to look out for is Niall Mclaughlin's ornate **Tapestry** development on the north-east side of Kings Cross. Following on from his work on the facade of a building at the Athletes' Village in Stratford, Mclaughlin here turns to Louis Sullivan's work (the Guaranty Building, Buffalo) and references to Semper (woven screens on the primitive hut) for another instance of witful branding inspiration (also see the Chipperfield office building). On the bottom left is the upper podium-level plan; on the right, a CGI of the elevation. (In construction in 2014 and located toward the north-west corner of the KX development.)

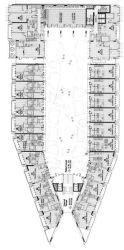

## 1B. Kings Cross Offices
Various architects. ongoing
Pancras Square, N1
Tube: St Pancras, Kings Cross

An office building is a three-part equation: an framing shell prepared for an scene-setting fit-out; common areas such as lobby and lift core, etc.; and an outer face presenting what is the most significant branded aspect of the entire exercise. The tectonic dimensions of such works have been settled over the last thirty years and are relatively straight forward for any competent architect. Developers now know exactly what they want in terms of floor-plate geometries and the like (e.g., a ubiquitous 1.5m grid), therefore the common areas and the façade are a crucial part of what the architect deals with. The latter is usually an empty, formulaic security lobby dressed out in pleasant materials, leaving the outside as an abstract challenge to communicate 'kerb appeal'. Of the seven office buildings around Pancras Square, two of the more significant are the realtively petite B2 (David Chipperfield Architects) and much larger B4 (Allies and Morrison). Other buildings are being designed by Studio Downie, Wilmotte and Associates, Porphrios Associates, Eric Parry and Bennett Associates, Completions will come during 2014.

All CGI's of Kings Cross courtesy of London Communications Agency

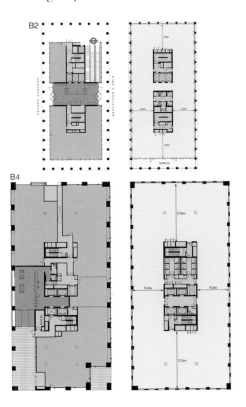

**Top and above left**: the Chipperfield design, with its strong branding pitch reliant upon cast-iron casings that wrap an inner concrete framing. And they have a woven texture – again, rather Semper-ish. Although much smaller than the A&M building (above right), it has significantly more presence.

**Right**: the Rab Bennett scheme for Five Pancras Square, to be used by Camden Council as their offices.

### 1C. Central St Martins
Stanton Williams Architects, 2012
1 Granary Square, King's Cross, N1
Tube: St Pancras, Kings Cross

The cultural flagship of the KX development: a major extension to the Granary building that employs the latter as a forecourt/lobby area leading into the mouth of a Turbine Hall-style atrium that serves as the heart of CSM's 40,000 sqm campus of studios, workshops, offices, theatre, etc. (for 5000 people). It's an impressive work in three senses: its role in the KX development; as a building in its own right; and as an exercise in sensitively retaining the 'marks' of history that are all around the historic fabric. Make a visit on an 'open' day.

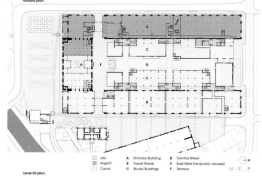
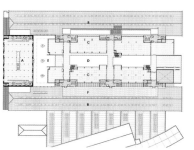

**Above**: the central atrium (with an inflated pillow roof) is the heart of institution and very much a lived-in space (end-grain wood flooring, for durability). The cross-bridges are wide enough to be work areas and a converted Airsteam caravan serves as a cafeteria servery point.

Photos of CSM courtesy of Stanton Williams Architects (John Sturrock)

## 1D. Kings Cross Station Concourse
John McAslan+Partners, 2012
Front piazza by Stanton Williams Architects, 2013
Tube: St Pancras, Kings Cross

This project was rushed ahead for completion serving the 2012 Olympic Games. Behind what you see are complex engineering issues that are neatly resolved into a new semicircular concourse area abutting the old KX rail station. Out front, some dreadful temporary buildings have been demolished and a Stanton Williams Architects design has taken their place, restoring the grandeur to the old (Lewis Cubitt, 1852) frontage (plus a McAslan canopy).

## 1E. St Pancras International
Rail Link Engineering, 2007
Pancras Road, N1
Tube: St Pancras, Kings Cross

There are three parts to this equation: the George Gilbert Scott hotel of 1868–76 (a favourite of Londoners); the impressive Henry Barlow train shed behind (same dates); and what Rail Link Engineering have achieved as the Eurostar train terminus. The meeting point (photo below) is at the upper level, but everyone meets downstairs in a more lively area where the shops and cafés are.

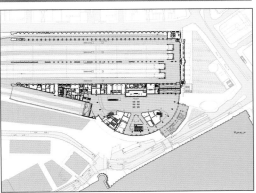

### 1F. The Filling Station
Carmody Groake, 2012
Goods Way, N1
Tube: St Pancras, Kings Cross

A redundant petrol station converted into a small restaurant with surrounding fibreglass screens that orient activities away from the road and toward the canal.

### 1G. Kings Place
Dixon Jones, 2008
90 York Way, N1
Tube: St Pancras, Kings Cross

Technically, not a part of KX, but the wavy west-facing glass screen-wall of Kings Place sits just opposite The Filling Station, on the canal. Mostly offices, Kings Place also includes an impressive concert hall. And there is a café here.

### 2. British Library
Colin St John Wilson, 1998
Euston Road, NW1
Tube: St Pancras, Kings Cross

Some 25 years in gestation, moving from one site to another at a late date in the design process, the British Library ended up as stylistically weird – not so enjoyably on the exterior, but much more pleasurably so in the interior: a homage to Alvar Aalto and an example of public spaces once found in hotels. As they say: they don't build public spaces like this anymore. Go inside, enjoy the restaurant and café, see an exhibition; become a member and join in the researches. It's an admirable place, despite its unfashionableness.

### 3. Gagosian Gallery
Caruso St John, 2004
6–24 Britannia Street, WC1
Tube: Kings Cross

A warehouse building conversion into the now-familiar equation of white walls and polished concrete floors. But impressively done.

### 4. Crick Institute
HOK and PLP, early 2015
Midland Road, NW1
Tube: St Pancras

A large biomedical research building housing 1250 researchers. Ground-level public facilities include an auditorium, exhibition space, teaching spaces, and conference and workshop facilities. Full completion will be April 2015. The architects tell us that:

> primary and secondary labs, arranged in four neighbourhoods over four upper floors, are linked by a sequence of interlocked double-height platforms set within the atria, which provide a variety of spaces and opportunities for casual and formal collaboration between research scientists pursuing diverse science programmes.

### 5. Lumen
Theis & Khan Architects, 2008
Regent's Square, WC1
Tube: St Pancras

A notable work that brought Theis & Khan into the limelight and dragged this neglected 1960s church into the proverbial 21st century. The mix of religiosity and mundane community facilities works well. It's a simple but articulate and refreshingly well-done project whose scale and proportions are eminently comfortable. The central cone within the main church body is clichéd, and yet it works well, both in itself and as a spatial divider. Try the café; go to the patio at the rear; use the community spaces, enjoy a service.

CGI courtesy of PLP

### 6. Brunswick Centre
Patrick Hodgkinson, 1972; Levitt Bernstein, 2006
Bernard and Marchmont Streets, WC1
Tube: St Pancras

Intended as private and then taken over for social housing. Intended to march on over Georgian terraces, but stopped after its first phase. Neglected and then revived as an excellent example of how such megastructural dreams can become loved works of contemporary architecture – after bits and pieces had been lopped off, the shops refurbished, new leases entered into, canopies added and an upmarket supermarket brought in as the 'anchor'. It's good, but still suffers from turning its back on the adjacent Marchmont Street. Note the Sant' Elia references in the original.

## 7. Angel Building
Allford Hall Monaghan Morris, 2010
407 St John Street, EC1
Tube: Angel

Derwent's radical conversion of a 1981 office building with a central court into what AHMM refer to as a 'white-collar factory'. As the architects explain:

> The reason Derwent London are confident in this new prototype is that the generosity of volumes and play of light ensures that it has a proven spatial character: that of a monumental piece of industrial production inspired by utility and the need for delight. Like its predecessors it is inherently convertible to something else, thereby embodying that most sensible maxim of enduring architectural quality, 'long-life/ loose fit'.

The concept has its roots in the TEA building in Shoreditch, but this particular 'factory' is more akin to high-technology assembly plant set in green surroundings and within an impressive central atrium manifesting distinct Louis Kahn influences, complete with a café to go with the high-specification raw concrete. Overall, it's an achievement with many project virtues. Have a look; have a coffee or try Jamie's Italian, on the corner.

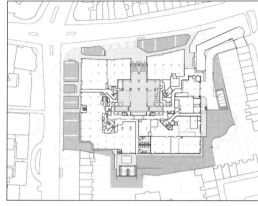

**Above**: the site plan of this over 33,200 sqm (gross) building (plus 500 sqm of retail and 2000 sqm of terraces, etc).
**Below**: the original 1981 building that was stripped back to its frame and reconstructed. The transmogrification is total.

Photo courtesy of AHMM

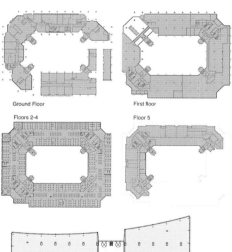

Ground Floor

First floor

Floors 2-4

Floor 5

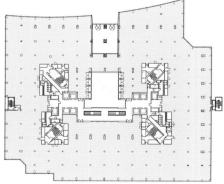

## 8. 10–4 Pentonville Road
Stiff & Trevillion, 2013
10-4 Pentonville Road, N1
Tube: Angel

A striking office building opposite AHMM's Angel building (both by Derwent), perhaps epitomising the return to confident restraint, brickwork and proportionality. The design "retains and connects the existing structural frames of two buildings, to provide six storeys and 55,000 sq ft (net)". The detailing (e.g. around the fenestration) is well considered and worthy of one's attention.

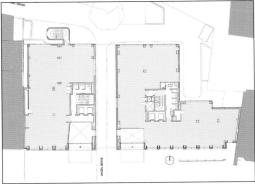

## 9. ITN
Foster + Partners, 1989
200 Gray's Inn, WC1
Tube: Russell Square

Now a somewhat forgotten Foster work featuring what was, the in those days, two novelties: an atrium and a storey-height revolving entry door. It's possibly better from the rear, east side, where large satellite dishes adorn the roof.

Photo courtesy of Foster + Partners

## 10. Sadlers Wells
Nicholas Hare Architects, 1998
Rosebury Avenue, EC1
Tube: Angel

Another almost forgotten scheme, in part because Nicholas Hare seems to have gone off the radar. Nevertheless, this is an impressive building.

## 11. Finsbury Health Centre
Lubetkin and Tecton, 1938
Pine Street, EC1
Tube: Angel

Not so much forgotten as neglected and worthy of not only your attention, but some TLC. The building is a fascinating piece of Modernist history from an émigré architect with a relatively short career – in this instance, his client being a 'progressive' left-wing local authority determined to do well in a borough with appalling health problems. Interestingly (this is the 1930s), this included bussing in school children down a rear ramp into a basement area, where they were deloused.

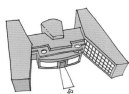

## 12. Moorfields Eye Hospital

Penoyre & Prasad, 2007
162 City Road, EC1
Tube: Old Street

A famous London eye hospital with a new children's wing and an exuberant south-facing façade seeking an alternative to the usual ways of sun-screening: a flock of birds. The projecting red box is a compositional cliché from an earlier period, but it almost works.

**Note**: the church to the south of the Baths is St Lukes (John James, Steeple by Nicolas Hawksmoor, 1728), converted in 2003 by Levitt Bernstein to provide London Symphony Orchestra rehearsal rooms.

## 13. Ironmonger Row Baths

Tim Ronalds Architects, 2013
1 Norman Street, EC1
Tube: Old Street

A listed baths building of 1938 reinvented for the 21st century. It's a fine, understated and technically complex conversion and refurbishment, complete with a distinctive Tim Ronalds signature on the repositioned entry façade. (Also see Hackney Empire.)

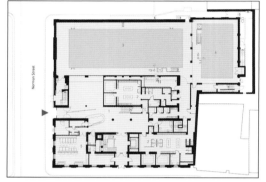

## 14. John Soane Museum

Sir John Soane, 1792–1834
Lincolns Inn, WC1
Tube: Holborn

You came to London and didn't visit the Soane Museum? Admittedly, it's a lot busier these days, but that is no excuse to miss this most famous of works by a man in love with architecture: at once Soane's home, office, museum and gallery. Go on a cold and grey Monday or Tuesday when it is less crowded.

Photos courtesy of TRA (Morley von Sternberg)

## 15. Gee Street
Munkenbeck+Partners, 2012
45–55 Gee Street, EC1
Tube: Old Street

Acombination of apartments and offices employing an inventive use of brickwork. Simple and effective.

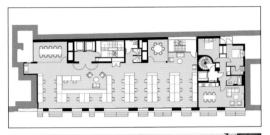

Photo courtesy of Munkenbeck+Partners

## 16. Somerset House
Dixon Jones; Inskip & Jenkins; Feilden & Mawson, 2001
Strand, WC2
Tube: Temple or Covent Garden

William Chambers' building was completed in 1776, housing learned societies and government departments. It now houses museums and galleries, provides  a fine central court and becomes an ice-skating venue in the winter. Both the river terrace (once at the river's edge) and well-used central court are by Dixon Jones.

## 17. LSE campus
Lincoln's Inn, WC2
Tube: Holborn / Temple

The notable works on this campus at the south-east end of Lincoln's Inn, WC2, includes the following:

### 17A. Library Foster+Partners, 2001
10 Portugal Street, WC2.

A simple spatial concept within an old shell given focus and grand effect by a large spiralling ramped staircase with a roof light above. However, there is a slight disjuncture between the impressiveness of this architectural gesture and the rest of the library.

## 17B. New Academic Building
Grimshaw, 2008
Lincoln's Inn, WC2

The conversion of a 1915 building that provides new lecture halls and lots of flow space in the guise of a dramatic and large, wide staircase where students can hang about as well as move up and down. Academic accommodation is on the top floor with a perimeter roof terrace that provides superb views over London.

Photo courtesy of Grimshaw (Jens Willebrand)

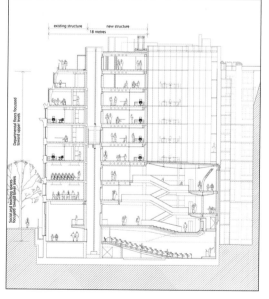

**Note**: there is a sheltered outdoor area on the LSE campus called John Watkins Plaza, designed by MJP (2003).

## 17C Saw Swee Hock Student Union
O'Donnell & Tuomey, 2013
Corner of Sheffield Street and Portsmouth Street, WC2
Tube: Temple

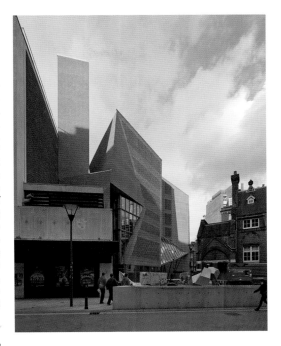

London's second work from this notable Dublin practice and a significant, enjoyable work prompting one's interest. However, not too helpfully, the architects tell us that: "This building does not feel like a hotel, an office, or an academic institution. It is fresh and airy, heavy and light, open and clear, sculptural and social." The reality is a somewhat agitated aggregate squeezed onto a tight triangular site and pushed up against an adjacent theatre whose principal feature (apart from trapezoidal façade shapes dealing with rights of light and reminiscent of Herzog & de Mueron at the Tate Modern) is a winding central staircase that wraps a lift core and spill out onto a series of open floor areas where one finds the building's cafes, meeting rooms, gym, bar, etc. (One imagines a lesson has been learned from Grimshaw's NAB, across the road.) The scheme's agitation is apt for LSE students, who appear to be very much at home in the place. Bizarrely, this keynote of restlessness reminds one of Farrell in the 1980s (similar agitation; different styling games).

Photos left and above courtesy of Dennis Gilbert / View

### 18. ME Hotel
Foster+Partners, 2012
336–337 Strand, WC2
Tube: Temple, Charing Cross or Holborn

A new 157-room hotel on the western corner of Aldwych, complete featuring a dramatic atrium and popular roof-top restaurant / bar. We are told that he design of everything, from the shell of the building to the layout of the public spaces and guest rooms – down to the smallest details of the bathroom fittings – has been undertaken by the Foster studio.

Photos courtesy of Foster + Partners (Francisco Guerrero)

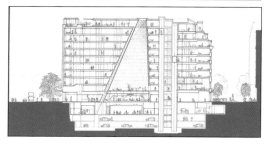

## 19. Royal Opera House
Dixon Jones, with BDP, 2000
Bow Street, WC2
Tube: Covent Garden

A large and complex project (tours are available) that extends E.M. Barry's original building of 1858 and required 80,000 drawings and 150,000 documents. Old, new and recreations are strangely intermixed. The pity is that the public areas simply aren't appropriate and don't work very well (apparently they are going to be altered). It's all a bit ponderous, although (ironically) the re-creation of Inigo Jones' Covent Garden arcade (of the 1660s) is quite pleasant. Have a look at Wilkinson Eyre Architects' contrasting twisting bridge link on the north side (above Floral Street).

## 20. City Lit
Allies and Morrison, 2005
Keeley Street, WC2
Tube: High Holborn

The City Lit is an adult education institution and we might look back upon it as A&M in transition from what they were to their current commerciality. Interestingly, the brickwork and offset windows exhibit what are still very much current fashions in 2013. It's the playful bits that one enjoys most: e.g., the West-End quotation of Alvar Aalto. The circular building opposite is again Col. Richard Seifert (for something similar, see his circular hotel in Knightsbridge, opposite RSH's One Hyde Park).

## 21. Comyn Ching Triangle
Terry Farrell & Company, 1984
Seven Dials, Covent Garden, WC2
Tube: Covent Garden

This Post-Modern exercise from Terry Farrell, fresh from his break-up with Nicholas Grimshaw and then at the heights of his Po-Mo enthusiasms, is actually a fine urbanistic exercise whose stylistic tropes are now so unfashionable that, some thirty years later, we still find it difficult to acknowledge the work. In part, this is because the Po-Mo period is considered to be as a peculiar interlude that only practices such as FAT have dared to continue to play with. For this reason alone, you should attempt to look at it on its own terms.

The Comyn Ching Triangle was formerly a rabbit warren of buildings and spaces, in part occupied by a notable ironmongery firm known to every architect in London. Its buildings originally dated from 1723 and Farrell took on this decrepid triangle as a challenge to his abilities for urbanistic mending, healing and revitalising. He cleared out a central courtyard and patched up the surrounding buildings, inserting new ones where necessary – especially on the three corners. Uses are mixed: offices, shops, apartments. The detailing is extraordinary: Hawksmoor on steroids (for example, see the courtyard entry point, bottom right).

**Note**: at the time of writing the Donmar Warehouse rehearsal and education space has just been completed very near here by Haworth Tompkins (Dryden Street, WC2).

## 22. Po-Mo Villas
Quinlan & Francis Terry (QFT), 1992
Outer Circle, north-east side, NW1
Tube: Swiss Cottage or Baker Street

Three of these villas (Veneto, Gothik and Doric) – at once HiTech and Po-Mo – were constructed in 1992 and later added to by three more, the last (the Tuscan) completed in 2004. It is regrettable that Terry's work has been derided more for being politically incorrect than any other reason, but there is little of the irreverent wit that John Outram brought to Neoclassical predilections.

## 23. London Zoo
Various architects
Outer Circle, north-east side, NW1
Tube: Camden Town

The principal works here include: the (Buckminster Fuller-influenced) Aviary by Cedric Price and Frank Newby, with Lord Snowdon (1964; it sits on the Regent's Canal and can also be seen from there), the Elephant House (Hugh Casson, Neville Conder & Partners, 1964 – an interesting Brutalist exercise), and Tecton's Penguin Pool of 1935 (which the penguins hated). There is also Joass' Mappin Terraces (1914), the partner of John Belcher. His design inspired the architects of the South Bank during the 1960s. A new work of particular interest is SHH's Terrace Restaurant.

## 24. Lord's Cricket Ground
Various architects, 1987–1994
St Johns Wood Road, NW1
Tube: Baker Street, Swiss Cottage

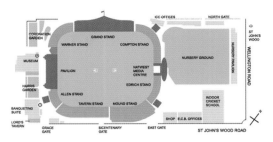

Change at Lord's has recently eased off, although there are now plans to enter another phase of major redevelopment (led by Populous). As Lords report:

"In May, MCC announced its Masterplan for the redevelopment of Lord's. The flexible plan, which has a proposed lifespan of 15 years, will commence with the redevelopment of the Warner Stand in the autumn of 2014, and finish with the reconstruction of the Compton and Edrich Stands. Before that, in the winter of 2013, MCC will refurbish the outside of the Nursery Pavilion, replacing the roof canopy." (Cf. http://www.lords.org/masterplanvideo)

All this began in the 1980s as an offshoot of international interest in cricket as potent international television content. Thus began an active period initiated with Michael Hopkins' **Mound Stand** of 1987, added to by the subsequent **Edrich Stand**, ending ten years later with Future Systems' (controversial) **Media Centre** in 1997 (with an original interior trying to be Las Vegas, 1966), Grimshaw's north **Grand Stand** (1998) and David Morely's the rather good **Indoor Cricket School** on St Johns Wood Road (1994). In late 2013 a new Lord's masterplan by Make Architects was approved (six phases of development works through to 2017.)

You can get tours around the grounds, but access to the Future Systems Media Stand (below) is not always possible. (Future Systems is now survived by Amanda Levete Architects.)

Mound Stand

Indoor Cricket School

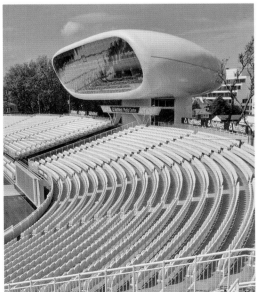

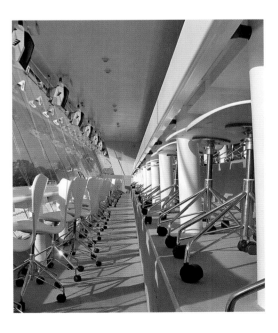

## 25. Regent's Place
Various architects, 1970-2013
Marylebone Road, NW1
Tube: Camden Town

An island of offices begun with the Euston Tower (1970) and ever more dense and vibrant. More recent parts at the west and east ends were masterplanned by Farrells, who have three works along the western edge: two office buildings, providing 37,000 sqm (lettable) over 9/10 storeys, together with a residential building consisting of 154 residential units over 20 storeys (all 2010). To the east, the complex has recently been adorned with Stephen Marshall's Triton Building (2013), with 70 affordable units fronting the main road and 98 private units in a 25s tower behind (neat planning; miniscule apartments), set around an inner court that also includes an 8s office building.

The newest office building (13,350 sqm) is 10 Brock Street, by Wilkinson Eyre Architects – a clever 3-core design of a faceted (mixed stealth geometry and Renzo Piano) character. The Triton Tower (2013) sports a rather Po-Mo reference to Semper in its inflated 'basket weave' cladding and the goal-post features at the penthouse level are not dissimilar to something tried by Marshall at Bermondsey Square. Earlier buildings here include one by Arup Associates, 1998 – a Stirling-influenced design now overwhelmed by neighbours. Carmody Groake have an elegant ornamental pavilion in Regent's Place.

Above: Marshall's Triton Tower of 94 apartments, together with 70 affordable units along the street edge.

Right: the Wilkinson Eyre Architects building – a typical floor plan at a lower level and a view to the south façade.

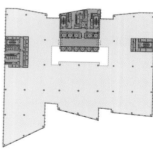

Bottom left: view to the Farrells buildings on the west side.
Top left: Site plan for Regent's Place. To left and right are residential buildings (in black; by Farrells and Marshall respectively). The square central building is by Arup Associates. The three central office buildings along Euston Road are by Sheppard Robson. The square on the far right is the original Euston Tower (Sidney Kaye, 1970).

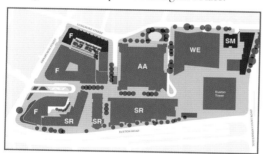

## 26. Fitzroy Place
Lifschutz Davidson Sandilands, and Sheppard Robson, 2014
Mortimer Street, WC1
Tube: Oxford Circus

A large, mixed-use redevelopment that tells you nothing less than what London is becoming: dense.

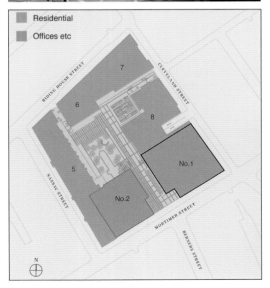

The scheme is somewhat obscurely described as "a modern reinterpretation of the Fitzrovia context" and comes complete with 'heritage façades'. It comprises three high-specification residential blocks designed by Lifschutz Davidson Sandilands, providing 237 apartments (three-bed approx. £15m) plus 54 affordable units, together with two office/retail blocks (by Sheppard Robson; see the typical floor plans below).

These are all set around an internal court (see the site plan, bottom left). The residential component incorporates an existing Edwardian terrace façade (rebuilt behind; it is located in front of the No.2 office building in the site plan). At the heart of the central court there is a retained chapel that formerly belonged to the hospital on this site – perhaps an intriguing reminder of what constitutes a no-go area in the game of major redevelopment.

**Above**: typical floor plans of the two Sheppard Robson office buildings.

**Left**: the overall site plan. The orange areas are the residential buildings.

## 27. Hopkins Studio
Hopkins Architects, 1985
27 Broadley Terrace, NW1
Tube: Camden Town

Since the mid-1980s the Hopkins studio has been within prefabricated 'Patera' buildings (designed by Hopkins in the spirit of the 1960s California Schools projects and a then-current concern with office park sheds) that have stood the test of time and been the practice's offices ever since their construction.

## 29. Royal College of Physicians
Sir Denys Lasdun, 1964
Outer Circle, St Andrews Place, NW1
Tube: Regents Park

This splendid building has the air of a youthful NHS buying off privileged physicians, even at this date. It is rather Corbusierian in influence, but uniquely Lasdun. Alvin Boyarsly once analysed the work in terms of blood flows, but it is also a human body: the head as library, lungs as the double-height central area; heart as an initiation room off to one side, a speech bubble off to one side as the lecture theatre ... Bizarre? It's not as if this would not have been within a long and great tradition of architectural references to the human body and it certainly lends a new dimension to the experience. Often open for Open House London.

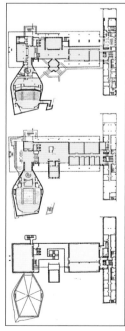

## 28. Regent's Park terraces
John Nash, 1812-25
Outer Circle, east and west sides, NW1
Tube: Camden Town

Regent's Park was intended as an aristocratic place of residence edged with terraces and infilled with villas. Of what was constructed the eastern terraces are the most impressive. The architect was John Nash, acting for the Prince Regent and other developers aiming to create a suburban royal park linked to the palaces of the Mall by a 'royal mile': Regents Street. It was an impressive speculative achievement, knitting together old and new as it wound its way south from Regent's Park.

## 30. Lisson Gallery
Tony Fretton Architects, 1991
Bell Street, NW1
Tube: Camden Town

An early Fretton work that people still want to see: a two-stage minimalist conversion, L-shaped in plan, wrapping an existing corner building.

## 31. 125 Park Road
Farrell Grimshaw, 1970
125 Park Road, NW8
Tube: Baker Street

From the days when a young architectural practice could set up a housing co-op and nominate themselves as tenants. More Grimshaw than Farrell (the practice partners who, of course, had the two penthouses). Now listed.

## 32. Marylebone Girls' School
Gumuchdjian Architects, 2008
64 Marylebone High Street, W1
Tube: Baker Street

A challenging extension to a large girls' school short on space, providing new classrooms and a rubberised playground above a deep underground gymnasium with a gallery and dance-practice rooms at one end. In the building above there are art and music rooms – in all, it is an excellent exercise in concrete and steel that possibly manifests the Rogers foundation to Gumuchdjian's architectural career. The architect notes that the project required "the removal of a predominantly 18th-century burial ground containing some 3000 remains including those of Charles Wesley, James Gibbs and George Stubbs."

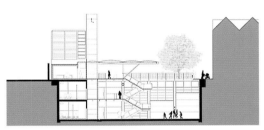

### 33. Regent's Park Open Air Theatre

Haworth Tompkins, 2011
Inner Circle, NW1
Tube: Regents Park

A London institution where you are provided with blankets, even in the summer (rather like the Globe). It was founded in 1932 and more recently had new facilities provided mostly back-of-stage, but with improvements in the public areas. Experiencing a performance in these settings, with aeroplanes above and the wind rustling the leaves of trees can be a pleasant experience.

**Right**: a rear area.
**Below**: entrance and ticket box.
**Bottom**: site plan (north end of the Inner Circle).

Photos courtesy of HT (Philip Vile)

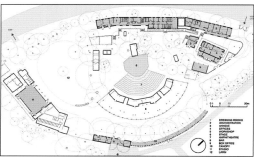

## 34. Wellcome Trust Gibbs Building
Hopkins Architects, 2005
215 Euston Road, NW1
Tube: Camden Town

Forget the battleship-grey exterior with a less than joyful character and go inside, where the daylit interior of this large office building (connected to the museum next door, also a refurbishment by Hopkins) is admirable and simply doesn't seem to age. You can get in by booking a visit to see an enormous and impressive Thomas Heatherwick sculptural installation (referencing a Germanic superstition of molten lead poured into water, which incongruously contrasts with all that the Wellcome represents).

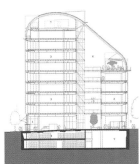

## 35. Unison Building
Squire and Partners, 2012
130 Euston Road, NW1
Tube: Euston Square

An HQ building for one of the few remaining large trades unions. It is a more complex project than it at first appears. For example, the listed building just to the left of the photo is an integral part of the scheme. To the north of the site is a small apartment building. Also see Squire's work at Reiss, 5 Hanover Square and 11 Baker Street (work that is invariably well designed).

## 36. Slavonic & East European Studies
Short & Associates, 2005
16 Taviton Street, WC1
Tube: Euston Square

This is rather too idiosyncratic for most people's tastes and so this rather characterful and interesting 'green' building (completed in the same year as the nearby Wellcome Trust building) has been largely ignored. Just think thoroughly 'green' with thermal chimneys, etc., and you've got what it's all about.

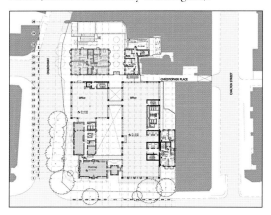

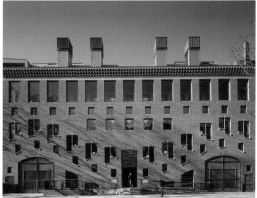

Photo courtesy of Short Associates (Peter Cook)

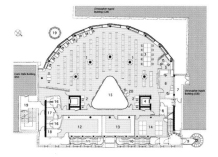

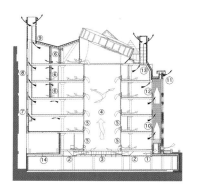

## 37. UCL Laboratories
Grimshaw; Hopkins Architects, 2007–12
Huntley Street, WC1
Tube: Euston Square

Two similar buildings, opposite one another, both by notable architectural practices. One (the O'Gorman Building, right), linked to an older neighbour (within which there is an atrium with a café covered by an inflated roof) and provided with waves of finely detailed ceramic fins that screen a work area adjacent to laboratories, by Grimshaw (2007). It works hard to relate to existing Georgian terraces in the area. The other building (the MacMillan Cancer Centre) is by Hopkins Architects (2012), its windows bearing hints of Portcullis House. Both have a very similar purpose: to facilitate cancer research.

Photo courtesy of Grimshaw

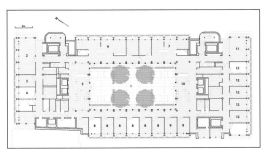

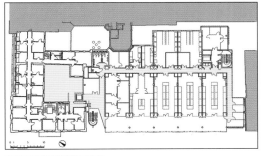

Photo courtesy of Hopkins Architects

### 38. British Museum
Foster + Partners; Rogers Stirk Harbour+Partners, 2000 –14
Great Russell Street, WC1
Tube: Holborn or Tottenham Court Road

There are two contemporary aspects of the Museum to see: (A) Norman Foster's Great Court (2000); and a new extension to be completed in 2014 by Rogers Stirk Harbour. The Great Court is possibly Foster's best London work which, with some simple moves taking place around the former British Library building at the heart of the central court, transforms the circulation of the Museum. The Rogers extension (B) provides for a special exhibitions gallery and conservation studios. Four 4-storey pavilions are above four underground levels of storage, together with a fifth research 'pavilion'.

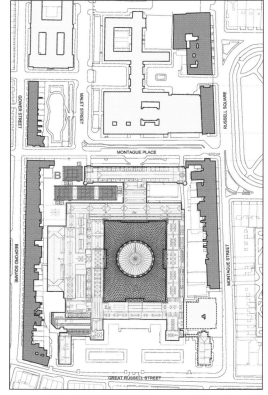

Photo courtesy of Denis Gilbert / View

CGI courtesy of RSH

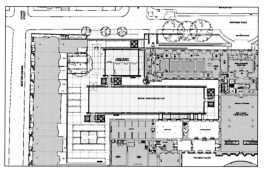

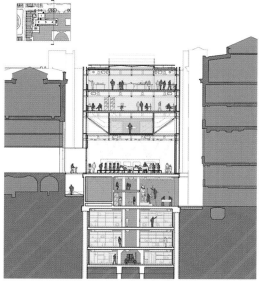

## 39. SOAS & The Institute of Education
Denys Lasdun, 1973
16 Taviton Street, WC1
Tube: Russell Square

The Institute of Education was completed in 1970, and the SOAS (the School of Oriental and African Studies) in 1973. They are both very Lasdun in character. The Institute, especially, is a marvellous megastructural statement whose march along the street may take a while to assimilate but gets evermore impressive as time goes by. Inside? Not so impressive.

## 40. Imagination
Ron Herron, 1989
Store Street, WC2
Tube: Gower Street

A relatively simple scheme forming offices for a creative concern from an Edwardian H-shape plan, made into two wings linked by bridges and covered over by a tensile roof that wraps over the lower of two roofs. The dramatic white atrium has become rather silted up, but is still impressive (if you can get in). Visible from all kinds of nearby locations (e.g. the AA). There is also a rather nice Seifert work just north of here (in Alfred Place).

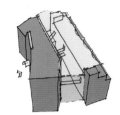

## 41. Brunei Gallery
Nicolas Hare Architects, 1995
Russell Square, WC1
Tube: Russell Square

This (a part of SOAS) remains in our minds as the first building of interest to emerge from the 1990–5 recession in construction, and an outcome of the Hi-Tech/Po-Mo rivalries of the previous decade. Its contexturalist brick façade on Russell Square is still very contemporary. Inside, there is a fine gallery and a roof-top garden space.

## 42. Congress House
David du R. Aberdeen, 1957
Great Russell Street, WC1
Tube: Tottenham Court Road

Then, symbol of the power of 9m trades-union members: *moderne*, looking to a bright post-war future (imagine Frank Sinatra singing about 'foggy London town' and you'll be in an apt mood). Compare with Squire's Unison building in Euston Road.

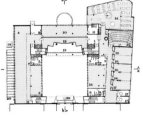

### 43. RADA

Avery Associates Architects, 2001
Malet Street, WC1
Tube: Gower Street

A theatre inserted into an older building that runs between Malet Street and Gower Street. At the former, there is an entry that leads into the Jerwood Vanburgh teaching theatre providing 203 seats and is loaded with the kinds of arcane geometries that fascinate Avery and take the theatre design back to Inigo Jones. In the foyer is a typical Avery conceit: a slot designed to capture a ray of sun on the summer solstice. It is a complex architecture of old and new attempting to be orderly as well as enjoyable.

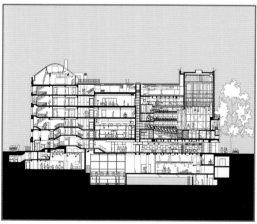

### 44. Gazzano

Amin Taha Architects, 2005
Farringdon Road, EC1
Tube: Farringdon

A corner apartment block above a retail store clad in a rain-screen of Corten steel panels. At once gritty and elegant, but with a hint of an enthusiasm for dark enigmatic boxes that we also see in Taha's building off Broadway Market, in Hackney.

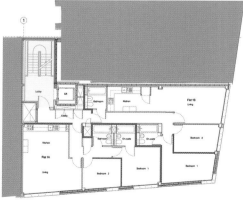

## 45. Rathbone Studios
Sergison Bates Architects Architects, 2011
7–10 Rathbone Place, W1
Tube: Tottenham Court Road

One scheme, three buildings, mostly studios but with some residential at the top of one of the buildings. These are also accessible from the rear, behind Lifshutz Davidson' Charlotte building (see opposite page). The principal part is simply a black mass.

**Above**: the striped building that is a part of the scheme dates from the late nineteenth century and gives expression to the bay-width already existing in this area from earlier Georgian speculative development. The mix of red brick and Portland stone and other features are quite common all over this area (Soho, Fitzrovia, etc.), as the remarkable Soho Square building on the right shows.

**Left**: the ground level of the Rathbone Studios scheme.
**Below**: the upper level at Rathbone Studios.

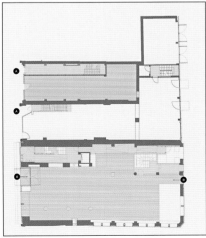

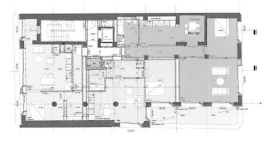

## 46. Centre Point
Richard Seifert, 1967
New Oxford Street, WC1
Tube: Tottenham Court Road

This tower at this notable road junction was once infamous as a tax dodge that made more money for the developer by being kept empty than rented out. And everyone detested the work of its architect. Now, everyone loves it and him. At the moment Centre Point is being converted into residential use (as are many former office buildings); the team is lead by Rick Mather Architects. The area all around is radically changing as the Crossrail station at Tottenham Court Road is completed and new buildings are constructed in the area (e.g., Number One Tottenham Court Road by AHMM; see image and site plan below). Such potential has spread into neighbouring areas, especially Fitzrovia and Covent Garden, where the landowners are attempting to upgrade the character of property tenancies.

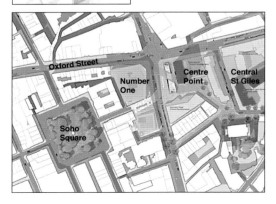

## 47. Charlotte Building
Lifschutz Davidson Sandlilands, 2010
17 Gresse Street, W1
Tube: Tottenham Court Road

An attractive, nicely detailed and height-constrained, media people-oriented office building in a changing part of town.

**Note**: there is also a characteristic CZWG converted warehouse at the northern end of Gresse Street (1983).

### 48. Central St Giles

Renzo Piano Building Workshop, 2011
St Giles High Street, WC1
Tube: Tottenham Court Road

St Giles stretches itself between all that is Covent Garden and the radical changes going on around Tottenham Court Road station. It's a clever work of architectural gamesmanship. The block to the west is residential – equally divided between private and affordable. The eastern U-shaped block looks like more than one building but is actually a single, large floor plate. Note the *de rigueur* roof terraces and also the louvred corner rooms that, one supposes, are technically outdoor and therefore good for smokers. As always: no car parking. The cladding is ... ceramic, of course. The colours? One gets used to them.

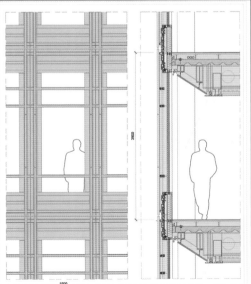

Photos courtesy of RPBW and Jones Lang LaSalle

## 49. 55 Baker Street
Make Architects, 2008
55 Baker Street, W1
Tube: Baker Street, Bond Street

The conversion of a large 1950s building, with residential to the rear (west side), providing 46,000 sqm of offices and 5700 sqm retail, plus 23 affordable housing units. The lobby displays some structural gamesmanship behind a dramatic entry façade that is mirrored to north and south, further along the massive street frontage.

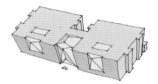

## 50. BBC
MJP Architects, 2013
Huntley Street, W1
Tube: Oxford Circus

An ill-fated project that saw the architects walk away from a design-and-build contract that was giving Bovis all kinds of problems. The project has a peculiar non-vitalistic quality about it, rather like Paternoster, but it looks very good from the air, especially at night (as on TV news). There is a café in the entry court. The Church of All Souls (John Nash, 1820s) that sits outside – which is a fraction of the BBC's size – still outshines its new neighbour and adds meaning to the way the site has been used and an entrance formed. Have a look at the church and its interlocking geometries – it's total urban theatricality and showmanship of a kind that we don't understand any more: ornamenting London rather than Nash's reputation (or that of the Prince Regent).

Photo courtesy of Make (Zande Olsen)

## 51. Hampden Gurney School
BDP, 2002
Nutford Place, W1
Tube: Marble Arch

An old school with a large central area playground had a contemporary idea: sell off the playground for residential uses and build a new school that incorporates playgrounds into the structure. The outcome has been an admirable success in every sense.

## 52. 11 Baker Street
Squire and Partners, 2011
11 Baker Street, W1
Tube: Bond Street

A three-part project: an office building of 7000 sqm facing onto Baker Street, and two apartment blocks behind, and retail at the front ground level. Smart (as are many Squire schemes these days).

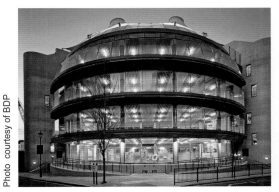

Photo courtesy of BDP

Photo courtesy of Squires (Will Pyre)

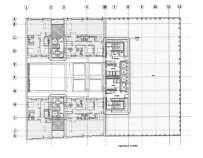

## 53. Wallace Collection
Rick Mather Architects, 2000
Manchester Square, W1
Tube: Bond Street or Baker Street

There is no longer such a thing as a secret anywhere, but when there was, the Wallace (like the Soane Museum) was a part of that scene. Here, the late Rick Mather covered in the central court to provide a café area.

## 54. Sedley Place
Fletcher Priest Architects, 2004
Sedley Place, W1
Tube: Bond Street

A small, unexpected oasis just off Oxford Street and also behind the main part of this project: a shop fronting Oxford Street itself – which is OK, but go down the alley to this small court for some relief from the clamour and pollution of Oxford Street itself.

## 55. Reiss

Squire and Partners, 2008
Barrett Street, W1
Tube: Bond Street

Flagship store and brand HQ, with retail at the bottom and offices above, plus a penthouse for the boss and some apartments at the rear. It's the south-facing façade that impresses: a glass layer behind an acrylic rain-screen with periodic openings that induce a stack effect cooling the façade. This is cut away by large vertical gauges of varying width and depth, within which are etched even finer vertical striations. The effect changes at night when the acrylic is edge-lit giving it the capacity to vary the building's appearance. Its impressive, although it divides opinion. (**Below**: third-floor plan.)

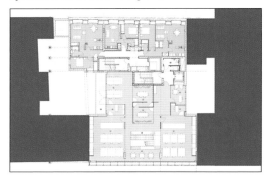

## 56. Photographers' Gallery

O'Donnell & Tuomey, 2012
16–18 Ramillies Street, W1
Tube: Oxford Circus

The first in London from this notable Dublin practice – a superb example of old and new intermixed (with a corner café having distinct undertones of Hopper's *Nighthawks*). It's an economic project, but has some nice, well-judged details. Better than the LSE building?

Photo courtesy of Dennis Gilbert / *View*

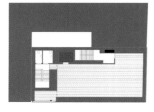

## 57. 10 Hills Place
Amanda Levete Architects, 2010
10 Hill Place, W1
Tube: Oxford Circus

Head east and then north along the alley behind the Photographer's Gallery, going toward Oxford Street, and enter Hills Place, where you will come across a refreshing façade (it's aluminium, like a suspended ceiling, set upon boat-builder's shaping). An inset door leads to an escape stair and lift, accessing upper-level offices. That's it. Soak it up.

## 58. Oxford Street façade
Future Systems, 2009
193 Oxford Street, W1
Tube: Oxford Circus

After getting from the Photographer's Gallery to 10 Hills Place, keep going around into Oxford Street and a bit east – on the south side of the road will be this façade. The crystalline structure seems rather un-Future Systems, but appears to work well (although there is the usual problem of occupiers pushing junk up against the glass). Odd, but one can sense the rationale behind this problem of designing an Oxford Street façade.

## 59. Regent Street W4/W5 sites
Allford Hall Monaghan Morris, 2014
Regent Street, W1
Tube: Oxford Circus

Not quite 'white-collar factory' (suited to Shoreditch media people) or a 'City-Slicker-House' (as per AHMM's Blackfriars Road building), nor even the 'Mid-Town-Worker House', as at Angel Islington, but a Mayfair equivalent that, no doubt, will be occupied by developers and hedge funds.

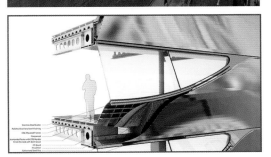

## 60. Bonham's
Lifschutz Dividson Sandilands, 2013
New Bond Street, W1
Tube: Bond Street

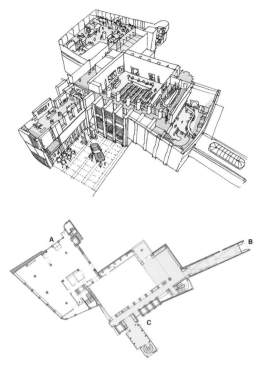

A complex new building for a famous auction house, inserted into an aged urban fabric at this end of New Bond Street:

> The scheme retains the historic façades on New Bond Street and Blenheim Street. A new building, accessed from the existing Bond Street entrance, creates three large new double-height sales rooms, preview galleries, a café and day lit space throughout. Brick, stone and faience provide a contextual response to the surrounding historic fabric.

Bonham's presents three faces to the world: to the north, a vaguely 1930s facade looking to Woodstock Street; on New Bond Street, a traditional, aged facade complete with large flag (the principal entrance); and, to the south and rear, in the aptly named Haunch of Venison Yard, a new façade from LDS (see the CGI on the right). Behind these three is a renewed house of facility and lots of flattery that one is a member of an élite purchasing clique.

Photo and CGI courtesy of LDS (Hufton & Crow)

## 61. 28 South Molton Street

DSDHA, 2012
28 South Molton Street, W1
Tube: Bond Street

An striking instance of 'flat-iron', ceramic-clad, amazingly designed and constructed in nine months building. The mixed-use building, which includes residential, office and retail houses, and is the first European headquarters of a Chinese menswear label. Also see their small Snowfields building, near London bridge.

## 62. 5 Hanover Square

Squire and Partners, 2012
Hanover Square, W1
Tube: Oxford Circus

Squire's are an intriguing practice whose designs manifest an interesting planning skill (here as a simple mix of offices and residential). But now they're in Mayfair it's as if the architect spent a lot of time in Saville Row: offering a smart, 'dolled-up' façade that won't be to everyone's tastes. In brief: 8500 sqm of accommodation, with the residential neatly set to one side.

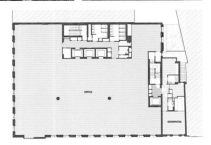

Photo courtesy of Denis Gilbert / View

Photos courtesy of S&P (Hufton & Crow)

### 63. Broadwick House

Rogers Stirk Harbour+Partners, 2002
Broadwick Street, W1
Tube: Oxford Circus

Simple, exhibiting a large curved roof over a tall upper-level galleried and terraced space with fine views, manifesting the usual served:servant equation so favoured by the Rogers team. Although lifting the quality of works in this area, it seems somewhat out of place adjacent to the Georgian terraces of the slowly dying Berwick Street Market (although other neighbours are a distinctly mixed and undistinguished group). It is interesting to compare Broadwick with DSDHA's South Molton Street building – ten years apart, and yet an entirely different agenda.

Concept sketch courtesy of RSH

### 64. Regents Palace Hotel (Quadrant 3)

Dixon Jones, with BDP, 2011
Glasshouse Street, W1
Tube: Piccadilly Circus

This complex project fills the whole of the triangular urban block, restoring parts of the hotel, providing new retail, residential and office spaces. Three different but similar façades poke through between retained neo-classical corner features in order to give presence to what is behind. This is Dixon Jones getting back on form.

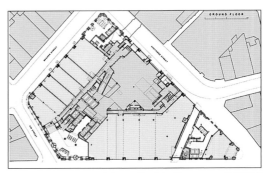

## 65. W Hotel

Jestico+ Whiles, 2013
10 Wardour Street ,W1
Tube: Piccadilly Circus

A 192-room hotel in a very central location, with a cladding that doesn't quite do the trick. Better at night, but one wonders how they would have done this in Tokyo, where an architecture of light is commonplace.

## 66. Asprey

Foster + Partners, 2005
167 New Bond Street, W1
Tube: Bond Street

Asprey is surprisingly tolerant of architectural tourists visiting this fascinating mix of Georgian, Hi-Tech and high-end shopping. Leave your credit card at home.

## 67. Economist Group
Peter & Alison Smithson, 1964
St James' Street, SW1
Tube: Green Park

Still heroes to many, this has to be their best work: three blocks carefully disposed around a piazza (with Boodles club to one side) on a hill (originally a bank, a residential block and an office block, all of different heights); a mini-Acropolis for London. What no one talks about is how remarkably un-1960s it is, except in that American and neo-Miesian sense of careful detailing and proportionality. Also see the St James' apartments directly across the road – the first private apartment block after WWII and best seen from within Green Park.

## 68. 198-202 Piccadilly
ADAM Architecture, 2013
198-202 Piccadilly, W1
Tube: Piccadilly Circus

ADAM, like Quinlan Terry and son, have never given up their market niche in what they call 'progressive Classicism'. This work (set next to the former Simpson's building, Joseph Emberton, 1935, and, on the other side, adjacent to Wren's St James' Church) is 11,340 sqm gross and appears to have revealed to the architects that office buildings are about making wraps to empty spaces. (Where have they been all this time?) In its own way, it is impressive, densely featured and even jolly, but one longs for the wit of John Outram in this kind of gamesmanship. London continues to live up to its reputation as a city of differences.

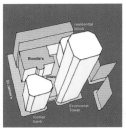

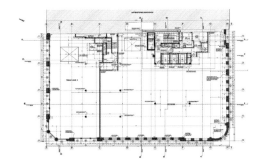

## 69. New Zealand House
Robert Matthew, Johnson-Marshall & Partners, 1963
Haymarket, SW1
Tube: Leicester Square

An early London high-rise, until recently coping with the sun by the provision of endless amounts of graceful internal curtains (now removed!). There is a fine top-level bar and terrace here (not public, unfortunately). The adjacent Pall Mall has some fine building, especially Barry's Reform Club and its strange neighbour by McMorran and Whitby (see their police station in Wood Street, in the City). Other salient clubs include the Athenaeum and the Directors (both by Decimus Burton, respectively 1830 and 1819) at Waterloo Place.

## 70. One Eagle Place
Eric Parry Architects, 2013
Piccadilly, W1
Tube: Piccadilly Circus

This fairly complex refurbishment and rebuilding of a block on the south-west corner of Piccadilly is as idiosyncratic and, to some, as upsetting as anything from ADAM (or Terry Farrell in the 1980s). But it is an expert job that has to be unpicked as one traverses the façades from Piccadilly all the way around to east Jermyn Street). The riotous façade cornice on Piccadilly is by Richard Deacon; the window reveals are Parry's own artistic endeavour. There is a vague Art Deco feel to the work and, although odd, it is surely a huge improvement on ADAM's version of late 19th-century Mannerism. The Jermyn Street blocks 'B' and 'C', below, are residential.

## 71. Sackler Gallery
Foster + Partners, 1991
Piccadilly, W1
Tube: Piccadilly Circus or Green Park

A skilled work from the partner-in-charge, Spencer de Grey and a wonderful historical jigsaw to explore (you can play at architective). The house dates back to Lord Burlington in the early 18th-century (and, before him, to the 1660s). It was turned into the Royal Academy and extended to the north (as galleries) and to the south (as an entry court) in the 1870s. The latter is by Charles Barry and R.R. Banks; the former is by Sydney Smirke – who put in a new 'bridge link' from the existing main stair (moved to this location by Samuel Ware sometime after 1815) and into the new galleries. Look to either side of William Kent's main stair, into what were light wells; see Colen Campbells's rear façade of the original Burlington House, where Foster's access stair rises to the upper-level Sackler Gallery (which replaces Smirke's original roof extension). Go up in the lift and come down via the new staircase – looking about you as you descend. The clarity of the Foster scheme may have been literally silted up and to some degree covered over; however, it is still discernible.

Photo courtesy of Dennis Gilbert / View

## 72. Embankment Place
Farrells, 1991
Villiers Street, WC2
Tube: Charing Cross

Farrells' riverside beast above Charing Cross Station is one of his principal Po-Mo works, complementing his MI6 building, on the riverside further upstream. It is quite a baroque and acrobatic exercise which, no doubt, he hopes will one day (like MI6) be ripe for listing status. And he's probably right: there are few Po-Mo works around that are less than execrable and the conservationists will be getting worried that decent examples are disappearing.

### 73. Sainsbury Wing
Venturi, Rauch, Scott-Brown & Partners, 1991
Trafalgar Square, WC2
Tube: Piccadilly; Charing Cross

Here we have an architect playing sophisticated architectural games. One might question them, but at least we are witness to gamesmanship of a deeply skilled and intellectual kind. Sometimes the work is heavy-handed (as on the staircase glazed wall), but the building invites one's deconstruction and there is lots to enjoy. The National Gallery entrance to the main building (Prince Charles' 'old friend') is by Dixon Jones.

### 74. St Martins-in-the-Field
Eric Parry Architects, 2008
Charing Cross Road, WC2
Tube: Charing Cross or Leicester Square

James Gibbs' church has been restored and the crypt converted into a restaurant, with additional spaces including a chapel where densely packed burial chambers – located on the north and east sides of the church – have been cleared. On the north side Parry's work obtrudes to the surface as a light well and an entrance pavilion. The lower level meeting room is rather fine, but it is rather bizarre eating lunch while sitting upon a memorial stone reading, 'In memoriam, died 1821 ...'.

### 75. National Portrait Gallery
Dixon Jones, 2000
St Martins Place, WC2
Tube: Leicester Square

Extensions and adaptations to the old Portrait Gallery building that not only work well, but provide a popular top-level restaurant with good views.

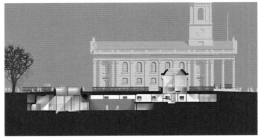

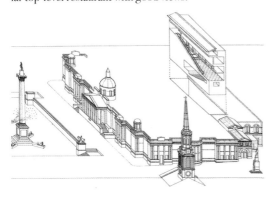

## 76. Portcullis House
Hopkins Architects, 2001
Victoria Embankment, SW1
Tube: Westminster

One thinks of contexturalism as a heritage from Po-Mo, but here is Hopkins again blurring categorical boundaries by giving us one of the most contextural works in London: on one side the Old Scotland Yard building by Norman Shaw (1890) and, on the other side, Barry & Pugin's Houses of Parliament. The building serves as offices and conference rooms for the Right Honourable Members and is linked to Parliament by an underground tunnel. The structure is largely prefabricated (everything you see is authentically tectonic) and the ducts on the exterior rise up to a huge metal roof and heat reclaim chimneys that mimic Shaw's roof and chimneys next door. At the heart of the building is a very large, glass-covered atrium. The structure has to cope with Underground tunnels below ground and you are advised to penetrate down the Jubilee Line to see how Piranesian it all becomes (photo below). It's clever, underrated and under-appreciated. Often open for Open House London.

## 77. Inn on the Park
Hopkins Architects, 2004
St James Park, SW1
Tube: Green Park

A timber-framed restaurant built into the landscape that is a welcome addition to St James Park. Whether the design is posing as hi-tech timber or sophisticated log-cabin is not clear. It certainly has none of the exuberance of Patrick Gwynne's Dell building in Hyde Park, designed in the 1960s (image middle left).

St James is a pleasant park which, around its perimeter, has the Mall (where John Nash's 'Royal Mile' from Regent's Park terminated), Buckingham Palace and Horse Guards Parade (with William Kent's rather fine buildings of 1757).

## 78. Cardinal Place
EPR, 2005
Victoria Street, SW1
Tube: Victoria

A rather sub-Foster set of buildings comprising some 49,100 sqm of offices and 8,400 sqm retail, but with a rather simple and good masterplan making reference to Westminster Cathedral (which is a basilica-style building with massive brickwork although, again, it is impressive rather than beautiful).

## 79. Green Park Tube Station
Acanthus, 2011
Piccadilly, W1
Tube: Green Park

A dmittedly odd, but unusual, well done and exhibiting use of the same Portland stone used on the Economist building in St James Street.

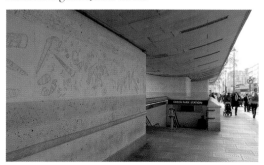

## 80. QEII Conference Centre
Powell & Moya, 1986
Broad Sanctuary, SW1
Tube: Westminster

The most dramatic feature of this rather splendid building is the tectonic gamesmanship that gives us giant projecting beams and suspending the principal conference floor. The stepped-back penthouse levels conceal

an inner courtyard, delegates' bars, etc., as well as secret parts that even the architects weren't aware of. Sadly, it is all rather unfashionable these days.

## 81. Wellington House
John McAslan+Partners, 2013
Buckingham Gate, SW1
Tube: Victoria

This is a 10s block (with the zinc-clad top storey set back) comprising 59 apartments above ground floor retail tenancies (from 55 to 222 sqm.). Two principal features stand out: the red Indian sandstone, with its projecting fins (see Plantation house, in the City; and the site plan. The former is artfully machined; the latter works well in the manner the principal façade provides a colonnade and the secondary façade does not. In general the block is intended to complement the many traditional London red-brick mansion blocks in the area.

**Above**: a typical, first floor, 3-bedroom apartment.

## 82. 62 Buckingham Gate
Pelli Clarke Pelli Architects; Swanke Hayden Connell, 2013
62 Buckingham Gate, SW1
Tube: Victoria

A rather dramatic, all-glass faceted/folding-planes office building around the corner from Wellington House. Also see AHMM at Blackfriars Road and Wilkinson Eyre at the Royal Docks.

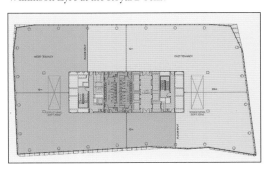

## 83. Asticus Building
Lifschutz Davidson Sandilands, 2007
Coxton Street, SW1
Tube: St James Park

A small but elegant 5220 sqm, 28 diameter office building with vaguely Richard Seifert undertones (see, for example, Centre point and, especially, Space House, opposite the City Lit). A lift and service core is 'strapped' to one side.

## 84. Channel Four
Rogers Stirk Harbour+Partners, 1994
124 Horseferry Road, SW1
Tube: Westminster or Victoria

This is a building that doesn't seem to age. One suspects this is because the design was not only the first 'normal' commercial building Rogers completed after the Lloyds 1986 building, but because it makes such a great play of branding, namely the acrobatics on the corner which serve to provide a dramatic entrance into the building – a function more lately emphasised by C4 itself (with a huge sculptural logo). The plan is simple enough: two office wings set off from the (peculiarly small and linear) entrance, with studios below ground. The principal features of the building can be seen on all subsequent Rogers works in London, from Lloyds Register to Tower Bridge House to 88 Wood Street, etc. However, none of these later buildings (perhaps apart from the one at Tower Bridge) seeks to concentrate an architectural superfluity so dramatically in one part of the overall scheme.

## 85. Home Office
Farrells, 2004
2 Marsham Street, SW1
Tube: Westminster

A sensible masterplan and tripartite arrangement to the buildings which house up to 4500 government workers, with through pedestrian routes linking to existing streets (ironically, often closed, for security reasons) and a residential strip along the western side. But then came the artfulness: coloured glass and suchlike which serve as lipstick to the architecture.

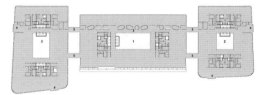

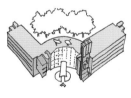

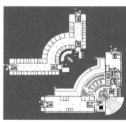

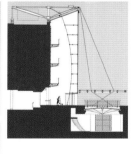

## 86. Millbank Tower
Ronald Ward & Partners, 1963
21–24 Millbank, SW1
Tube: Westminster or Pimlico

A fine example of the tower-and-podium typology imported from the USA. Cf. SOM's Lever House, New York, 1952 (although, admittedly, this is hardly as elegant). There is an 'Altitude' viewing gallery on the top floor (but it is not free).

## 88. Tate Britain
Various architects
Millbank/Atterbury Street, SW1
Tube: Westminster; Pimlico

Subtle alterations designed by Caruso St John were instituted at the Tate in late 2013, including an uncharacteristically nice but vaguely kitsch and neo-Deco staircase near to the entrance. These changes reorganise some of the circulation and provide new facilities, addressing a variety of original buildings. The original is by Sidney Smith, 1897; the Duveen Galleries extension is by Romaine Walker & John Russell Pope, 1937; the now ignored Clore Gallery extension is by Stirling Wilford, 1986; more recent works are by John Miller

(Atterbury Street side), with on the external landscaping (who removed the Stirling pond), 1991. The adjacent river shuttle pier outside is by Marks Barfield, 2003. The Clore is actually an intriguing work manifesting an architect constrained on the interior and left to do whatever he wanted on the exterior, where he seems to have retreated in order to play his games. The entrance area is an external room worthy of study and as a place to quietly soak up what is going on.

## 87. Chelsea School of Art
Allies and Morrison, 2005
Atterbury Street, SW1
Tube: Pimlico

While some are into patterned surfaces, offset grids, curves, stealth and crystalline geometries, etc., Allies and Morrison have continued along a consistent design path. Here, they have refurbished and extended to an existing old military hospital complex with a set of 'interventions' that interplay old and new, producing the retention of 'scarring' and the like one also sees at Central St Martins (Stanton Williams Architects). Whether wrapped in intellectual references to memory or not, the resulting textural affects make an admirable difference to one's experience.

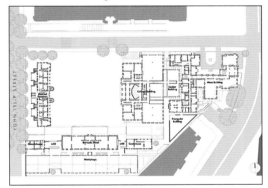

## 89. Lillington Gardens
Dabourne & Darke, 1971
Vauxhall Road, SW1
Tube: Westminster or Pimlico

A now ignored housing scheme from a period when housing concerns had shifted from towers to friendly low-rise complexes. The police hate them and it is possibly only now – as London densities increase – that schemes of this nature manifest their attractions (too late for a similar D&D scheme in Islington). This fascinating and maturing period in London's housing was short-lived and soon to be cut off by Margaret Thatcher. The adjacent church is George Street's St James-the-Less (1861). Across the road, alongside Vauxhall Bridge and along the River Thames, is the scheme that brought a young Nicholas Lacey to fame: Crown Reach (1984). (See it from the bridge or the other side of the river.)

## 90. MI6
Farrells, 1992
Albert Embankment, SW8
Tube: Vauxhall or Pimlico

Sister to Farrells' building that sits on top of Charing Cross Station, the MI6 building manifests Farrells' then-current enthusiasms for 1930s American Modernism: a mix of New York skyscrapers and Frank Lloyd Wright. Will it be listed as London's most notable Po-Mo building, strutting its stuff and adding glamour to 007 movies? We suspect it will.

It is perhaps again worth emphasising that one can walk considerable distances along the riverside – including (as below) in front of MI6.

## 91. Vauxhall Bus Station
Arup, 2005
Wandsworth Road, SW8
Tube: Vauxhall

Hey, look, it's me! A dramtic oddity whose efforts to cope with MI6, railway lines, St George's Wharf housing huge volumes of traffic and the like is not without its merits (but which hardly include the provision of shelter).

## 92. St George's Wharf
Broadway Malyan, 2005
Vauxhall Road, SW1
Tube: Westminster or Pimlico

Some of the most prominent, oddest and expensive housing in London (nearly 1100 units), now added to by the tallest residential tower in the UK (223 units): Vauxhall Tower, 50s, 180m, and topped by a wind turbine (bottom photo). (Strata Tower sports a similar feature.)

## 93. Evelina Children's Hospital
Hopkins Architects, 2005
Lambeth Palace Road, SE1
Tube: Waterloo

A specialist, 140-bed facility, the first purpose-designed children's hospital in London for more than a century. The architectural concept and section are not dissimilar to that of the Wellcome Trust in Euston Road. (The hospital is difficult to access.)

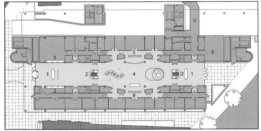

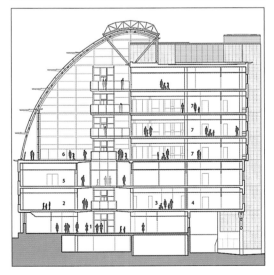

## 94. One Centaur Street
dRMM, 2004
1 Centaur Street, SE1
Tube: Waterloo

A simple and interesting house-type designed in accord with a set of values that dRMM have more recently taken to the scale of upmarket housing in Kings Cross and Battersea, as well as for affordable housing schemes. The architects describe the building as:

> a hybrid of the European horizontal apartment and the English vertical terrace house. Each apartment enjoys a Raumplan interior organised as a large, open double-height living space, interpenetrated by adjacent enclosed bedrooms and stairs, which form a concrete buffer to the

## 95. H10 Hotel
Maccreanor Lavington Architects, 2010
284-302 Waterloo Road, SE1
Tube: Waterloo or Embankment

This is a strange project: an attractive building that started out as an apartment block but, we're told, the client decided to let it become a hotel – while avoiding the pain of planning permissions concerning the façade. So the function was transformed (although still a place of habitation) and the façade was retained. In other terms this again represents a recent turn to brickwork and simple (but skilled), proportional play.

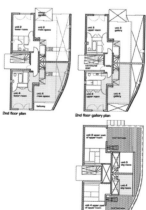

railway. Construction consists internally of high exposed concrete economically over-clad externally with insulated rain screen. Other than in site concrete, all components are prefabricated, specified from international sources according to dRMM's catalogue design methodology.

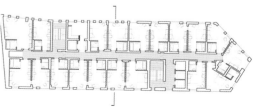

242

## 96. Eurostar Station, Waterloo (former)
Grimshaw, 1993
Waterloo Station, SE1
Tube: Waterloo

Eurostar trains used to come here before going to St Pancras. It is a fascinating but now obsolete structure over a set of platforms now being converted for use by local commuter trains.

## 98. Southwark Jubilee Station
MJP Architects, 2000
Blackfriars Road, SE1
Tube: Southwark

One of the best of the series of Jubilee Line stations provided for the extension completed in 2000.

Other notable stations include: Westminster (Hopkins), Canary Wharf (Foster) and North Greenwich (Alsop). The design champion for the stations may have got his fingers burned, but these stations still set a design standard for similar infrastructural works (such as Crossrail).

## 97. Coin Street
Haworth Tompkins Architects, 2001 and 2007
Belvedere Road, SE1
Tube: Waterloo or Embankment

Two schemes filling an urban block: a housing project of 2001, later fronted by a community centre, of 2007. The latter is a colourful statement from HT (courtesy of artist Antoni Malinowski), apparently "inspired by the façades of Venetian palazzi"), providing a creche, conference rooms, permanent offices for the client, etc. The housing is a restrained housing block, looking rather Spanish: 59 dwellings (inc. 32 that can accommodate eight persons) around a private inner sanctum for residents. Also see Lifschutz Davidson Sandiland's nearby Broadwall housing of 1994 (one-bed flats located in a nine storey tower, and two-bed flats and family houses in an adjacent terrace).

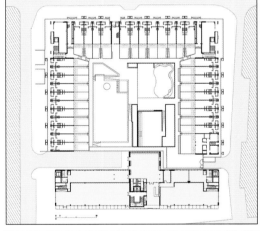

## 99. OXO
Lifschutz Davidson, 1997
Belvedere Road, SE1
Tube: Waterloo or Southwark

The conversion of the former OXO building into mixed uses (inc. studios and 78 apartments), including restaurants on the top floor – which are, unfortunately, north-facing (good views, but no sun).

Photo courtesy of HT (Edmund Sumner)

## 100. The Young Vic
Haworth Tompkins Architects, 2007
The Cut, SE1
Tube: Waterloo

The keywords for this controversial reinvention of a 1970 theatre by Bill Howell are ad hoc, temporary, ordinary, provisional, patched, basic, informal, loose-fit, ... The architects say: "The ad-hoc temporary aesthetic, use of the most basic materials [and] recycling of an ordinary Victorian shop as the public foyer became emblematic of the Young Vic's identity and values – demotic, light-footed and classless." They add:

> Transformation and provisionality are the key theatrical ideas on which the new design is founded. To respect the personality of the street and maintain a sense of informality, the project has been conceived as a connected group of distinct elements, each with a specific materiality: the totemic butcher's shop, locally significant as a wartime bomb survivor as well as the old foyer, has been salvaged, its familiar tiling and signage unsentimentally patched; the existing auditorium has been significantly adapted and re-skinned in a composite of unique, hand-painted cement board panels [...] and silver mesh held away from the painted surfaces and uplit, so that the transformation between the understated, working daytime and celebratory night-time modes of the theatre is made explicit and the one-off, live activity inside alluded to; the new large studio theatre is texturally related to the auditorium by the use of a similarly scaled 'weave' of dark, profiled brick; the support spaces and smaller studio are subsumed within an enveloping skin of concrete blockwork that wraps the rear of the site and emerges onto the Cut as the scenery workshop; and the public foyer is expressed as an informal, lightweight timber and steel structure that covers the resultant courtyard formed by the principal performance studio and the butchers shop, both of whose exterior walls bracket the double height interior. Materials throughout are basic and detailing informal and loose-fit, so that a provisional, low cost aesthetic prevails and the theatre's technical production team can easily adapt the building in the future.

Photo courtesy of HT (Edmund Sumner)

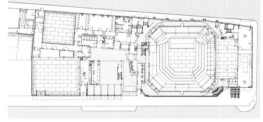

Behind all this was a concern that:

> many theatre artists feel alienated by new theatre architecture, particularly when existing, well-loved buildings have been replaced; that theatre re-builds often appear too resolved, too polished or too unyielding to adaptation by theatre makers. [...] Despite upgraded facilities, existing loyal audiences often feel over-managed or manipulated by new buildings in a way that previous, less well-appointed theatres avoided.

Interestingly, the Young Vic's 'adhoc' aesthetic agenda has become increasingly fashionable as a mode of fit-out for a host of London bars, cafés and restaurants,

## 101. Rambert
Allies and Morrison, 2013
Belvedere Road, SE1
Tube: Waterloo or Embankment

## 102. National Theatre
Denys Lasdun, 1977
Upper Ground, Embankment SE1
Tube: Waterloo or Embankment

This, together with the Royal College of Physicians, are Lasdun's masterpieces. But while the RCP is relatively pristine, the National has suffered all kinds of alterations (notably the silting up of its interior spaces). The diagonal planning toward Waterloo Bridge (Lasdun considered the building to be an extension of the bridge) tells you volumes about the character of this site at that time, before the embankment along the southern side of the Thames was created (bringing what was the rear of the National to the foreground).

Photo: John Donat

Another interesting work from A&M, this time up against it on their budget. The project is simply described as:

> Three large dance studios share changing, workshop and technical areas alongside space for administration, while a dance archive and reading room are open to the public. The sectional arrangement exploits the required mix of single and double-height spaces and allows permeability and views between them. Key spaces are grouped around an internal courtyard which acts as a social focus for the life of the building while also maximising natural light and ventilation. The building's concrete structure is exposed and two of the dance studios project beyond the precast concrete panels of the front façade as large glass and aluminium-clad boxes, clearly expressing their function to the street below.

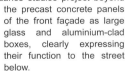

As ever with A&M, this is a nice design, but the entrance lobby is curiously constrained for a building crying out for a touch of public generosity.

## 103. Southbank Cultural Centre
Various architects
Upper Ground, Embankment SE1
Tube: Waterloo or Embankment

The Royal Festival Hall at the Southbank is all that remains from the 1951 Festival of Britain. The Hayward, Queen Elizabeth and the decks came in the 1960s, courtesy of the GLC, and more recent additions along the abutment to the railway tracks (and refurbishment of the RFH) were made by Allies and Morrison (2007); note their light reflector/vent feature.

### 104. Hungerford Bridge
Lifschutz Davidson, with WSP Group Engineers, 2002
Victoria Embankment, 2002
Tube: Waterloo or Embankment

The pedestrian walkways are wonderfully strapped onto the old railway bridge (1864) like alien beasts. Note that this bridge (with its buskers, etc.) is much more socially friendly than the Millennium Bridge. Let us hope Heatherwick realises his proposed 'green' bridge.

### 105. London Eye
Marks Barfield, 2000
Jubilee Gardens, Belvedere Road, SE1
Tube: Waterloo or Embankment

Meant to be temporary, the Eye has become one of London's finest tourist attractions – with views that are arguably better than the Shard. The design is witness to background experience within the Foster office.

### 106. IMAX theatre
Avery Associates Architects, 1999
Belvedere Road, SE1
Tube: Waterloo or Embankment

A 500-seat cinema set into the heart of the roundabout that leads onto Waterloo Bridge. The façade varies and the plants keep growing around the building's base. The drum is now usually adorned with advertisements, but it was probably better when plain and stark (as an enigmatic naked drum). A nice concept.

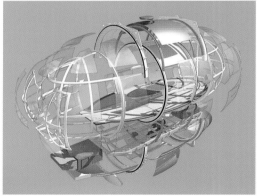

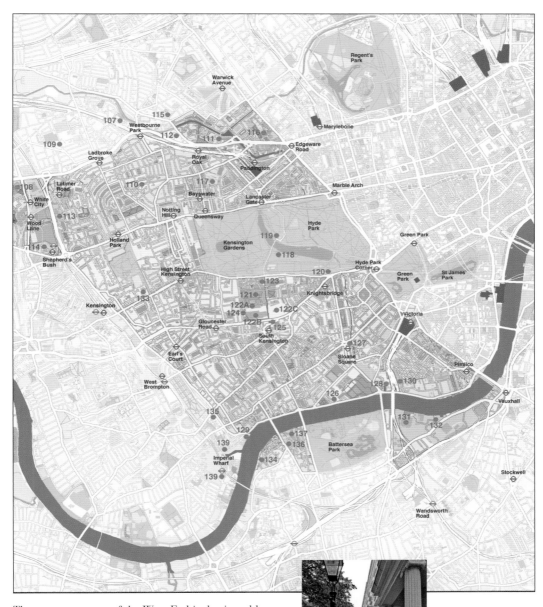

The westermost part of the West End is dominated by southern parts of the Royal Borough of Kensington & Chelsea – which boasts the wealthiest, most long-lived and healthiest residents in the UK. As the name suggests, this derives, in essence, from the area's historic associations with royalty and its court. The shopping centre of Knightsbridge, together with the (largely uninhabited) apartment block One Hyde Park, designed by Rogers Stirk Harbour+Partners, epitomises the controversial nature of the area's more expensive locations.

## 107. Trellick Tower
Erno Goldfinger, 1973
7 Golborne Road, W10
Tube: Ladbroke Grove

A London favourite from the man who so upset Ian Fleming that this author's arch villain was so-named (Goldfinger). Its stacked maisonettes, etc. are very popular among architects, who read the Brutalist character as aptly robust and heroic. The building gets more fashionable by the day, especially as the general area improves.

## 109. St Mark's Road housing
Dixon Jones, 1979
St Mark's Road, W10
Tube: Ladbroke Grove

Still interesting because of an attempt to continue a terraced, semi-detached London typology in a contemporary (then vaguely Po-Mo) manner. Otherwise belonging to another era not to be repeated.

## 110. Toilets/Flower shop
CZWG, 1993
Westbourne Grove at Colville, W11
Tube: Notting Hill Gate

One of the smallest and surely the most enjoyable of CZWG's varied output over the years. The Francophile glass canopy and use of glazed tiles was an idiosyncratic and distinctive CZWG touch at that time.

Photo courtesy of CZWG

## 108. BBC White City
Allies and Morrison, 2003
White City, W12
Tube: White City

A complex of corporate buildings, witness to a time when the BBC was expanding its accommodation. The master planning and architecture is by A&M (the latter being subject to security guards preventing photography). A&M should soon be on a nearby site with a 1600-unit residential scheme.

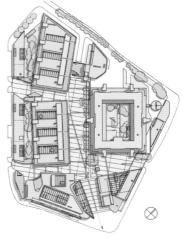

## 111. Paddington Waterside

Various architects
Paddington Basin, W2
Tube: Paddington

A large, mixed development stretched out along the Regent's Canal, mostly using former railway lands (as at Kings Cross). It includes works by various architects, but the most interesting design work is perhaps the Rolling Bridge, by Thomas Heatherwick – an ingenious device that, however, has no other purpose than to entertain tourists. Overall, the area feels like an office island, although recent works by Nicholas Grimshaw at the station have greatly improved access.

**The architects of some of the buildings:** A. Farrells; B. Rogers Stirk Harbour+Partners; C. Munkenbeck & Marshall; D. Siddell Gibson; E. Kohn Pedersen Fox Associates; F. Sheppard Robson; G. (Novotel) Dexter Moren; H. Grimshaw (PII station extension – much less fussy than PI).

## 112. Westminster Academy

Allford Hall Monaghan Morris, 2007
255 Harrow Road, W2
Tube: Royal Oak

One of London's more dramatic and impressive academy schools, but which upsets some architects, who see it as a built diagram and more like a corporate office building than a school. However, this diagrammatic quality may be the point: simple, economic, and on-target – but, of course, that 'target' depends upon one's values. The interior, as with many AHMM buildings, relies heavily on super-graphics.

### 113. Monsoon & Talk Talk buildings
Allford Hall Monaghan Morris, 2008
Nicholas Road, W11
Tube: Shepherd's Bush

Two instances of AHMM's 'white-collar offices' concept: deliberately cheap 'n' cheerful and slightly raw. The interior of the Monsoon building makes a determined attempt to impose a tectonic characterfulness, but little of this is evident on a rather less than satisfactory exterior that bears little relation to internal dynamics (which, in turn, needed a Lloyds-style escalator).

### 114. Bourbon Lane
B+C Architectes (Fr.), with Cartwright Pickard, 2007
Nicholas Road, W11
Tube: Shepherd's Bush

An interesting example of affordable housing squeezed onto a difficult urban site that backs onto the Westfield shopping centre, exhibiting some rather large cantilevers. The nearby Westfield? Yes, it's interesting if you are into shopping malls. (The White City area had a masterplan that somewhere in it included OMA, but there is no evidence of this in what is constructed.)

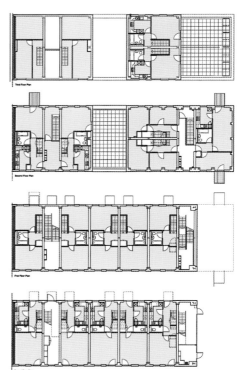

## 115. Yaa Centre
Foster Wilson, 2012
Carnival Village, 1 Chippenham Mews, W9
Tube: Westbourne Park

A hidden community building incorporating 19th-century parts described as a new home for Yaa Asantewaa, the Association of British Calypsonians and Ebony Steel Band. Facilities include workshops for making costumes and floats for carnival and the tuning of steel pans, a dedicated steel pan rehearsal room, together with offices, arts and IT education rooms, a café and an informal central performance space for carnival artists and the local community.

## 116. City of Westminster College
Schmidt Hammer Lassen, 2011
Paddington Green, W2
Tube: Baker Street

An impressive college with an equally impressive central atrium, around which student activities are gathered.

Photos courtesy of FW (James Morris)

## 117. Hallfield School

Denys Lasdun, 1954; Caruso St John, 2005
Inverness Terrace, W2
Tube: Bayswater

A classic school building from Lasdun, more recently given two new pavilions designed by Caruso St  John, which provide six new junior classrooms and three infants classrooms. The overall site plan is given below.

## 118. Princess Diana Memorial

Gustafson Porter, 2005
Hyde Park, W2
Tube: South Kensington

An excellent design that has now overcome its initial problems. The remaining problem is that it needs good weather in order to be enjoyable. But when the sun shines the computer-formulated undulations and texturing engender all kinds of pleasantries. Make it a summer visit, perhaps when the Serpentine Gallery (just opposite) has one of its annual architectural pavilions on display (mid-summer to October).

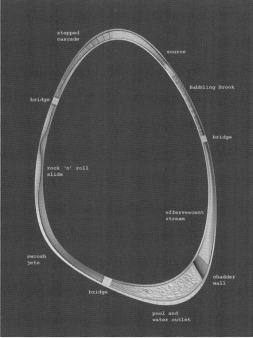

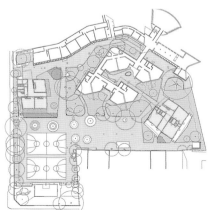

Photos courtesy of CSJ

### 119. Serpentine Sackler Gallery
Zaha Hadid Architects, 2013
Kensington Gardens, W2
Tube: South Kensington

The art has stepped outside as if to have a quick cigarette whilst looking glamorous as it leans up against the neo-classical, 1805 Magazine gunpowder store. The work is, of course, gloopy. It houses a restaurant and social space covered by an undulating white membrane roof, punctuated with dramatically elegant roof lights. However, this is, in fact, an adjunct to the contrasting adjacent gallery spaces that have been created the 1805 neo-classical building. Both buildings are impressive (Liam O'Connor Architects were consultant on the historic parts), although the Hadid part will not be to everyone's taste. The engineers were Arup.

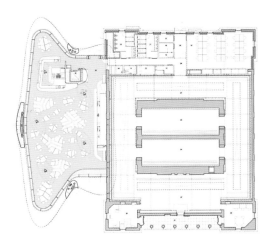

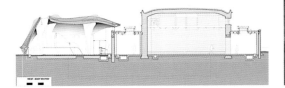

All Images courtesy of Serpentine Sackler Gallery (© Zaha Hadid Architects)

## 120. One Hyde Park
Rogers Stirk Harbour+Partners, 2011
60 Knightsbridge, SW1
Tube: Knightsbridge

The irony about One Hyde Park everyone points to is that this incredibly expensive building is designed by architects with distinct left-wing concerns who have long sought to positively influence urban policy-making in London. We're told that, on being put onto the market, an affluent Ukrainian purchased three apartments at One Hyde Park for £40m each and then threw in another £60m in order to convert them into a single unit. And a penthouse went for £140m. And that the place remains largely uninhabited, thus making a negligible contribution to community life.

In design terms the architects provide a strongly contextural argument:

"In recognition of the context [...] a series of interlinked pavilions was conceived to allow permeability and offer views of Hyde Park from Knightsbridge. The separation of the pavilions was conceived to create a stronger visual connection between Knightsbridge and the Park than had previously existed. The relationship of the pavilions with each other and with neighbouring buildings follows a radial pattern emanating from a central point well within the Park. This has resulted in a complementary alignment with the immediately adjacent buildings of Wellington Court and Mandarin Oriental Hotel, as well as reinstating – as close as possible – the sweep of the original road and pavement alignment to Knightsbridge.The shaping of the pavilions – which widen towards the centre of the site and taper towards the perimeter – allows for oblique lateral views from each pavilion towards Knightsbridge to the south and the Park to the north. The passenger cores are used by residents for primary access to the apartments and penthouses, and service cores are used for secondary access by staff and for providing service access to the apartments.

The project (of 86 residential apartments and duplexes and three upmarket retail boutiques within four interlinked pavilions) is best thought of simply as an addendum to the adjacent Mandarin hotel (the life-support machine), from which servicing is available 24/7 by an underground passage that leads to the above-mentioned service lifts. The latter are another instance of the remarkably consistent application of Louis Kahn's served-and-servant spaces concept (elaborated by Reyner Banham and exemplified at Lloyds) that has characterised this practice's history. Now, however, the servant dimension is again people rather than (or, as well as) articulated machinery. In essence we are witness to a fascinating reinvention of the Edwardian upstairs-downstairs equation now married to enhanced technological servicing.

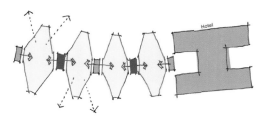

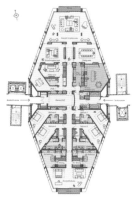

**Above**: the basics of the served:servant equation informing the architectonics, one that creates a symbiotic relationship with the hotel. **Left**: an 880 sqm, full-floor apartment. The three-bed apartments are 330 sqm.

## 121. Imperial College
Foster + Partners, 2001–04
Exhibition Road, SW7
Tube: South Kensington

Among the recent buildings here you will find four Foster buildings.

The first is the **Alexander Fleming Building** of 1998, described as a research forum wrapped around an atrium (as at the Blizzard Building by Will Alsop), plus research facilities.

A second is the **Flowers Building** of 2001.

The third is the blue **Faculty Building** (2004; below left). This has a diagonal ramp that cuts through the building. The building is located more deeply within the campus, but being such a striking blue it can't be missed.

The fourth is the **Tanaka Business School** (2004) – a building that fronts Exhibition Road with a frame of giant-order columns that brace the facade glass. One forgets how fashionable this recently was as a mannerism for enlarging a building and establishing presence. (Below right; ground plan bottom.)

**Note**: a principal feature of the area is the pedestrianisation of Exhibition Road, designed by Dixon Jones (2012).

## 122. Exhibition Road Museums
Various architects
Exhibition Road, SW7
Tube: South Kensington

### 122A. Wellcome Wing, Science Museum
MJP Architects, 2000
Science Museum, Exhibition Road, SW7

A version of the Rogers/Piano Pompidou or Foster's Sainsbury, transmogrified for this site and purpose, namely two walls of circulation and servicing to either side of galleries, all facing out to a large west glazed area. The exhibitions themselves were by Wilkinson Eyre Architects.

### 122B. Darwin Centre, Natural History Museum
C.F. Møller, 2008

Perhaps more architectural gesture than notable exhibition content. Also see the Museum's Dinosaur Room (a rare instance of Ron Herron, 1992) and Ecology Gallery (Ian Ritchie, 1991).

### 122C. Victoria & Albert Museum

There is a set of galleries by notable designers here: Ceramics Gallery (Stanton Williams Architects, 2009); Jewellery Gallery (Eva Jiricna, 2009); Medieval Gallery (MUMA, 2009), Fashion Gallery (6A Architects), Clothworkers' Centre (Haworth Tompkins, 2013), etc. Oddly, the Museum promotes historic design but doesn't make a public celebration of the design of the galleries.

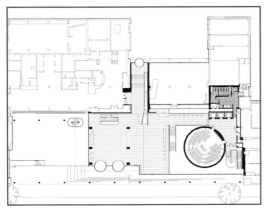

## 123. Royal Geographic Society
Studio Downie, 2004
1 Kensington Gore, SW7
Tube: South Kensington

A notable small extension to Norman Shaw's building of 1875, providing an exhibition space supplementing work on a 750-seat theatre, etc.

## 125. Ismaili Centre
Casson Condor, 1983
Cromwell Gardens, SW7
Tube: South Kensington

An unusual building with a fine Islamic roof garden, not as celebrated as it should be (in truth, the exterior is better than the interiors). The first floor provides a large prayer hall.

## 126. Red House
Tony Fretton Architects, 2006
Tite Street, SW3
Tube: Sloane Square

A house for an art collector set into a street noted for its historical associations with artists. Behind the upper parapet are facilities described as a retreat for hedonistic pleasures, complete with an outdoor 'tropical hot-tub'.

## 124. Dana Centre
MJP Architects, 2004
165 Queen Anne's Gate, SW7
Tube: South Kensington

A collaboration between the British Association for the Advancement of Science (BA) and The European Dana Alliance for the Brain (EDAB). As a venue the Dana offers information, debates and the like – and comes with a café. The architecture makes an interesting contrast to its neighbours, old and new, and bears recognisable MJP tropes that can also be seen, for example, on a very different building: Warwick Court, Paternoster. The Centre says about itself: "The Science Museum's Dana Centre is an adult-only venue that lets you explore issues in contemporary science through dialogue, interaction, performance and art whilst enjoying food and drinks in our fully-licensed café-bar."

## 127. Royal Court Theatre
Haworth Tompkins, 2000
Sloane Square, SW1
Tube: Sloane Square

A key part of the HT portfolio comprises theatre conversion and design that aims to enhance ambience rather than become lost in formalism. This venue (describing itself as "London's coolest theatre"), the Bush Theatre and the Young Vic, are all good examples of this practice's sensitivities and expertise.

## 129. Cremone
Sarah Wigglesworth, 2006
Lots Road, SW10
Tube: Fulham Broadway

A small riverside project from Wigglesworth: two Corten steel pavilions providing office, canoe store, changing rooms, etc. Simple; neat.

## 128. Grosvenor Waterside
Various architects, to 2012
Ebury Road, SW1
Tube: Sloane Square

A more upmarket 'residential village', masterplanned by Broadway Malyan, set around a former dock basin, with contributions from a set of notable architects: Make Architects, Sheppard Robson, Allies and Morrison and Twigg Brown (see the site plan below; note the Peabody estate on the far right).

The three A&M buildings (one affordable and two private) serve as a symmetrical 'gateway' from the Thames. The two SR buildings (see the more salient one opp. page, bottom right) are at the northern end. The two Make buildings (illustrated in this column and overleaf) are perhaps the most striking and located on the eastern side, with one block (of 196 affordable housing) serving as an acoustic block against the railway lines heading into Victoria Station. The unusual etched artwork stretched across the metallic façade is by Clare Woods – and note the unexpected balcony edge detailing, below right (a tree trunk). Unfortunately, everything in this development appears to be single aspect. On the other hand, note how the A&M scheme offsets its corridor planning with varied apartment plans and three lift cores.

We are told there are plans to have house boats in the lock, but so far they haven't appeared.

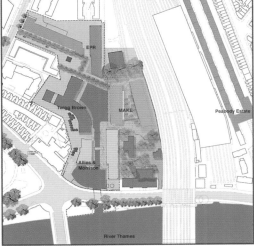

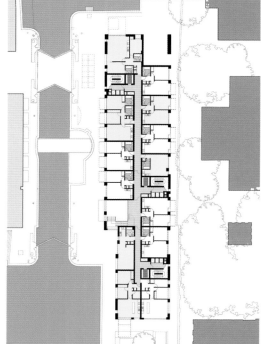

## 130. Peabody Estate
Haworth Tompkins, 2012
Lupus Road, SW1
Tube: Sloane Square

It is easy to underestimate projects like this: a subtle supplement to an existing 1878 Peabody Estate that runs along the eastern side of railway lines going into Victoria. One end of the scheme received bomb damage in WWII and this was the basis of the HT repair project.

In the architect's words:

> The scheme was developed in close, formal collaboration with residents, to create a sense of enclosure and completeness within the estate.[...] The entrance to the estate – a wide, double height opening entered form a small public open space – provides a clearly recognisable, secure threshold and allows long views down the Avenue to be maintained. Generated around three stair and lift cores, the circulation pattern seeks to minimise travel distances, reinforce clusters of apartments with defensible space, and provide optimal, double aspect daylight to all units. The cores are designed to be generous, daylit spaces with a high degree of transparency. Family maisonettes occupy the ground and first floors, with apartments for disabled people exploiting high-level views over the city and river from the top floor. Large external balconies cantilever over the western façade, with roof terraces to upper units. A new community room, landscaping across the whole estate, and a new ball court and children's play area completes the project.

Unfortunately, the western is not easy to see.

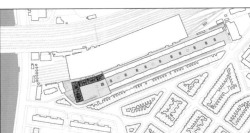

Photos courtesy of HT (Philip Vile)

## 131. Battersea Power Station (BPS)
Various architects, 2016 onwards
Battersea Park Road, SW8
Rail: Battersea Park

After decades of neglect, the Battersea redevelopment is underway for three key reasons: a transport link is to be provided (an extension of the Northern Line; the Nine Elms area is, now that the American Embassy is to move there (2017), undergoing massive redevelopment; and the world wants to invest in London. The first BPS scheme is Circus West, designed by Ian Simpson and dRMM for a site between the Power Station and the railway bridge into Victoria (estimated for completion in 2016). The planning difference between these two schemes reflects the Mayor's shift away from double-loaded corridors and single-aspect apartments. The final scheme at BPS is probably best thought of as an upmarket version of Stratford, supplemented by the conference hall, hotel, etc. one would expect in such a location.

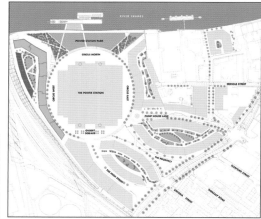

The overall BPS site plan is by Rafael Viñoly (above), indicating the Simpson scheme in orange and the dRMM scheme in red. The Power Station building will have its chimneys rebuilt and be infilled with shopping, a station, conference centre, and other leisure facilities. Phase three (by Gehry and Foster; for completion 2017) will provide 1200 residential units, a 200-room hotel overlooking both the town square and the Power Station (being handled by Wilkinson Eyre Architects), retail and restaurant space, a library and further leisure space.

## 132. Riverlight
Rogers Stirk Harbour+Partners, 2014
Nine Elms Lane, SW8
Tube: Vauxhall; Rail: Battersea Park.

Son of NEO (at Southwark): a scheme in the rapidly changing Nine Elms area of Battersea comprising 18m-wide buildings that are appropriate to residential and hotel uses. These are set which are perpendicular to the river and are arranged in a rising form of composition, from a height of 12 to 20 storeys, thus providing the development with a varied skyline. Unfortunately, it is clear that Rogers had nothing to do with the detailing.

*Images courtesy of Battersea Power Station*

## 133. New Design Museum
RMJM, 1962; John Pawson, 2014
Kensington High Street, W8
Tube: High Street Kensington

Due to open in late 2014/early 2015, John Pawson's conversion of the former Commonwealth Institute galleries beneath its hyperbolic paraboloid roof will provide a transformation of the Design Museum's facilities. Three adjacent residential buildings are being handled by OMA and Allies and Morrison. West 8 will design the landscaping.

## 134. Montevetro
Rogers Stirk Harbour+Partners, 2000
100 Battersea Church Road, SW11
Overground: Clapham Junction

One of the first of a now commonplace series of tall (now relatively modest) residential buildings along the river frontage, sitting adjacent to St Mary Battersea (1777), which benefits from a riverside walkway created as a part of the planning-gain. It has 103 double-aspected units and is organised as a slim block divided into five parts. All the apartments have west-facing balconies, toward the River Thames.

## 135. K&C College
Dixon Jones, 2012
Hortensia Road, SW10
Tube: Fulham Broadway

Two sites, rationalised and redeveloped as residential use and a new 3550 sqm Hortensia Centre college building. A dramatic long staircase rises through the heart of the building, linking social and teaching facilities.

Image courtesy of Design Museum (Alex Morris Visualisation)

### 136. RCA Sackler & Dyson Buildings
Haworth Tompkins, 2009–12
1 Hester Road, London SW11
Tube: South Kensington. Overground: Chelsea Harbour

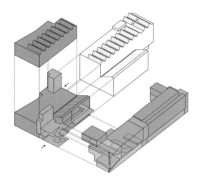

Two academic buildings for the Battersea Royal College of Art campus. The earlier building is the Sackler. To paraphrase the architects: purpose-made accommodation was provided for all the Painting students, uniting them on one site, providing a minimum of 46 studio spaces with capacity for expansion to 60, with spaces of varying scale and character. The **Sackler** was conceived as the conversion of an old single-storey factory transformed into a series of new daylit spaces under a new roof, inserting a new independent steel structure in order to increase the height of the building, provide several double-height, 7m-high studios along with a mezzanine level housing a

number of smaller top-lit, 3.5m high studios. The profiled roof allows north light to be achieved throughout. The large studios are almost cubes: 8m x 7.5m in plan and 7m high, and can be subdivided into as many as six individual studio spaces if required. While the Sackler is a simple building (see the model cutaway, left), the later **Dyson** is more complex (see isometric above), providing engineering workshops, a 220-seat lecture theatre, a public gallery and the College's business incubator, etc. The building is, we are told, conceived as a 'creative factory' both in the industrial sense (as a place of industry), and through the reference to Andy Warhol's Factory as a place of art production. At the time of writing, a third building by HT is going ahead.

Photos courtesy of HT (Philip Vile)

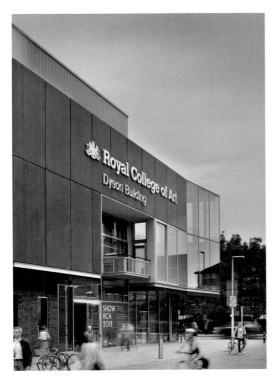

### 137. Foster studios + Albion
Foster + Partners, 1990–2003
Hester Road, SW11
Tube: South Kensington; Overground: Chelsea Harbour

The Foster riverside studio development from 1990 and an idiosyncratic, up-market residential building (2003; the ground level has commercial spaces) whose massive front–backside equation works rather well. Foster used to have the penthouse above the studios.

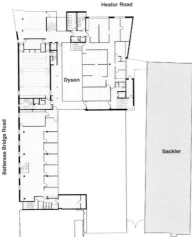

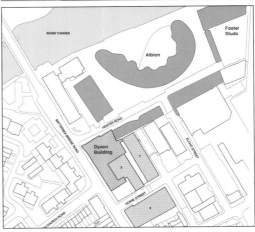

**Above**: the relationship of the Dyson and Sackler buildings.
**Right**: site plan for this overall group of buildings. The Foster-designed buildings are in mauve, with the embryonic plan of the Albion residential building facing the River Thames. The Foster studios are immediately to the east of this. The RCA buildings are in orange/beige, with the Dyson north of the Sackler.

### 138. Chelsea Academy
Feilden Clegg Bradley Studios, 2011
Lots Road, SW10
Overground: Imperial Wharf; Tube: Fulham Broadway

An urbanely polite, brick-faced academy of 1060 pupils in years 7 to 13, on a tight site of 5500 sqm and built area of 11,000 sqm. The school fills two-thirds of an urban block and neatly (and densely) complements its context. Also see St Mary Magdalene, at Highbury.

### 139. ROCA showroom
Zaha Hadid Architects, 2012
Station Court, Townmead Road, SW6
Overground: Imperial Wharf; Tube: Fulham Broadway

Chelsea Harbour is somewhere to avoid, but you have to go there in order to enjoy this unique, high-end, voluptuous branding exercise from Hadid – here out to sell Italian toilets, baths and basins. It's impressive (how much did it cost!?), but does one notice the hardware on sale? ROCA hould try Clerkenwell next time.

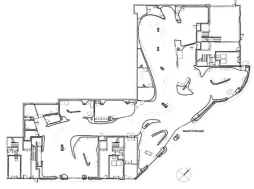

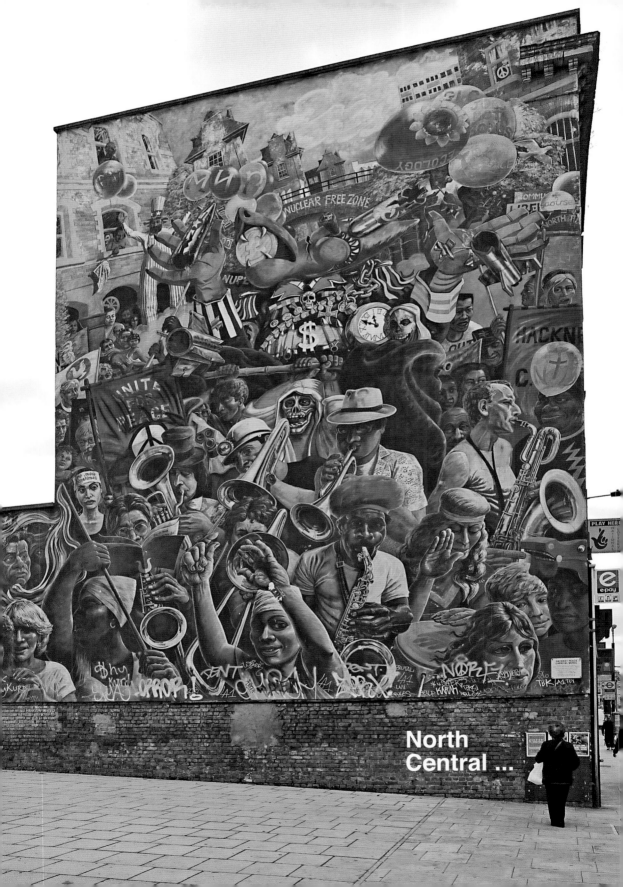

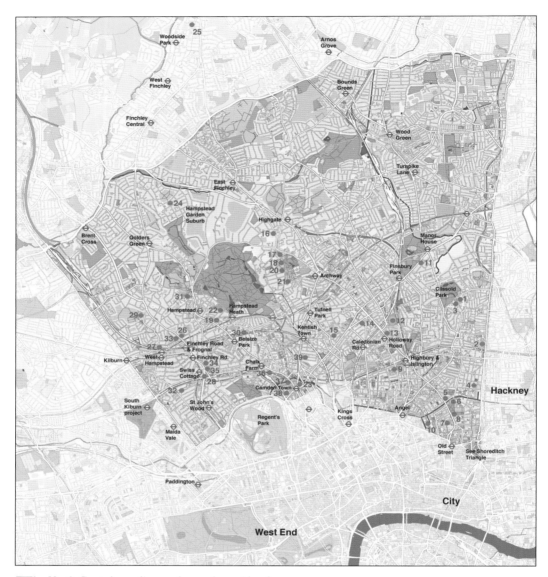

The North Central area lies on the northern side of the Marybone/Euston Roads and Regent's Park, bounded on the west by Edgeware Road and, on the east, Kingsland. It reaches northward up to the North Circular Road that roughly defines Inner London from outlying suburban areas.

**Previous page**: the Hackney Peace Carnival Mural (1985), at Dalston, adjacent to the entry of the Eastern Curve Garden and opposite the Overground station.

## 1. Stoke Newington School
Jestico+ Whiles, 2011
Clissold Road, N16
Rail: Stoke Newington

This Stoke Newington School and Sixth Form rede-velopment tackles the neglect of existing 'Brutalist' buildings and is 20 per cent new build and 80 per cent refurbishment: three key new-build additions include a new entrance building of additional teaching accom-modation, a dining hall, and a link at second-floor level which resolves a variety of circulation issues.

## 2. Gillet Square
Hawkins Brown, 2005
Gillet Square, N16
Overground: Dalston Kingsland

Already, it would perhaps be done differently, with more ambition and certainly more density, but Gillet Square is quite a success: a Victorian terrace was saved and converted into workshops, etc.; the Cultural House offers good jazz; the square itself is used for all kinds of community events; and the string of small shop cabins down one side of the square facilitate local entrepreneur-ial activity.

## 3. Clissold Leisure Centre
Hodder Architects, 2001
Clissold Road, N16
Rail: Stoke Newington

An ill-fated project that was eventually sorted out, providing an excellent local facility: a familiar mix of main pool, teaching pool, squash courts, crèche, café, etc. The Stoke Newington school sits opposite.

If it is still there, try the **Eastern Curve Garden** (13 Dalston Lane, E8), put to-gether by MUF and Exyzt (2009–10).

### 4. Ed's Shed
Adjaye Associates, 2007
75 de Beauvoir Road, N1
Overground: Haggerston

Another black number, now in solid engineered timber with hemp insulation: almost a cube, very simple and rather nice – for the photographer Ed Reeve. The entire house has been excavated down to basement level, creating a sunken patio at the lower level. (Often open for Open House London.)

### 5. Gainsborough Studios
Munkenbeck & Marshall, 2003
Poole Street, N1
Tube: Highbury & Islington

A 14-storey scheme of 280 new-build apartments, B-1 space on ground level, a restaurant and the refurbishment of the old movie studio space. One quarter of the residential area is affordable housing (all constructed on the site of a former power station and film studios). Nice sculptural piece in the centre court. But silly balconies.

Photo courtesy of Ed Reeve

## 6. Bridport House
Karakusevic Carson, 2012
Bridport Place/Poole Street, N1
Tube: Highbury & Islington

A two-phase redevelopment of the canal-side Colville estate. The first phase delivered eight four-bed maisonettes, topped by 33 other sized apartments. The eight storey and five storey blocks are constructed in engineered timber panels in order to reduce weight on the existing foundations.

Photo courtesy of Karakusevic Carson (Ioana Marinescu)

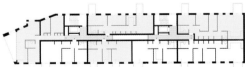

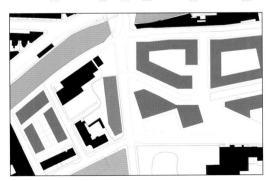

## 7. Nile Street
Stephen Marshall Architects, 2006
Nile Street, N1
Tube: Old Street

A combination of tenancies. The architect claims: "the density is very high and to increase amenity space the roofs of the buildings contain densely planted gardens. The central courtyard contains a zen water garden which acts as a backdrop to all the flats." However, the triangular balconies are peculiarly wilful. See this architect's more recent Triton scheme at Regent's Place.

## 8. Rushton Medical Centre
Penoyre & Prasad, 1996
Rushton Street, N1
Tube: Old Street

A Cullinan-like exercise housing four practitioners that remains a quite refreshing addition to this area.

## 9. St Mary Magdalene Academy
Feilden Clegg Bradley Studios, 2009
Liverpool Road, N7
Tube: Highbury & Islington

Another school building from FCB, this time for 1360 pupils and designed on a tight urban site at Highbury whose area was about the same as the internal gross area – hence features such as a play-field on the roof. An excellent, compact design.

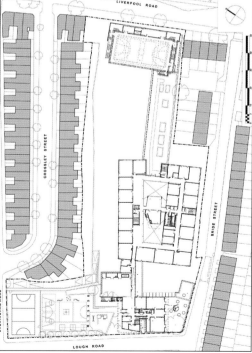

## 10. Victoria Miro Gallery

Claudio Silvestrin 2006; Trevor Horne, 2000
16, Wharf Road, N1
Tube: Old Street or Angel

A warehouse converted in two stages: first by Trevor Horne (who retained a wonderful collection of roof timbers), and then by Silvestrin, who created the huge (800sqm) white, roof-top gallery spaces accessed via a long, exhilarating staircase continued up from how Horne left it, going to the second floor.

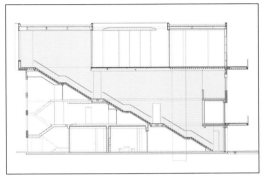

## 11. Brand Close

Sergison Bates Architects, 2008
378–384 Seven Sisters Road, N4
Tube: Finsbury Park

A well-planned mixed-tenure, housing scheme of three blocks. The rear block is social rented; the other two are a mix of social-rented and shared ownership. They are deliberately designed to look "solid and substantial" – which, interestingly, is not to everyone's taste. They're good, even if they lack kerb appeal.

## 12. Emirates Stadium

HOK Sport (now Populous), 2006
75 Drayton Park, N5
Tube: Holloway Road

This 60,000-seat Emirates Stadium is surrounded by redevelopment schemes (mostly residential). The architects say:

"The challenge was to create a master plan which could fit the new stadium on this difficult site, deliver the maximum area for residential development and meet the local council's requirements for the provision of social housing. [...] The roof is supported on just eight cores, allowing the slender roof plane to float above the robust façade of the building below. [...] The curved glass, concrete and steel mesh panelled façades of the stadium rise between the terraced streets, offering a series of dramatic views of the venue to the approaching visitor. Above, the roof is supported on just eight cores, allowing the slender roof plane to float above the robust façade of the building below. Within the grounds, our brand activation team have brought their innovative approach to way finding and signage, as part of a major naming rights sponsorship."

This expression of concern with branding is still (surprisingly) rare among architects.

An example of new housing (from CZWG) is given below (Drayton Park: 277 apartments).

## 13. Graduate Centre

Daniel Libeskind Studio, 2003
166–220 Holloway Road, N7
Tube: Holloway Road

Apparently a bemused Libeskind could find no contextual reference for this 700 sqm scheme that neatly links onto existing North London University buildings (fronted by a Rick Mather building), but he looked up and noticed the constellation of Orion – and so he offered this as a lighting pattern in the main lecture room. The striking intersecting forms have, until recently, worn well. However, time passes and now these forms increasingly remind one of a docked ship, abandoned, its back broken. Time passes.

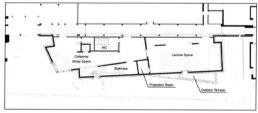

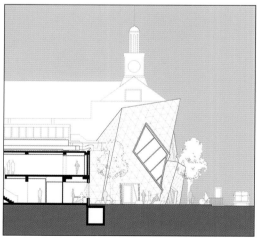

## 14. City & Islington College
Wilkinson Eyre Architects, 2006
44 Camden Road, N7
Tube: Holloway Road

The refurbishment of a 1960s building, plus a four-storey extension (see the red areas in the plan below). The most dramatic (and successful) aspect of the scheme is the long Camden Road frontage, with its branding signage apparently propping up the façade. It has presence. (See how HHbR do similar things with roots in the 1960s LA strip, via Venturi.)

## 15. Straw Bale House
Sarah Wigglesworth & Jeremy Till, 2001
9–10 Stock Orchard Street, N7
Tube: Caledonian Road

The home that established the talented Wigglesworth's reputation: born of economy, necessity, inventiveness and wit, exhibiting vaguely Schindler-esque notes. Its sand-bag frontage (admittedly very un-Schindler) facing toward passing express trains is not to everyone's taste, and its generally shocking character is somewhat different to the housing developments on the other side of the tracks (in Hornsey Street, off Holloway Road – which is a good location from which to get a view of the house). Still unique on the London scene.

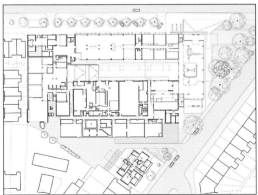

### 16. Highpoint
Tecton, 1935–38
North Road, N6
Tube: Highgate or Archway, then bus

Lubetkin and Tecton helped bring Modernism to London, here in the guise of two apartment blocks. Highpoint One offers us Le Corbusier's five points, but Highpoint Two (having 12 luxurious maisonettes instead of the originally intended 12 more ordinary flats, in order to satisfy the local conservation body) suddenly upsets the purists with a caryatid supporting the drop-off canopy. The internal details of both buildings contrast with the relatively limited influence of architects now. Also see the Lawn Road flats.

### 19. Hopkins House
Hopkins Architects, 1975
Devonshire Hill, NW3
Tube: Hampstead

It was done nearly 40 years ago, so no one takes notice any more – which is a shame, because this was a remarkable house then and still is now, even though its vaguely post-war, Californian Case Study House concerns are now well out of fashion. Or are they? Perhaps current media enthusiasms for low-cost self-build and the like will see a return to these exemplars.

### 20. John Winter House
John Winter, 1969
81 Swain's Lane, N6
Tube: Kentish Town and bus to Parliament Hill or Highgate

Built on the site of a custodian for the adjacent Highgate Cemetery, this design exercise would be unlikely to obtain planning permission today: a unique 3-storey, Corten steel clad Modernist exercise with an upper level living room overlooking the cemetery and Waterlow Park. Now listed and hopefully to be genuinely protected.

### 17. The Lawns
Eldridge Smerin, 2001
South Grove, Highgate Village, N6
Tube: Archway, then bus

Designed as a clever wrap around an existing Leonard Manasseh house. As a considerate interweaving of old and new, the work is clever and impressive.

### 18. Swains Lane House
Eldridge Smerin, 2008
Swains Lane, N6
Tube: Kentish Town or Archway, then bus

A replacement for an undistinguished John Winter house, making great play of glass and concrete in order to overlook the cemetery. However, the break in a tall and long existing brick wall that runs along the western side of the cemetery is the house's weakest aspect.

## 21. Chester Road housing
Rick Mather Architects, 2014
Chester Road, N19
Tube: Kentish Town, then 214 or C2 bus

A dense, mixed tenure scheme arranged in two blocks around a central court and designed to Passivhaus standards. It's impressive and nicely detailed, although one knows that, inevitably, the apartments will be small. The architects comment that site constraints resulted in

a block form consisting of stacked maisonettes with all dwellings having access to their front doors from the street. This strategy has meant that we could limit the number of circulation cores required and [...] maximise the efficiency of the site. Given the site restrictions and density this strategy has also meant that all units are dual aspect and all family units have generous private gardens or terraces.

Not many recent housing schemes can say as much.

## 22. 1–3 Willow Road
Erno Goldfinger, 1938
2 Willow Road, NW3
Tube: Hampstead

A marriage of 1920s Parisian Modernism plus an enchantment with the traditional Georgian terrace: what looks like four units, but is the Goldfinger home (in the centre) and two end flats made for sale. A marvellous example of Modernism and how a 1930s architect and his family expected to live in even a small home with servants. If you carefully study the elevations you shall find them loaded with geometric and proportional concerns. It is now owned by the National Trust and is readily accessible.

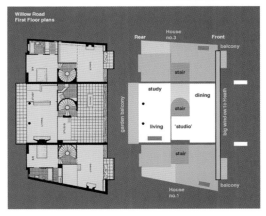

## 23. Sainsbury supermarket
Grimshaw, 1988
Camden Road, NW1
Tube: Camden Town

TLC would go a long way to changing opinion about this intriguing exercise in Hi-Tech married to historical contexturalism. Note, for example, the relationships between the front façade – where a massive structure presents itself (one that copes with a lack of columns in the supermarket hall) – and the elegant Georgian terrace opposite. Also note the terrace of town houses to the north, along the Regent's Canal.

## 24. Henrietta Barnett School
Hopkins Architects, 2011
Central Square, Hampstead Garden Suburb, N11
Tube: Golders Green

A controversial building within a very conservative setting, adding two wings to a building by Edwin Lutyens and arousing the ire of local inhabitants. (There had been 17 previous schemes that failed all the hurdles.) Actually it is a fine work that greatly enhances the area and admirably complements Lutyens' work.

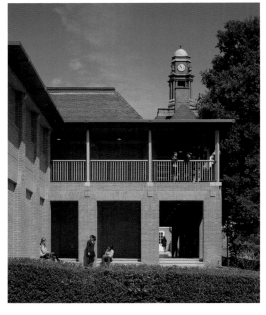

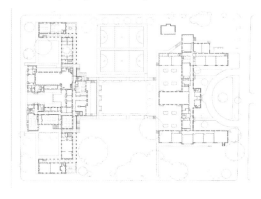

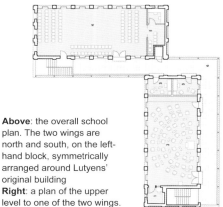

**Above**: the overall school plan. The two wings are north and south, on the left-hand block, symmetrically arranged around Lutyens' original building
**Right**: a plan of the upper level to one of the two wings.

## 25. North London Hospice
Allford Hall Monaghan Morris, 2013
47 Woodside Avenue London, N12
Tube: Woodside Park

A refreshing, simple and nicely detailed design for a hospice from AHMM, looking like two houses in a suburban context. That the work is a hospice imposed a huge demand on the architects, but the core issue is simply one of consideration. So why can't the housing in such dreaty parts of London be more like this?

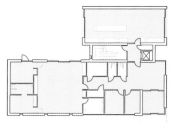

Photos courtesy of HA (Richard Brine)

Photos courtesy of AHMM (Rob Parrish)

## 26. Camden Arts Centre
Tony Fretton Architects, 2004
Arkwright Road, NW3
Tube: Finchley Road

A neat remodelling of an existing building to provide a new entry hall, café, etc. The central feature is the handling of the ground floor areas: entry, bookshop, café linked to side garden, etc. Typical restrained Fretton and quite refreshing.

## 28. Swiss Cottage Library
Basil Spence, 1964; John McAslan+Partners, 2003
Finchley Road, NW3
Tube: Swiss Cottage

A library from Sir Basil, with a superb interior, refurbished by John McAslan. Neils Torp loved it when we took him there, so perhaps you should give it a try as well. Not only are finishes and details different to contemporary new libraries (e.g. Peckham, Clapham and Canada Water), but the spatial feel and concern is different. It's refreshing.

## 27. West Hampstead Thameslink
Landolt & Brown, 2012
Rail: West Hampstead Thameslink; Overground: West Hampstead; Tube: West Hampstead

A part from the clunky roof detail, this is a pavilion with neo-Miesian touches, striving for stand-alone elegance ... plus a rather nice, long and bright green glazed wall.

Lower two photos courtesy of Landolt & Brown

## 29. Fortune Green Road
CZWG, 2010
37–43 Fortune Green Road, NW6
Overground: West Hampstead

A striking and ambitious apartment building with a retail ground floor, basement parking and penthouses with green roofs (but mostly single aspect again). Not unimpressive, but the plan has a familiar single-aspect problem. Nice penthouse level.

## 30. Isokon Apartments
Wells Coates, 1933
Lawn Road, NW3
Tube: Belsize Park

Style and social experiment: a famous Modernist community building of 22 'minimum' flats accessed by open cantilevered balconies, four double flats located at the south end, and three studio flats at the north end above the kitchen, staff quarters and garage, plus a large penthouse included for the Pritchards. Walter Gropius, Marcel Breuer, Agatha Christie, Moholy-Nagy, Adrian Stokes, Egon Riss and Arthur Korn all lived here. The building was more recently renovated and converted by Avanti.

## 31. Branch Hill
Benson & Forsyth (Camden Architects Department), 1977
Spedan Close, NW3
Tube: Hampstead

A marvellous hidden exercise in hillside social housing that prompts rumination on today's housing inadequacies. They could do it then; why not now?

## 32. Alexandra Road
Neave Brown, at Camden Architects Department, 1978
Bartholomew Road, NW8
Tube: Swiss Cottage

Completed in 1978, in the spirit of megastructures, providing 520 homes plus a school, community centre, etc. One 8s block (see bottom section) acts as a barrier against the railway. Impressive but scary.

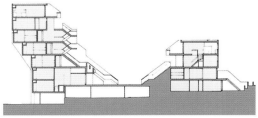

## 33. JW3

Lifschutz Davidson Sandilands, 2013
341–351 Finchley Road, NW3
Tube: Finchley Road

A Jewish community centre that strives to be open to everyone, providing a wide range of cultural activities (and lots of carefully disguised security measures). The scheme is an equation of podium+tower+sunken piazza – the latter crossed by a bridge that emphasises a distancing taking place from the busy Finchley Road. It is all well detailed and exhibits some equally well-considered compositional and material moves; however, this oddly includes turning the tower toward the road, away from the piazza, so that the latter has a blank (south-facing) wall.

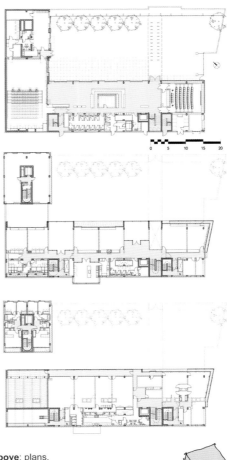

**Above**: plans.
**Right**: schematic diagram of the scheme.

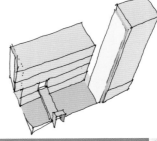

## 34. Central School of Speech & Drama
Jestico+ Whiles, 2005
Eton Avenue, NW3
Tube: Swiss Cottage

A simple building (providing a variety of rehearsal and performance spaces) at a very busy location that has a degree of bulk and presence Bennetts' Hampstead Theatre (sitting opposite) eschews. Ironically, early 2013 saw a row over large advertising hoardings outside that brought in funds to the school. The interior is very simple.

## 35. Hampstead Theatre
Bennett Associates, 2003
Eton Avenue, NW3
Tube: Swiss Cottage

An excellent theatre building that, for some reason, is thoroughly timid on the exterior and fails to throw itself at the public and offer the kind of enjoyment one finds on the inside. If anything, that exterior should have been even more simple ... or wild. It is too self-effacing. However, don't let this issue put you off visiting the place.

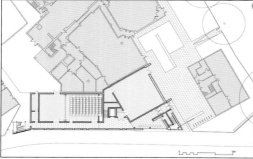

**Above**: the lobby of the Theatre.
**Below**: the outside of the Theatre.

## 36. The Roundhouse
John McAslan+Partners, 2006
Chalk Farm Road, NW1
Tube: Kentish Town

Once a shed where train engines were turned around, now a famous north London venue for all kinds of cultural events, accommodating 1800 seated and 3000 standing. The McAslan renovations and alterations made significant differences to the place most Londoners have enjoyed at one time or another. There is a café here, which serves as an alternative to Camden Market stalls.

Photo courtesy of The Roundhouse (Hufton & Crow)

## 37. Glass Building
CZWG, 2000
Hawley Crescent, NW1
Tube: Camden Town

CZWG have a long line of one-liners seeking to make an impact. And, occasionally, these are effective. This one in Camden – set amidst the market area – is a series of interlocking drums of varying heights, with commercial uses on the lowest level and 25 shell apartments above – works quite well in this setting. Also see Camden Wharf buildings across the road (2001).

## 38. Latitude House
Allford Hall Monaghan Morris, 2005
Oval Road/Parkway, NW1
Tube: Camden Town

A block of 12 apartments: elegant with vague Stirling & Gowan hints, but the patterned façade is thin, tectonically unconvincing and therefore slightly disturbing. A touch of robustness would have made all the difference.

## 39. Kentish Town Community Centre
Allford Hall Monaghan Morris, 2009
Bartholomew Road, NW5
Tube: Kentish Town

This design is not dissimilar to Sunshine House in Camberwell and done at about the same time. It is simple, economic, but with a bit of dash, colour and bold graphics from Studio Myserscough.

West
Central ...

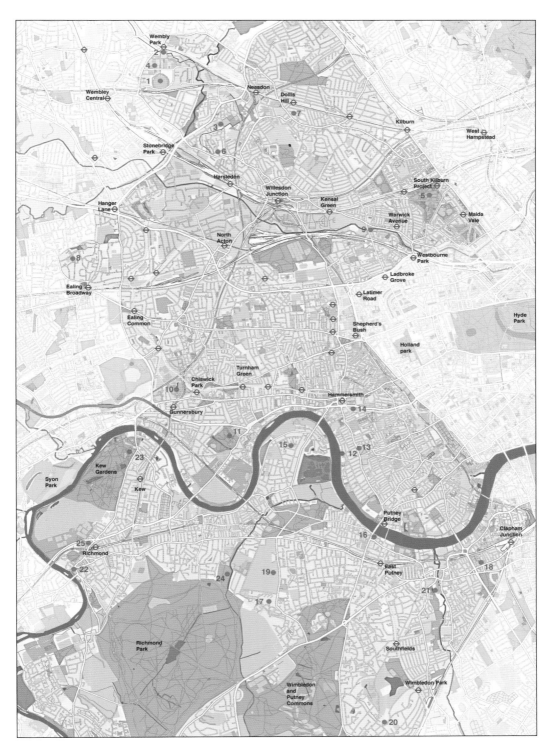

**Previous page**: Alsop's Fawood Nursery

## 1. Wembley Stadium

Foster + Partners (with HOK Sport), 2007
Olympic Way, HA9
Tube: Wembley Park

The huge 133m-high arch of this 90,000-seat stadium is visible from all over London. It's impressive, but not very pretty and best seen at night, perhaps from a distance – but at last the area round about is undergoing redevelopment (see the Hopkins-designed civic centre).

Photo courtesy of Wikipedia (Jbmg40)

## 2. Victoria Hall

CZWG, 2012
North End Road, HA9
Tube: Wembley Park

This isn't great architecture, but is one of the few buildings of interest around here. The 20-storey Hall provides 435 student rooms – big business these days (but not without criticism with regard to rooms sizes, outlook, etc). A typical CZWG instance of their concept of cheerfulness. Disconcertingly, one looks at the plan and immediately thinks of a prison typology. Such places are nowadays big business.

## 3. Shri Swarminarayan Mandir

C.D. Sompura, 1995
105–119 Brentfield Road, NW10
Tube: Neasdon

Visitors are very welcome to this Hindu community temple, in a bizarrely relocated traditional style. Amazing and utterly incongruous that raises all kinds of issues pertaining to craftsmanship. Another temple – the  Sri Guru Singh Sabha Gurdwara – exists in Southwall. And, of course, there are now many mosques (especially the Regent's Park London Central Mosque, designed by Frederick Gibberd (1978)).

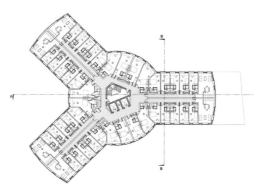

284

## 4. Brent Civic Centre
Hopkins Architects, 2013
Engineers Way, HA9
Tube: Wembley Park

Bearing parallels with a similar building designed by Hopkins for Hackney, the Brent Civic Centre is a bold design for an austere era, designed to house 2000 staff in offices around a grand atrium. The circular Drum clad in timber fins houses a multi-purpose community hall, library, one-stop shop and civic chamber. (And the interiors are also by Hopkins.) Overall, the Centre makes a significant addition to the regeneration of this area around Wembley Stadium.

## 5. South Kilburn regeneration
Various architects, 2012–23
Brent, NW6
Tube: South Kilburn

South Kiburn is a very large regeneration project concerning a district that ranks within the top ten of most deprived areas in the UK. Its scale bears parallels with what is happening at Elephant & Castle and at other sites of large social housing estates from the 1960s and 1970s. For example, Brent borough's aims include: 2400 homes of which around 1200 will be made available to existing South Kilburn residents; a new park; a health centre; improved environmental standards; a neighbourhood energy policy, etc. The project will last from about 2012–23.

The architects involved include Lifschutz Davidson Sandilands with Alison Brooks (see the CGI below), Rick Mather and Levitt Bernstein (the latter two in the eastern sector of the area). A masterplan was completed by PRP Architects in 2009. Watch it develop.

Photos courtesy of Hopkins (Morley von Sternberg)

CGI courtesy of LDS)

### 6. Fawood Children's Nursery
Will Alsop, 2005
Fawood Avenue, NW10
Tube: Harlesdon

Why some people are shocked at the idea of children kept behind wire in a shed stocked with old containers and a yurt is beyond us. In fact, this is one of Alsop's best works and thoroughly within the Cedric Price tradition to which he is allied. If you want to be more pretentious it is possible to construe the building as a take upon a Greek temple, now transmogrified into a mundane children's nursery ... OK: or an animal cage. And, yes, the external decorations are frivolous. But it's clever and London needs more buildings like this.

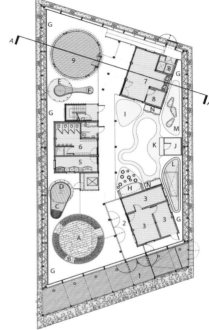

## 7. Villiers Road
Peter Barber Architects, 2009
192–198 Villiers Road, NW2
Tube: Dollis Hill

R ecognisable Barber. In the architect's words:
"three timber clad, single occupancy cottages situated in the rear yard of an existing homeless hostel. The proposal is conceived as move-on accommodation as residents progress towards independent living. Each home is accessed through a courtyard overlooked by an open plan living/kitchen with full height glazing. Stairs lead up to a first floor bedroom under a spectacular vaulted roof with large windows overlooking the communal garden area.[...] The relationship to the neighbouring gardens behind the development was key and drove the design of the vaulted roofs to reduce the impact along the boundary. [...] Traditional masonry and lightweight steel construction was utilised with insulated acrylic render finish to the courtyard façades and timber rainscreen cladding to the front façade and curved roof. A single ply membrane was used to waterproof the roof surfaces beneath the timber. Green painted timber windows were used."

VILLIERS ROAD

## 8. St Benedict's School
HHbR, 2008
Eaton Rise, W5
Tube: Ealing Broadway

A n expert insertion into a existing complex of buildings that at once organises and revitalises them, supplements them and greatly enhances them – and it does so by employing a monastic typology: the cloister – here, enclosed, thus forming a central meeting hall, but a recurring Simon Henley theme (see the Akerman Centre).

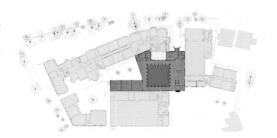

### 9. Portobello Dock
Tom Dixon, 2008; Stiff & Trevillion, 2008
Ladbroke Grove at Harrow Road, W10
Tube: Ladbroke Grove

There are three projects here, on either side of a canal basin on the Regent's Canal: Tom Dixon's restaurant and shop, and Stiff & Trevillion's Canal Building for Innocent drinks. The former is a conversion and addition to existing warehouse buildings that revels in its grungy feel. The latter is a gleaming new tower on the corner of the site. Across the road is an interesting converted water-tower

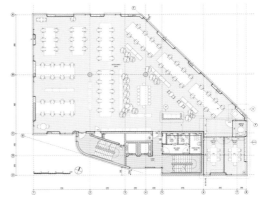

## 10. Chiswick Business Park
Rogers Stirk Harbour+Partners, 2000–13
566 Chiswick High Road, W4
Tube: Gunnersbury

Twelve buildings on an 'urban island' – a remarkable long-term design exercise with similar building types that are at once elegant, well detailed and economic, and with splendid landscaping in between the deep-plan buildings. A business park as they should all be (if, that is, you like business parks).

## 11. Chiswick House restaurant
Caruso St John, 2010
566 Chiswick High Road, W4
Tube: Gunnersbury

An ostensibly simple pavilion in the grounds of Chiswick House – restrained (as one would expect from this practice), beautifully detailed, but not the greatest interior and, in that sense, no match for Lord Burlington's house – on the subject of which: it is not to be missed. Think of it as a gentleman's (seven-eighths full size) den, set away from the main family house (now demolished). From this point of view the Caruso St John work repeats a past relationship but, of course, upon an entirely different basis (not a private indulgence, but a public convenience). See the two together.

## 12. Thames Wharf Studios

Rogers Stirk Harbour+Partners, 1994
Rainville Road, W6
Tube: Hammersmith

Aconverted 1950s warehouse to which upper levels have been added (actually by Lifschutz Davidson, then sharing the building), a café provided next door (the famous River Café) and some supplementary terraced housing added along the adjacent river edge (which remains surprisingly contemporary).

Foster did something similar further downstream. (See page 267.)

## 14. The Ark

Ralph Erskine, 1992
Talgarth Road, W6
Tube: Hammersmith

What you see now is the outer form to an interior that has been gutted and converted into something considerably more conservative and predictable

than Erskine intended – what was once the most idiosyncratic and exciting office building in London. However, it was completed in the midst of a deep recession and became ill-fated ever afterward. Facility managers (in those days) couldn't cope with Erskine's curves.

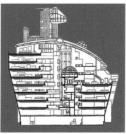

## 13. Maggie's

Rogers Stirk Harbour+Partners, 2008
Charing Cross Hospital, Fulham Palace Road, W6
Tube: Hammersmith

This series of cancer care centres are conceived as informal, semi-domestic settings and architectural showcases. This one fits the bill, but then the architects couldn't resist turning the idea of a 'floating' roof into a 'Hey Ma, look at me' roof. Otherwise, it is an excellent building whose entrance sequence neatly engenders a separation from the business of the outside world.

Photo courtesy of RSH (Richard Anderson)

## 15. Lowther School
Patel Taylor, 2009/2012
Stillingfleet Road, SW13
Tube: Hammersmith

Two new pavilions either side of, and linked into, an existing school building. The work involved a consideration of the whole school's organisation, demolition and remodelling works which provided a new hall for the older children (below left in the site plan, and bottom photo).

Photo courtesy of P&T

## 16. Putney Wharf Tower
Patel Taylor, 2003
Brewhouse Lane, SW15
Tube: Putney Bridge

The remodelling and extension of a 1960s office tower into an apartment building with lower level restaurants, etc. set against a new public space onto the river frontage. This kind of conversion has, as a matter of government policy, now become commonplace.

Photos courtesy of Patel Taylor

## 17. Roehampton flats
LCC, 1959
Highcliffe Drive, SW15
Rail: Barnes

A row of concrete high-rise flats famous for their setting and their imitation of Le Corbusier's somewhat similar blocks in France. One gets the impression of a disparity between the parkland and internal realities, but the

reality that such flats, as middle-class apartments, would be highly desirable underscores a strange aspect of Britain's class structure and what has happened to social housing estates since the Thatcher era.

## 18. St John's Health Centre
Henley Halebrown Rorrison, 2007
162 St John's Hill, SW11
Rail: Clapham Junction

One of a series of health centres designed by this practice, making use of enlarged signage integrated into the architecture.

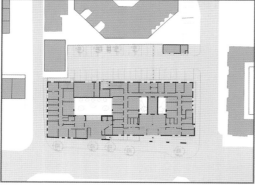

Also see Akerman Health Centre, Baldry Road Health Centre, and Waldon Health Centre. All make great play upon a significatory element and/or familiar typological references that, together, enhance the readable meaning of the work which is over and beyond mere aesthetic value.

## 19. The Yard, Roehampton University
Henley Halebrown Rorrison, 2007
85 Roehampton Lane, SW15
Rail: Barnes

The first project within HHbR's masterplan for the university, intended as a virtuoso exercise in the use of brick landscaping that knits together a mix of historic and more recent buildings.

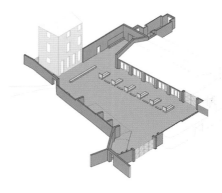

## 20. St Mary's Church Garden Hall
Terry Pawson Architects, 2002
30 St Mary's Road, SW19
Rail: Wimbledon

The project provides a nearly square 230 sqm hall divisible into two parts for use by church and community. Details draw material clues from the church itself, including a knapped flint wall and limestone.

Also see Pawson's house at 82 Arthur Road, SW19.

Photos courtesy of Terry Pawson

## 21. Wandsworth Workshops

Sergison Bates Architects, 2004
86–96 Garratt Lane, SW18
Rail: Wandsworth Town

Sergison Bates Architects have quite a European following. This work of theirs refurbishes and extends a 1930s paint factory, providing apartments, a health centre and some workshop units. Like A&M and similar architects they stick to their values.

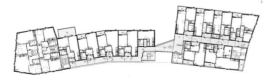

## 22. Richmond Riverside

Quinlan & Francis Terry, 1988
Hill and Bridge Streets, Richmond
Tube: Richmond

A theatrical exercise in 'progressive classicism' that upsets many architects, but whose underlying intentions (at once urbane and picturesque) are not disagreeable. It simply looks to be everything – stylistically and tectonically – that it isn't (10,000 sqm of offices).

The scheme provides for offices, flats, shops, two restaurants, community facilities, two underground car parks, and riverside gardens. In Terry's words, it seeks to exhibit "some of the rich variations of English 18th-century architecture, using red and yellow bricks, pantiles, plain tiles, slate and lead, sash and casement windows, and all the five Orders." He adds:

> In order to provide the variety that is needed on a project of this size on a sloping site, it is desirable to have many different buildings juxtapositioned, rather than one grand scheme; many of the buildings pick up the characteristic details of English and Italian architects, in particular Palladio, Longhena, Sansovino, Hawksmoor, William Chambers and the Gothic revival of the 19th century.

Complicated. Also see the Terry villas at Regent's Park and Robert Adam's work at the Oval (an entry frontage) and in Piccadilly (an office building). A third notable Neoclassicist on the English scene is Porphryios Associates (who have a 119-unit affordable housing development toward the southern end of Holloway Road (celebrated by Prince Charles), and have also designed one of the central office buildings at Kings Cross – an interesting addition to the aesthetic mix at this important site by the developers. Clearly, each of these architects has a following despite them being fashionably unfashionable.

## 23. Royal Botanical Gardens
Various architects
Kew Road, Richmond, TW9
Tube: Kew Gardens

The X-Strata tree walk (Marks Barfield, 2008), the Sackler Bridge (John Pawson, 2008), the Shirley Sherwood Gallery of Botanical Art (Walters & Cohen, 2008), a herbarium by Cullinan Studio (2010) and an Alpine House (Wilkinson Eyre Architects, 2006) are among the more recent works at Kew Gardens. Older buildings include the Palm House (Decimus Burton, 1848), the Pagoda (William Chambers, late 18th century) and Ham House (17th century). Overall, it is a pleasant place to visit. But note that Kew Gardens makes a charge for entry.

**Top right**: the Alpine House.
**Right**: the Palm House by Decimus Burton.
**Bottom right**: Pawson's Sackler Bridge.
**Below**: the X-Strata Walk in the trees.

## 24. Lawn Tennis Association
Hopkins Architects, 2008
100 Priory Lane, Roehampton, SW15
Rail: Wandsworth Town then bus

Not easy to get to or get in, but a notable Hopkins work, providing tennis training facilities including indoor courts (a large barrel-roofed shed), and residential facilities (along one side of the shed). The entry is a more extravagant gesture: a tensile-roofed area.

## 25. Richmond Adult Community College
Duggan Morris Architects, 2014
Parkshot at Twickenham Road, TW9
Tube and Rail: Richmond

A conversion and extension project that aims to create a world-class campus at Parkshot for the arts and theatre. Thus, as the architects say, "at the centre of the architectural programme is the need to create a sense of identity for the site, and the curriculum departments within. This was achieved by providing

"a cluster of simple cubic forms of varying mass and height, generated from old and new buildings, all gently wrapped in a softly textured brick skin and articulated with over sized picture windows and topped with metallic roof level lanterns intended to signify the special uses associated with certain buildings volumes within the cluster [and concealing saw-tooth roofs]."

This 'cluster' forms a central courtyard to the overall scheme. The architects go on to state the characteristic manner in which they tackle projects:

"a reduced palette of materials used in inventive and unusual ways, a reliance on the material quality, rather than an applied finish, to create interest and articulation, and above all an ambitious desire to create uplifting spaces which harness the quality of natural light through careful design of glazing and windows."

(In construction at the time of writing.)

South
Central ...

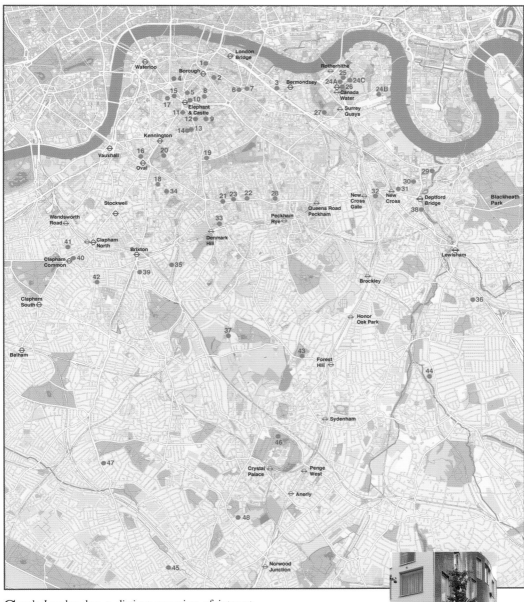

South London has a distinct grouping of interesting recent works around the Elephant & Castle area (much of it housing) and the enthusiast may be disinclined to travel further south than gentrified areas such as Clapham and Brixton. However, there are interesting works in development as far south as Croydon that justify an excursion.

Surrey Quays was developed during the 1980s as a suburban area, but is now rapidly maturing into somewhere far more dense. Use Canada Water (Jubilee Line) and Surrey Quays Overground stations.

## 1. Valentine Place Offices
Stiff & Trevillion, 2013
1 Valentine Place, Blackfriars Road, SE1
Tube: Southwark

A simple but elegantly handled office building of about 2900 sqm which, as a development, pushes what is happening at A&M's 123 Bankside, Alsop's Palestra and AHMM's Blackfriars Road building further south, indicative of this area's continued changes. Its features reflect current fashions: projecting fins, offset grids and simple proportions interplaying glass and solid panels (plus a contextural note in the relations to immediate neighbours (left, below).

## 2. Empire Square
Rolfe Judd, 2006
Long Lane, SE1
Tube: Borough

This project creates 572 apartments (212 affordable) centred around a public square with a sculptural pavilion (rather sub-Ronchamp, and rather like a flea in plan) at its centre, surrounded by shops, offices and retail space, gym, crèche, etc. A 22-storey tower is topped by a glowing barometer that changes colour according to the atmospheric pressure incongruously described by the architects as a landmark for the development and a beacon for regeneration of this Borough area.

Photos courtesy of S&T

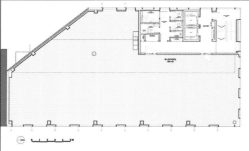

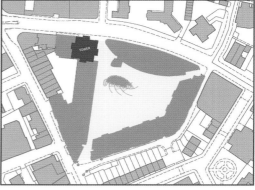

### 3. Bermondsey Spa
Levitt Bernstein, 2009–2013
Jamaica Road, Spa Road, SE1
Tube: Bermondsey

A large development for the Hyde Housing Association. The first phase (St James' Square) was 211 mixed-tenure apartments in two courtyard blocks (far right below). Eyot Heights is 114 apartments and the Bolonachi Building provides 138 apartments and has the novelty of many being entered through a common naturally ventilated but covered atrium (also see the later Alyesbury scheme). Here, family maisonettes are located at ground level on the west of the site and have ground-floor gardens and first-floor terraces. All dwellings either have ground-floor gardens/ terraces or, on upper floors, balconies of at least 6 sqm. The final phases (3+4) deliver another 319 'blind tenure' apartments along Jamaica Road (2013).

### 4. Muro Court
Metaphorm, 2011
Library Street, SE1
Tube: Elephant & Castle or Borough

A scheme providing 34 apartments and six three-storey terraced townhouses with between five and six units to each floor, each with its own private balcony. Tenancies are a mix of affordable flats for rent, sale or shared ownership. A landscaped roof garden provides shared amenity space. Slim Belgian facing bricks and precast concrete panels give variety and scale, responding to the red brick and stonework of the surrounding Victorian buildings.

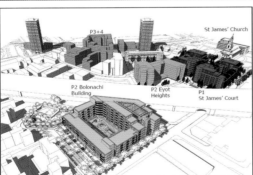

Cgi courtesy of LBA

Photo courtesy of Metaphorm

299

### 5. Keyworth I and II
BDP, 2004, Grimshaw, 2010
Southwark Bridge Road, SE1
Tube: Elephant & Castle

Keyworth I (centre photo) has a dreary exterior but a more exciting interior atrium witness to its designer's enthusiasms for Ralph Erskine's work. Keyworth II (right and bottom photos) has a quite different character but is linked through, so that the University's facilities have been extended into one linear arrangement stretching along the street.

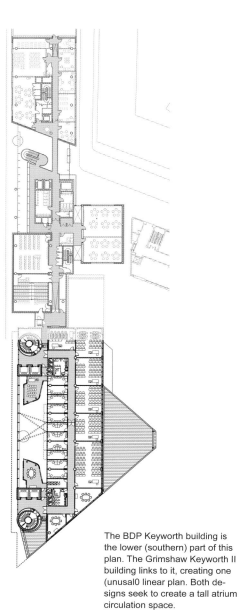

The BDP Keyworth building is the lower (southern) part of this plan. The Grimshaw Keyworth II building links to it, creating one (unusal0 linear plan. Both designs seek to create a tall atrium circulation space.

Photo courtesy of Grimshaw

## 6. Bermondsey Square
Munkenbeck & Marshall, 2008
Long Lane, SE1
Tube: Borough

Bermondsey Square is worthy of attention. To the architect it "involves the creation of a new heart in Bermondsey". To one journalist it "is intended to seduce the young and trendy with its take on inner-city living: and, one confesses that the developer's marketing team do lay it on thickly and implausibly."

The triangular Square is defined by three 8s blocks and the development comprises a mix of 76 apartments, offices, cinema (internal and external), a 100-room hotel, restaurant and bars. The problem starts with East's landscaping and its conception as "a carpet upon which are scattered an array of simple design elements – benches, bollards, cycle hoops and boules pitch like trinkets".

One of these 'trinkets' is Sarah Wigglesworth's store for 76 bicycles (2008). Others include painted icosahedra bollards intended to deter vehicles and claimed "to provide seating and bring extra delight to the square". Oak sleepers on stainless steel rotating legs act as additional seats and vehicle barriers. And the boules pitch "adds to the relaxed, playful ambiance ...". Meanwhile, street-lights hang in a neo-Japanese manner from overhead cables and are described as 'urban chandeliers'.

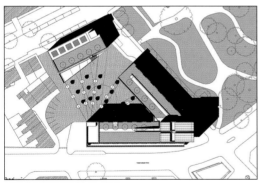

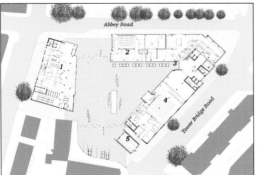

Photos courtesy of Stephen Marshall

## 7. Bermondsey Island

Urban Salon, 2012
Long Lane, SE1
Tube: Borough or Bermondsey

The 'Island' – a stand-alone building – sits opposite Bermondsey Square. Two façades (facing the busy roads) are in a 'brick tile'; the other two are rendered. The ground floor is retail and the top level has an array of solar panels (feeding underfloor heating). Inside, the 'Island' provides 13 new affordable rented one and two-bed units. And, as the architects remark: "Each face of the building expresses a different balance of window to wall to animate the scheme provide views out and protect privacy" (which includes the brick tiles for acoustic reasons). It's rather good.

Photo courtesy of Urban Salon (Gareth Gardner)

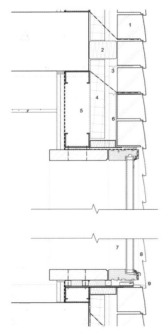

Key

1. Ibstock Tilebrick
2. Cavity fire barrier
3. Ancon wall tie channel system
4. Rigid insulation
5. Light-gauge steel with rockwool insulation
6. IG single skin lintel
7. Krone window
8. Fairfaced Tilebrick
9. Powdercoated sill

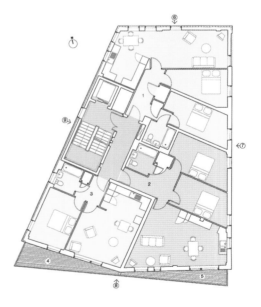

## 8. Harper Square
dRMM, 2013
Harper Road, SE1
Tube: Elephant & Castle

Whatever one thinks of their aesthetic concerns and the problems of contractor details, dRMM deliver housing witness to care and consideration. This is a scheme of 72 social rented and intermediate affordable homes, car-free and set around a shared central space. The site – described as an 'island' of low-density housing surrounded by older and higher density blocks – was construed to be complicated and requiring a design that would reconcile the conflicting architectural expression of a 1960s four-storey apartment building, an 11-storey slab block, an eclectic assortment of school buildings and public open space.

The architects say their aspiration was to create a high-quality housing scheme referencing traditional 'London Squares' and Eric Lyon's Ivor Cunningham's landscaped SPAN developments. Perhaps more importantly, they add:

"In order to foster a sense of community, apartments have been clustered in small groups of two or four apartments per floor to allow residents to meet and for neighbourliness to flourish. Apartment typologies have been developed to maximise the feeling of space and light through full height glazing and big views. Two main typologies were developed: a 'through apartment' (east/west orientation) with dual balconies and a 'prime aspect apartment (north/south) with a screened outside room. All of the apartments benefit from dual aspect."

With regard to the rear façades we are told: "The architectural expression of the buildings has been informed by the landscaped heart, which has been conceptually reflected onto the façades through the application of a series of green glazed terracotta tiles." A terrace of five-bed and four-bed, 3-storey units form the northern edge of the development.

2-bed prime aspect

2-bed through plan

3-bed prime aspect plan

4.bed townhouse level 0

4-Bed townhouse level 01

4-bed townhouse level 02

### 9. Brandon Street housing
Metaphorm, 2010
Brandon Street, SE1
Tube: Elephant & Castle

Two blocks of apartments with an access court in between, providing 18 socially rented apartments. The surprising and refreshing gesture is the Brandon Street façade, where a set-back has been created, trees planted and seats set against a coloured-tile backdrop provided for local children. And all this was on a low budget. (Also see Library Street by the same architects.)

## 10. Arch Street housing
S333 Architecture and Urbanism, 2011
Arch Street, SE1
Tube: Elephant & Castle

A scheme of 52 apartments (18 affordable) up against a railway viaduct. The street cladding is a matter of taste, but the planning (below) sets up a successful (brick-faced) communal area between two apartment blocks. The stepped massing (from two to six storeys) is, says the architect, "a literal articulation of the sunlight path".

## 11. Strata Tower
BFLS, 2010
Elephant & Castle, SE1
Tube: Elephant & Castle

We have to get used to these things: a tall residential tower of 40 storeys and 408 apartments, with generating turbines on top, with 25% of the apartments owned by a housing association. But did it deserve to be named the ugliest building of 2010? (What constitutes 'ugly'?) However, while it appears that the turbines never work (too much noise and vibration), were they such a bad idea?

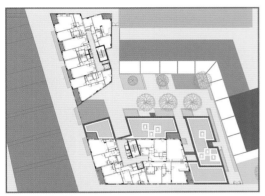

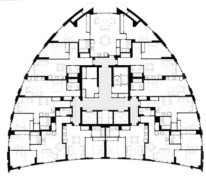

## 12. Wansey Street housing
dRMM, 2006
Wansey Street, SE1
Tube: Elephant & Castle

A clever scheme in itself and in its self-conscious rela-tion to neighbours: on one side a large red brick building; on the other a traditional early Victorian terrace in yellow London brick. The scheme is quite differ-ent on the northern side (where it responds to adjacent neighbours) and on the rear, southern, side where large aluminium louvres are employed and the apartments look down upon a communal garden area.

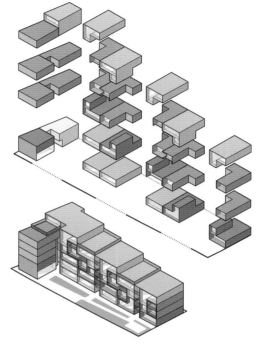

The apartments are skilfully interlocked (diagram top right) and the considerate step-down from one end of the block to the other (i.e., from the large community building to the Victorian terrace) facilitates the provision of upper-level roof terraces. On the other hand, dRMM's characteristic employment of materials such as cement board imitating timber irritates some people. As ever, details and some internal fit-out arrangements were de-termined by the contractor.

## 13. Printworks

Glenn Howell Architects, 2010
22 Amelia Street, SE1
Tube: Elephant & Castle

Printworks is the other (more commonplace) face of current London housing provision: a long 9-storey block whose main challenge"was to achieve a relatively high density on a site with constraints such as the adjacent railway viaduct and a small frontage to the public road." The architects add: "Printworks represents a modern interpretation of the London mansion block, and acts as a catalyst for the overall regeneration of the area. Its bronze anodized aluminium cladding was chosen to reflect the industrial history of the site." It's a decent development with a clean aesthetic (although it has single-aspect flat and why would one want to be reminded of the industrial history of the site?).

## 14. O'Central

Space Craft Architects, 2007
Crampton Street, SE1
Tube: Elephant & Castle

O'Central comprises three blocks of housing – two affordable, on Crampton Street, and one long private block along the railway viaduct, on the opposite side to Printworks. In all, there are 202 apartments and the long block has commercial uses on the ground floor. The architects claim: "The scheme respects the scale and form of the 19th Century Victorian tenements opposite placing the 'affordable housing' element of the scheme in the most desirable location, along Crampton Street, with the higher value apartments adjacent to the railway line." The former, they claim, "creates an urban boulevard with the four storey housing of the Pullens Conservation Area, as a re-interpretation of the original Victorian street form." It will either intrigue you or repulse you.

Photo courtesy of GHA

## 15. Wardroper House
Sarah Wigglesworth, 2010
St George's Road, SE1
Tube: Elephant & Castle

In the architect's words: this 15-apartment block aims:

> In an ordinary urban environment" to "demonstrate how new housing can respect and enhance its context through good design. [...] Generous shared spaces, careful layout and a quiet courtyard garden provide a friendly and attractive environment. A timber screen around the building contains private balconies and gives acoustic protection from the busy road outside. The screen's grid pattern echoes neighbouring buildings, while rendered panels within it add eye-catching burst of colour. Elsewhere a wall of vivid green glazed bricks provides colourful reflections.

The split cores reflect different tenures and (as always) the tight space allowances engender a living-room that is really a dining-kitchen area with a sofa (now commonplace). Some of this is the result of a problematic project history also affecting S333's scheme around the corner. In the words of a *Building Design* journalist both schemes were compromised by the financial crisis, subjected to changes in council personnel, and forced to accommodate the prosaic expectations of a housing association. At another level, we are witness to the outcome of a local authority initiative that began in 2005 with the intention to build 1000 homes designed by 15 young practices – which came down to 500 homes by a much reduced list. So far as Wardroper was concerned the story continued in this vein, i.e., one difficulty after another – which is regrettable for its occupants and also for the architect, who has proven herself to be a very good designer (see, for example, Siobhan Dance). The lesson? Apart from the issues plaguing the E&C redevelopment as a whole, all spin has to stop at some point, enabling us to see the achieved reality of current housing procurement policies which include the peculiarities of limiting the design architect's role and placing a contractor in control of delivery – including the detailing and internal fit-out – while employing another architect in an executive role.

## 16. Oval
ADAM Architecture, 2012
Harleyford Street, SE11
Tube: Oval

As an instance of 'progressive classicism', this is an improvement on what the façade was before ADAM added the steps, portico, etc. It's certainly a contrast with the Populous/Miller partnership work around the corner (2005).

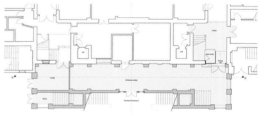

## 17. Siobhan Dance
Sarah Wigglesworth, 2005
St George's Road, SE1
Tube: Elephant & Castle

## 18. Vassell Road housing
Tony Fretton Architects, 2008
Vassell Road, SW9
Tube: Oval

One turns from Wardroper to an earlier Wigglesworth scheme to see a more successful design that delights in its own inventiveness. A Victorian school has been converted and added to at roof level in order to provide facilities for an independent dance school. This top level studio is an impressive space, but so, too, are the stair details, the first-floor gallery and the mix of materials and new with old. Overall, this is a hugely enjoyable scheme of a kind that pops up now and then in London, but is all too rare.

A contextual exercise making reference to neighbouring Victorian villas, but now in the guise of a private 3-storey terrace of seven two-bed maisonettes and a doctor's surgery. The end of the terrace terminates in a four-storey block of apartments. The brickwork of the whole is overpainted with (in Fretton's words) "Keim mineral paint to simulate the aged quality of the brickwork in the surrounding villas".

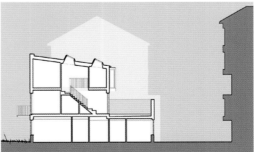

## 19. Aylesbury Estate Renewal
Levitt Bernstein, 2011–13
Westmoreland Road, SE1
Tube: Kennington

An admirable four-stage redevelopment project of the decaying Aylesbury estate: 261 mixed-tenure homes are being provided (affordable rent 39%, intermediate 13%, private sale 48%) as part of a project to rehouse the 7500 people on the neglected estate – a situation similar to the Heygate Estate at the heart of the redevelopment at Elephant & Castle. In both cases once admirable instances of 1960s rehousing became places of decay, deprivation and crime. The controversial answer to this mix of social and physical prob-

lems has been the same: demolish and rebuild. At least the replacement is of good quality. Block B in the site plan is considered the 'anchor block' and features a covered central courtyard (top right photo and plan at bottom of page; elevation, right; the court is the central lateral area; some plans are coloured in order to suggest the vari-

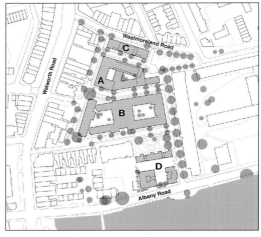

ations existing). Block D (red in the diagram above) is private (facing onto the adjacent park). Block A includes a community building. The scheme provides a mix of one-, two-, three- and four-bedroom homes evenly split across affordable rent, intermediate and private tenures and at a density close to 700hr/ha that almost doubles that currently on the site (at space standards that are Parker Morris plus 10%, which is generally similar to current London Housing Design Guide standards). This is achieved in six new buildings, ranging in height from two to ten storeys.

All images courtesy of LB

## 20. Royal Road housing
Panter Hudspith Architects, 2013
Royal Road at Otto Street, SE17
Tube: Kennington

Another unusual and admirable development resolutely striving against a familiar contractual arrangement constraining the architectural input (a cooperative builder and client helped the outcome). Four blocks of affordable units are unevenly set around an inner private court, the whole clad in brickwork and articulated so as to ensure that maisonettes are evident and each unit has a unique façade – and yet done so in a simple, slightly irregular and cohesive manner.

As an affordable housing scheme, Royal Road consists of 96 homes, 20 of which are shared ownership, and one-third are family homes with three or four bedrooms. In the architect's words:

> A main driver for the scheme was the desire to retain the healthy, mature trees on the perimeter of the site. The plan consists of four open air cores, ranging in height from four to nine stories, about which flats radiate in a cruciform plan. This allows the footprint of the buildings to step around the existing trees and results in over 40% of the homes being triple aspect, and all remaining are dual aspect. This provides excellent cross-ventilation and daylighting for all rooms.

Those rooms – together with their balconies – are about 20% larger than normal for such a scheme (making a huge difference). The photo below is indicative of this consideration: a room-sized balcony, lined in sawn oak, directly off the living-room (even the builder's sometimes disappointing detailing fails to detract from the generosity of the design).

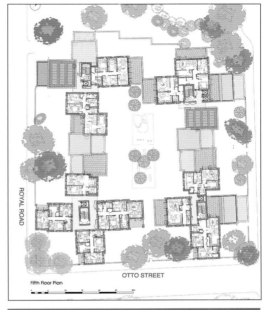

Fifth Floor Plan

ROYAL ROAD

OTTO STREET

**Note**: PH have a not dissimilar scheme on the corner of Bromley Road and Southend Lane, in Lewisham, being completed in mid-2014. (117 units and 400 sqm of commerical space.) However, on this scheme they had no control over detailing.

Photos except of balcony courtesy of PH (Morley von Sternberg)

## 21. Sunshine House

Allford Hall Monaghan Morris, 2008
27 Peckham Road, SE5
Rail: Denmark Hill

Typical AHMM: a health centre that is simple, straight-forward, economic, no nonsense but incorporating moves that tell you an architect is at work (note the cantilever and the graphic qualities, as well as the art inside (Jacqui Poncelat and Milou van Ham). As other modern London health centres, Sunshine provides a whole range of services.

## 22. South London Gallery

6A Architects, 2010
65 Peckham Road, SE5
Rail: Denmark Hill

A gallery that occupies and extends a Victorian house (with an artist's residence at the upper level) and links through to the adjacent Camberwell Art School. Good architectural design and somewhere pleasant for breakfast.

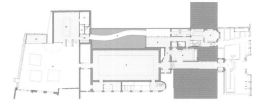

### 23. Employment Academy
Peter Barber Architects, 2013
29 Peckham Road, SE5
Rail: Denmark Hill

Exactly that: an institution whose aim is to assist South London youth in finding employment. It is aptly housed in an Edward Thomas Hall building from 1904 which once housed the offices of the Poor Law Guardians of Southwark, now extended by Barber in a brick (rather than render) exhibition of his picturesque architectural concerns. (Thomas also designed the Liberty store, 1924.) A key feature of the scheme is the new rear courtyard, with its 'mihrab' (or, if you want, an exedra) which comes complete with random windows (inc. a false one, which is square, as are most of the windows in the scheme). And everything is in a textured cream brick. Such enthusiasms – a mix of the Italianate and North African, which harmonise well with Hall's concerns – are worth comparing with those of Simon Hudspith (Royal Road and Bear Lane), who similarly enjoys such effects. The 'house' below (compare with Donnybrook, etc.) is actually an office. Barber has gone beyond white render.

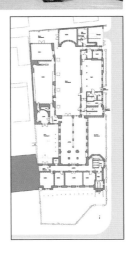

## 24. Surrey Quays
Various architects
Lewisham Way, SE14
Overground or Tube: Canada Water

Surrey Quays was developed post the docks closure that released a vast quantity of land in this area during the 1980s. Those concerned had a good idea: increase that quantity by infilling most of the docks and creating a suburban development. Ironically, this was about the time that London was turning around, in upon itself and becoming more dense and urbane.

The Canada Water station on the Jubilee Line (2000) brought the entire area within minutes of the West End and from Canary Wharf. Consequently, Canada Water has been targeted by the London Mayor for densification and there is a masterplan for providing approximately 3300 new homes near to the Underground station. Developers are now constructing large blocks of flats that give variety to the area and achieve a more sensible density, e.g. Glenn Howells' **Maple Quays, (31)** which includes a tower called **Ontario Point** (both 2012–2023). Overall, Surrey Quays is to become more mature and what it always should have been: more urbane. (See the development masterplan on the right.)

Among the older buildings in Surrey Quays there is the **Canada Water bus station (30A)** above the Jubilee Line station, both designed by Eva Jiricna (2000), and CZWG's impressive new **Canada Water Library (32)**.

Over on the north-east side of the area (**30B**), where docks were retained, you will find some interesting 1980s housing such as **The Lakes** (Shepheard Robson Epstein & Hunter, 1990), off Redriff Road, SE16; **Finland Quay** (Richard Reid, 1990), also off Redrill Road; **Greenland Passage** (Kjaer & Richter, 1989), again off Redriff Road.

Adjacent to the Canada Water Library, sitting alongside a small canal that runs through the area, is **Wolfe Crescent (30C)**, by CZWG (1990). This is accessed from Quebec Way. How times have changed in 20 years.

On the north-west side of Surrey Quays you will find the older village area of Rotherhithe. It is worth visiting in order to see the 18th century church of St Mary, and the Brunel Engine House Museum (built to serve the Thames Tunnel of 1843, through which the Overground now travels under the River Thames).

Also see Walter Menteth's converted church-cum-art gallery in Southwark Park (although you should check uncertain opening times).

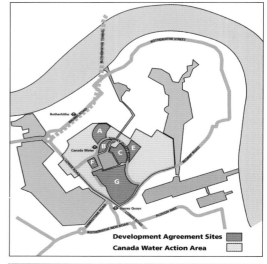

**Development Agreement Sites**
**Canada Water Action Area**

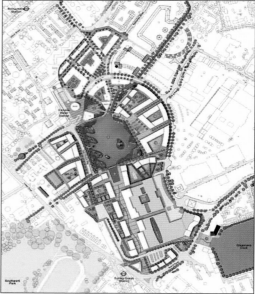

## 24A. Canada Water Station
Eva Jiricna Architects, 1990
Overground or Tube: Canada Water

Completed in 2000 as a part of the new Jubilee Line that runs out to Stratford, the Canada Water Station expresses some typical Eva Jiricna tropes, particularly her love of glass. The circular building is the Jubilee Line Station; the adjacent parts are a bus interchange.

## 24B. The Lakes, Finland Quay, Greenland Passage
Various architects
Finland Quay, Redriff Road, SE16
Tube: Canada Water

The Lakes was designed by Shepheard Epstein & Hunter (1998–1996) and comprises 175 houses and flats arranged around the former Norway Dock. It is described in *The Buildings of England Guide to London Docklands* as a scheme that:

... draws water into its heart by using part of the old Norway Dock [...] built in 1813 with wooden walls, though the central lake has been created above the level of the infilled dock. [...] As if moored round the irregular lake, neat hipped-roofed double villas rest on almost freestanding timber decks. There is nothing like this elsewhere in England: the peaceful watery effect evokes Scandinavia.

## 24C. Wolfe Crescent
CZWG, 1990
SE16
Tube: Canada Water

A development of apartments that sits alongside a small (and pleasant) canal running through the heart of Surrey Quays. The towers and terrace feature some typically quirky CZWG details.

## 25. Maple Quays
Various architects (ongoing)
Canada Water, SE16
Overground or Tube: Canada Water

The Maple Quays scheme is the first phase and a major part of the redevelopment and densification of the Canada Water area. The developers comment that: "900 mixed-tenure apartments, 28,500 sq. ft. of retail and community facilities and £9.5m of community and public realm benefits." The architects employed on the scheme include: Maccreanor Lavington, PKS Architects, Hawkins Brown and Glenn Howells (the latter on the 26 storey Ontario Tower).

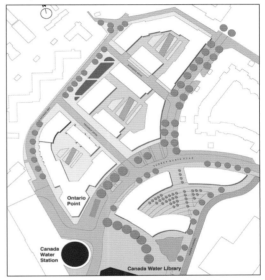

## 26. Surrey Quays Library
CZWG, 2011
21 Surrey Quays Road, SE16
Overground or Tube: Canada Water

It's surprising to find new libraries being built in London. This impressive one is a large building stuck with a small site between a road and some water – hence the unusual geometry. Inside, a dramatic central stair leads from a ground-floor café and community performance space to more private study areas at the top level – an arrangement that really does work. The striking exterior is clad in bronze expanded-aluminium sheets. The architect's description makes strong contextural claims for this changing area:

> The idea of a free standing object in space is quite appropriate for a library, since it is a portal to the discovery of other worlds. As a piece of sculpture it binds together a tube station, a stretch of open water and a plaza and makes the precursor landmark of a substantial new development on London's Canada Water.

The design can be compared with Alsop's Peckham Library (which is an obvious precedent and reference, with its upper-level main space, canted columns, etc.), Adjaye's Idea Store, Bissett Adam's Idea Store, Studio Egret West's Library in Clapham and Sir Basil Spence's older Swiss Cottage Library. Also see CZWG's Wolfe Crescent (1990) immediately around the corner.

## 27. Dilston Grove Gallery
Walter Menteth Architects, 2010
Southwark Park, SE1 (south-east corner)
Tube: Canada Water

A pre-WWI converted church and community hall converted into an art gallery with an inventive hydraulically operated new side wall to the hall.

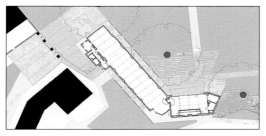

## 28. Peckham Library
Alsop & Stormer, 2000
Peckham Hill Street, SE15
Rail: Peckham Rye

It's dating and has been the inspiration of newer libraries such as that at Canada Water (CZWG) and Clapham (Egret West), but Alsop's (now partly altered) library still impresses. Its key move is the extraordinary one of shifting the principal accommodation up to a high level, leaving a (contentious) public piazza beneath. The internal pods are a 1960s hangover and very enjoyable; the red 'tongue' can be read as an irreverent gesture. At the lower level is a 'one-stop' social services facility (altered) and, above that, administrative areas. However, it should be noted that, almost in every case of new London Libraries, the key achievement is social, e.g. somewhere for school children to do their homework.

# South Central

## 29. Trinity Laban Dance
Herzog & de Meuron, 2003
Creekside, SE8
DLR: Greenwich

On the outside the Laban is a shed set back within a green defensive perimeter, together with a tall security fence. Inside is another story. One expects a two-storey set of spaces, but it is much more complex and clever than that. Interestingly, Herzog & de Meuron found it necessary to find contextural references but could come up with nothing except Thomas Archer's splendid baroque St Paul's Church of 1713–30 (see site plan, right, and plan below right). To get around you will need to book a tour or visit one of the public dance performances.

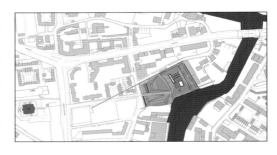

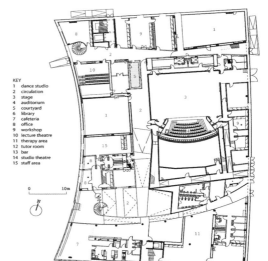

KEY
1 dance studio
2 circulation
3 stage
4 auditorium
5 courtyard
6 library
7 cafeteria
8 office
9 workshop
10 lecture theatre
11 therapy area
12 tutor room
13 bar
14 studio theatre
15 staff area

Photos courtesy of Trinity Laban

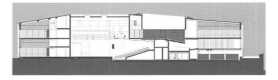

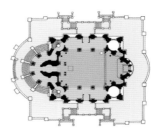

318

## 30. Deptford Lounge/Tidemill Academy
PTEa, 2012
9 Giffin Street, SE8
Rail: Deptford

A remarkably dense, up-beat and rather clever combination of library, studios, school and residential units. The architect's describe the scheme as a visionary concept "combining a replacement primary school with a state-of-the-art district library and other community facilities, including a school/community hall, a rooftop ball court and refectory, with separate access points from within the school and from the public realm." It is worth comparing with two BDP schemes: Hampton Gurney school at Marble Arch; and the Bridge Academy at Haggerston.

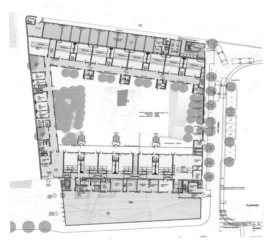

Commercial units
Residential
Teaching Areas
School ancillary
Circulation / service
Community space
Library Services
Resource centre

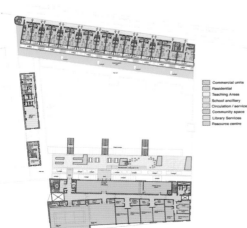

## 31. Waldron Health Centre
HHbR, 2008
Stanley Street, SE8
Rail: New Cross

One of a fine series of community health centres from this skilled practice: two long wings arranged around a new urban square at the entrance. It is worth comparing with others in the series, particularly Akerman – the last and possibly most playful design in the series. Here, it is characteristic of HHbR that they clad the Waldron with lacquered timber veneer panels because they "sought an association with a fine piece of furniture or a musical instrument". We need more 'fine pieces of urban furniture' in London.

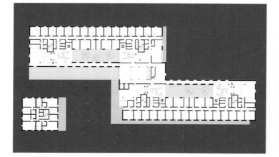

## 32. Goldsmiths Ben Pimlott Building
Alsop Architects, 2005
Lewisham Way, SE14
Rail and Overground: New Cross

Will Alsop playing at being Frank Gehry – doing it rather well and as the only British architect ever to work for an art college and have sufficient kudos that he can stick a very large sculpture on the roof. On the other hand, there is something sad about a set of low-budget art and craft studios that look like a cheap office building with an expensively redundant entry canopy: cheap-'n'-cheerful + gestures, a la Venturi, without a north-light in sight.

There is also a small library by Allies and Morrison (1997) on the Goldsmith's campus – overall, a fascinating place: one walks along a residential terrace only to find every house is a university department. Wonderful.

## 33. Maudsley Ortus Learning Centre
Duggan Morris Architects, 2013
82-96 Grove Lane, SE5
Overground: Denmark Hill

A relatively small but well-crafted building (1550 sqm, and including a public café) within a psychiatric research institution. It is described as housing "learning facilities, café, exhibition and ancillary spaces" with a focus upon creating "a totally immersive learning environment through networking, social media and Wi-Fi technologies such that each individual user can tune the learning process to his/her needs".

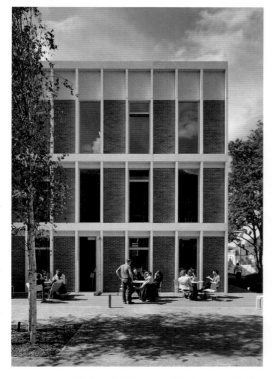

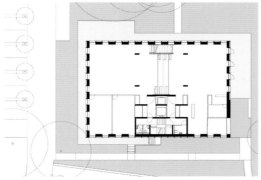

Photo courtesy of Ortus (Jack Hobhouse)

## 34. Akerman Health Centre
Henley Halebrown Rorrison, 2013
60 Patmos Road, SW9
Tube: Oval

An idiosyncratic building, if only because one hardly expects its gamesmanship to arise within such a contractural context. The 4 storey scheme with an 80m long façade makes strong references to church design:

> The building, on the ground, first and second floors, is rectangular in plan. The third floor describes an extended cruciform plan in effect mimicking that of a Gothic minster with its nave, aisle, transept, crossing and choir. This same cruciform motif is evident in all four elevations. The building is a hybrid, taking its cue from both the plan form and massing of the minster and homogenous façade of the 18th Century London terrace. [...] The foyer itself is divided into four quadrants, one of which incorporates the main stair. Overhead, four storeys above the foyer, a cruciform skylight illuminates a painted frieze. [...] Two GP practices share the first floor and another two the second floor. Each pair shares a linear waiting space directly opposite the central stair and lifts. [...] In effect the architectural hierarchy evident on the outside is borne out in the logic of the first floor piano nobile and second floor interiors.

Clearly, someone was having fun. Note: there is a large new housing project in construction next door (the Oval Quarter of 1000 new homes; PRP Architects).

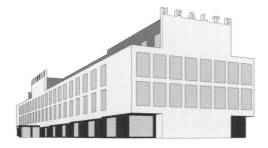

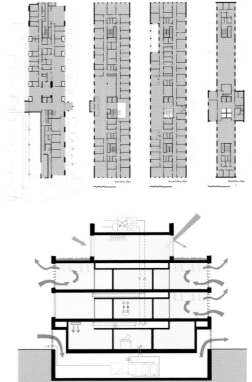

## 35. Evelyn Grace Academy
Zaha Hadid Architects, 2011
255 Shakespeare Road, SE24
Tube: Brixton

Hadid's first London building: a large academy school on a constrained site and a relatively low budget, displaying lots of concrete and familiar zesty diagonals, but no curves. Organisationally, the school is split by a denied 'desire-route' between two parallel streets that crosses the site and has been transformed into a running track. In terms of classrooms, etc., the organisation is basically symmetrical, plus two end addenda for art, music and gymnastics, etc. Internally, it is not what you might expect and one wonders about an aesthetic programme that requires a grey palette and double walls with insulation in between, simply so that exposed concrete can be displayed.

**Note**: London schools are not easy to access, especially during term time and school hours.

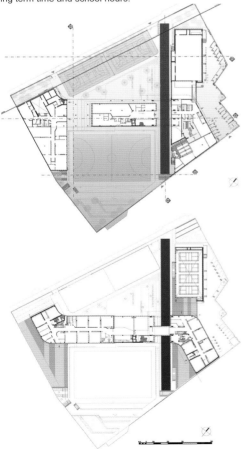

## 36. Spring Gardens Centre
Peter Barber Architects, 2009
1 Arlington Close, off Ennersdale Road, SE13
Rail: Hither Green

A 40-bedroom homeless hostel, one of a series of notable buildings of this kind completed by Barber. As Barber comments: "Our aim was to design a building with no air locks or corridors which traditionally separate and segregate residents and staff."

## 38. Stephen Lawrence Centre
Adjaye Associates, 2007
39 Brookmill Road, SE8
DLR: Deptford Bridge

Two 3-storey linked pavilions clad in expanded aluminium. Inside, the centre provides educational facilities for local children, community rooms to hire, etc.; however, unfortunately there is an air of lost-role about a design that unavoidably suggests keen defensiveness rather than openness.

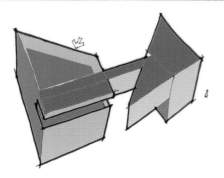

## 37. Dulwich Picture Gallery
Rick Mather Architects, 2000
Gallery Road, Dulwich Village, SE21
Rail: West Dulwich or North Dulwich

An extension to Soane's gallery that creates a partially cloistered space and cries out to be completed. A simple new brick gateway pavilion provides a café and offices; and an equally simple glazed corridor leads from here into the Soane rooms. It's very good.

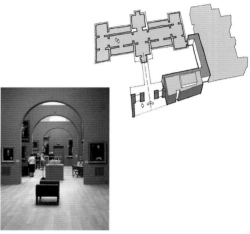

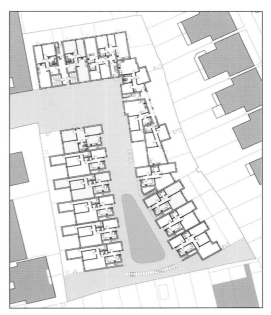

### 39. Effra Road Housing

Inglis Badrashi Loddo Architects, 2013
63 Effra Road, Brixton, SW2
Tube: Brixton

Another affordable housing scheme on a tight, inner block site in a relatively suburban part of south Brixton, one that appears to indicate a nod toward Peter Barber's work. The site is developed as an instance of perimeter geometry around a shared central space.

A perimeter geometry arguably allows a maximum of units on the site, but at a cost of density that is veritably akin to that of an aged Italian village, raising a variety of issues regarding privacy, social relations and the contentions that can arise from such proximity. The Pete Barber influence is evident in the stacking of ground and upper maisonettes, with separate front doors and outdoor spaces. (See, for example, Hannibal Road, Donnybrook and Tanner Street.)

### 40. Clapham One

Studio Egret West, 2013
Clapham High Street, SW4
Tube: Clapham Common

White and glossy, the positive, in-your-face qualities of this complex of housing, health centre and library can demand adjustment. The apartments are actually fairly standard for London these days (apart from some curved living-rooms), but the design does attempt to provide shared roof terraces as well as a good range of flat types and access points. The Library is unusual and conceptually impressive (the ramp and its side-rooms overlooking the tall central space really does work); however, it is let down by detailing resulting from the budget and familiar design-and-build issues. Note the Victorian suburban context – the contrasting reality of most of inner London that is now undergoing change.

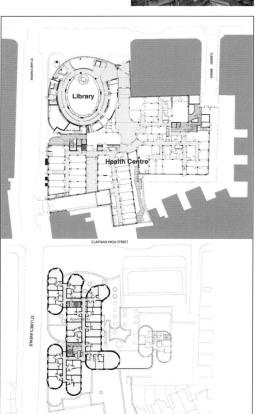

## 41. Clapham Manor School
dRMM, 2009
1 Arlington Close, off Ennersdale Road, SE13
Tube: Clapham Common

A polychromatic pavilion extension to a Victorian school building, with cladding that neatly infects internal shelving arrangements, etc. Matters such as the location of voids and links to the existing building, and the colour variations are well considered – a simple and uplifting design. Note, for example, the alignment with the neighbouring property in a manner that engenders a link serving as an entry foyer.

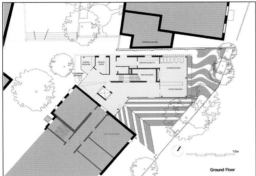

The colours of the school form a polychromatic loop: reds and yellows next to brickwork, green where the façade emerges onto the playground, etc. In addition, the storey heights are quite concealed. Internally the cladding provides for shelving, views, privacy, etc., depending on the context.

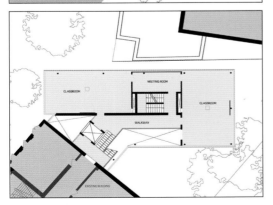

## 42. Slip House

Carl Turner, 2012
Peckham Hill Street, SE15
Rail: Peckham Rye

This project has been on Grand Designs and is readily viewable from the street: a house that, for once, doesn't nod toward its neighbours, muttering about context. They are Victorian and what they are; Carl Turner's house is what contemporary life suggests it can be. On that basis it is worth quoting the architect about this house built at the bottom of a garden of a derelict house:

> Three simple 'slipped' orthogonal box forms break up the bulk of the building and give it a striking sculptural quality. The top floor is clad in milky, translucent glass planks which continue past the roof to create a high level enclosure for a private roof terrace. Designed to Code for Sustainable Homes Level 5, Slip House features 'energy piles' which use a solar assisted ground source heat pump integrated into the pile foundations, PVs, a green roof, rain water harvesting, mechanical ventilation with heat recovery and underfloor heating. A prototype brownfield development offering dense, flexible, urban living – the house is a vehicle for in-house research into sustainable design, seamlessly integrating the often conflicting aesthetic requirements of architecture and alternative low energy systems.

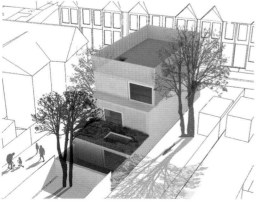

## 43. Horniman Centenary Building

Allies and Morrison, 2002
100 London Road, SE23
Rail: Forest Hill

Extensions and renovations to the original building by Charles Harrison Townsend (1901). That original is now a set of pavilions – one is a linear building complementing Townsend's work; another (earlier) work is entirely different in character to either: a design by Archetype exhibiting eco-friendly pretensions. Notice the similarities between A&M's tectonics and its Abbey Mills pumping station (1997).

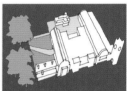

## 44. Barmeston Road

Duggan Morris Architects, 2009
100 London Road, SE23
Rail: Forest Hill

A strikingly inventive scheme from a practice to watch:

This [speculative] project regenerates a redundant commercial site in a residential conservation area in Catford, previously occupied by two commercial buildings. The scheme consists of two different flat typologies. The first a series of two-bedroom 'strip' units arranged laterally on the roof of the foremost brick commercial building. The second typology being two open plan 'loft' units arranged one on top of the other in a free standing building at the front of the site. This new structure represents an opportunity to 'plug' the gap within the urban fabric, and in turn create a new communal amenity in the space between blocks.

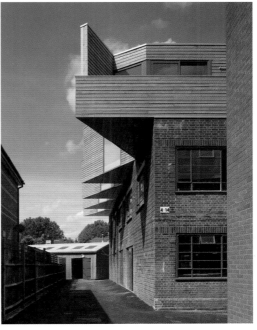

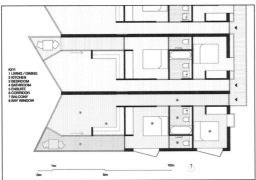

KEY:
1 LIVING / DINING
2 KITCHEN
3 BEDROOM
4 BATHROOM
5 ENSUITE
6 CORRIDOR
7 BALCONY
8 BAY WINDOW

Photos courtesy of DMA (James Brittain)

## 45. Thornton Heath Library

FAT, 2010
190 Brigstock Road, Thornton Heath, CR7
Rail: Thornton Heath

Another new London library, this time as an incongruous addition and extension to an existing building, as if Venturi had a secret project down here in a somewhat dreary part of south London, where it's a moot point as to whether such areas can cope with FAT's wit. That the practice has now closed its doors without more work in London is regrettable.

## 46. Crystal Palace Bandstand
Ian Ritchie Architects, 1997
Crystal Palace Park, SE26
Overground: Crystal Palace

It looks like some WWI leftover: a wonderful Corten steel structure that substitutes for what is still, in many parks, the Victorian bandstand. It sits on a concrete plinth in a pond of water, accessed by a small bridge at the rear, flanked by two speaker columns.

## 48. South Norwood Hill Centre
Erect Architecture, 2012
21 Cypress Road, SE25
Rail: Norwood Junction or Crystal Palace

There are many recent schools to see in London, some new, many refurbished and extended, with little to see without access. This is one of the better ones and can be seen and understood from the street. It is a children's centre within an infant school, designed as an addendum to some existing buildings. In the words of the architects:
    "The typology of the existing pitched roof nursery inspired the extension, which was designed as a series of folded roof planes. The roof gives identity, a strong form and generous height to rooms of different sizes, ranging from smaller meeting and consultation rooms to the large multi-purpose space."

## 47. Baldry Gardens Health Centre
Henley Halebrown Rorrison, 2012
Corner of Streatham High Road and Baldry Gardens, SW16
Rail: Streatham

One of the series of well-considered centres by HHbR (Waldron, St John's, Akerman). It is described as follows:

> ground floor flexible use suite with group room and staff and office accommodation; first floor reception & waiting, GP/nurse consulting rooms; second floor plant room. [...] The building plays on its simple massing [...] The third storey brickwork plant room rises above, and marks, the entrance where the two wings converge. [...] Multifarious brickwork elevations forge a connection between the brickwork colours used in this eclectic street of period and modern houses, and the white render system recently used to overclad the housing estate immediately south of the Centre. Baldry Gardens has been designed to create a calm and therapeutic healthcare environment, a considerate working environment for staff, and for ease of adaptability.

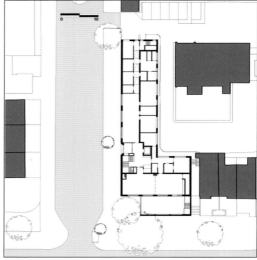

## South and West: off map

Places that are quite far south and west, but which you may want to visit.

### 49. Terminal Five

Rogers Stirk Harbour+Partners, 2008
Heathrow Airport
Tube: Terminal Five

Controversial, but the star of Heathrow: a giant processing machine getting you to the shopping areas between you and the aeroplanes, but worth lingering over. Fifty-minute Tube ride from central London.

### 50. Waterside

Niels Torp, 1998
Bath Road, Heathrow outer perimeter road, north-west of the airport; take Junction 14 if you are on the M25

The 114,000 sqm head office of British Airways in the UK, which brought together 2500p from 14 locations. When we last went there with the architect he was hailed like a returning hero. How many others are received like that 10 to 12 years after a building's completion? However, being relatively isolated and not easily accessible, the building falls off the radar. If fact, its central street is a exemplar for any kind of building complex of this type – perhaps retail as well as university or offices.

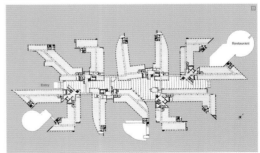

## 51. BedZed
Bill Dunster Architects, 2002
Beddington, Sutton (A237, Hackbridge)
Rail: Hackbridge or Mitcham Junction tramlink

An experiment in expressive eco-housing, BedZed was phenomenally successful. However, green has turned into an invisible issue and you should look at the development as much in terms of housing estate design as anything else. On that basis it is too suburban to be very relevant to current trends. Don't drive; take a Rail from Waterloo.

## 52. Stockley Park
Various architects, 1986–2000
Furzeground Way, Hillingdon, north side of Heathrow Airport.

This was once the future: the suburban, next to an airport business park, here put together with buildings by Foster, Troughton McAslan, Ian Ritchie, Geoffrey Darke, SOM, Arup Associates and Eric Parry. It's all about tight developer control, lots of landscaping and security cameras, i.e., somewhat sanitised and weird, but nonetheless interesting if you are in the Heathrow area.

## 53. The Homewood
Patrick Gwynne, 1930 onward
Esher
See National Trust website for details

If you are interested in Lubetkin, Goldfinger *et al.* and their work between the wars, then this might shock you: gay young man builds house for parents at age of 24, then working with Lasdun at the office of Wells Coates; inspired by Le Corbusier's Five Points, but as an English interpretation; modified in the 1950s and 1960s in a James Bond style. Access only by booking through the National Trust. **Note**: a Gwynne restaurant still exists in Hyde Park.

## 54. Bedfont Lakes
Michael Hopkins; Ted Cullinan, 1992
New Square, Bedfont Lakes.

A small business park on the south side of Heathrow. In 1988 Hopkins completed a building here and was matched by Ted Cullinan, then coping with Post-Modernism and commerciality. As Hopkins describes it: "The masterplan was a high density, formal solution – a single square, the same size as Berkeley Square, in the West End of London, surrounded by six, three storey air-conditioned office buildings, with car parking underground." Ageing, but interesting.

**Index of
Architects
and
Buildings**

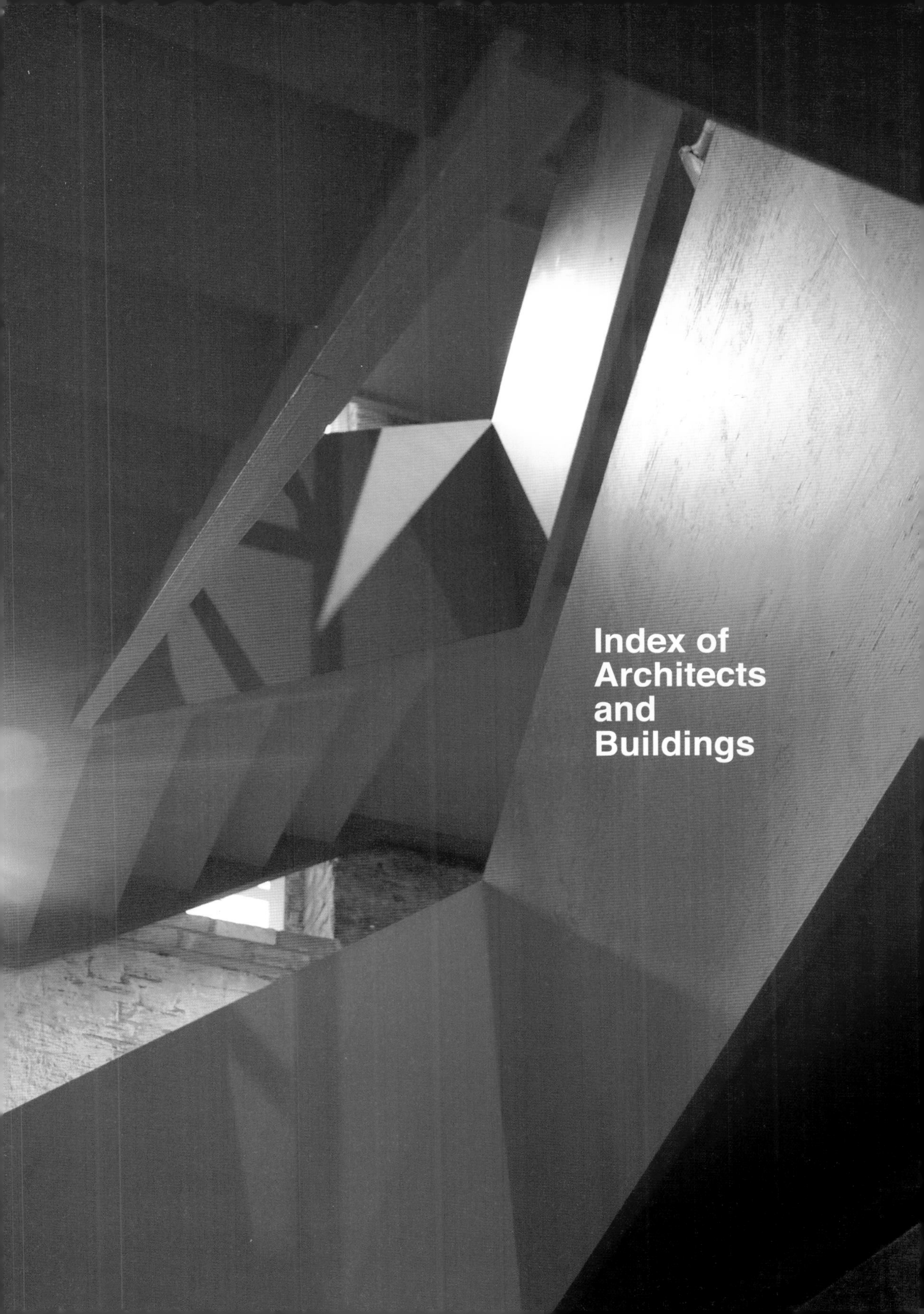

**Photo on the previous page**: a polychromatic staircase within the Domar Warehouse rehearsal, education and administration centre, Dryden Street, Covent Garden, WC2, designed by Haworth Tompkins (2014). The staircase is hand painted by Haworth Tompkins' regular collaborating artist Antoni Malinowski, It is interesting and topical that Haworth Tompkins tell us:

As for many of Haworth Tompkins' creative working spaces in existing buildings, the personality of the historic architecture has been allowed to set the tone, with a provisional, loose-fit language of new additions setting up a fluid, adaptable relationship of new and old. Materials added have been simple and straightforward – whitewashed plywood, painted timber beams and wall coverings, waxed mild steel – to complement the richly patinated texture of the found surfaces. The aim is very much for a benign occupation rather than an obliteration of the original fabric.

## Index of Architects and Buildings

## Index of Architects and Buildings